ROUSSEAU

Selections

THE GREAT PHILOSOPHERS

Paul Edwards, General Editor

ROUSSEAU

Selections

Edited,
with Introduction, Notes, and
Bibliography by

MAURICE CRANSTON
University of London

A Scribner/Macmillan Book

Macmillan Publishing Company
NEW YORK

Collier Macmillan Publishers
LONDON

Macmillan Publishing Company
866 Third Avenue, New York, New York 10022

Collier Macmillan Canada, Inc.

Library of Congress Cataloging-in-Publication Data

Rousseau, Jean-Jacques, 1712–1778.
    Rousseau selections.

    (The Great philosophers)
    "A Scribner/Macmillan book."
    Bibliography: p.
    1. Philosophy. I. Cranston, Maurice William,
1920–   . II. Title. III. Series.
    B2132.E5 1988   194   87-28151
    ISBN 0-02-325521-8

Printing: 1 2 3 4 5 6 7   Year: 8 9 0 1 2 3 4

ACKNOWLEDGMENTS

The translation of Rousseau's *Confessions* is reprinted from an unexpurgated edition privately printed in London in 1896.

The translation of the *Discourse on the Sciences and the Arts* is adapted from an edition originally published in Edinburgh, Scotland, by Alex Donaldson in 1774.

The translation of the *Discourse on the Origin of Inequality* is published by permission of Viking Penguin, Inc., and A.D. Peters and Co., Ltd. Copyright © 1984 Maurice Cranston.

The translation of Chapters 9–20 from the "Essay on the Origin of Languages" from *The First and Second Discourse* and *Essay on the Origin of Languages* by Jean-Jacques Rousseau, edited, translated and annotated by Victor Gourevitch is copyright © 1986 by Victor Gourevitch. Reprinted by permission of Harper and Row, Publishers, Inc.

The translation of the letter to M. d'Alembert on the Theatre is reprinted with permission of The Free Press, a Division of Macmillan, Inc., from *Politics and the Arts* by Allan D. Bloom. Copyright © 1960 by The Free Press.

The translation of *Émile: General Principles of Education* and *The Education of Women* by William H. Payne was originally published by Edward Arnold, London, in 1893.

The translation of the *Profession of Faith of a Savoyard Priest* by M. Nugent was originally published at Edinburgh by W. Coke in 1773.

CONTENTS

ROUSSEAU

Selections

Introduction

Jean-Jacques Rousseau was born on June 28, 1712, in Geneva, at that time an independent state surrounded by fortified walls, a city dedicated to virtue, both republican and puritan. Geneva was, moreover, a city built on a hill, so that people who were equal in their rights but unequal in their condition could be decently divided, the upper classes living on the upper slopes, the humbler families crowded into wooden dwellings on the damp shores of the lake. Rousseau was the second son of a marriage between high and low Geneva; his mother, Suzanne Bernard, belonged to the academic *élite*, and his father, Isaac Rousseau, was an artisan. The patrician house where Rousseau was born was owned by his mother; at the time of his birth, she was already in her fortieth year, and within a week she died of a puerperal fever. In an early draft of his *Confessions*, Rousseau wrote, "I cost the life of the best of mothers," although in later versions he removed the hyperbole. What perhaps he had done, and was certainly made to feel he had done, was to rob his father of the best of wives.

Soon after Rousseau's birth, his father went down in the world, moving literally from the elevated district of Geneva to the low-lying working class parish of St. Gervais, where Rousseau, the son, was proud to boast that the manners of the family "distinguished it from the people."

The boy's grandfather, Daniel Rousseau, was a political activist, a supporter of the opposition to the patrician monopoly of power in Geneva, and he seems to have been happy enough in the milieu of artisan-radicals. But Jean-Jacques' father was not; Isaac felt himself to be a superior person who had been cheated of his rights. Rather than protesting with the radicals against the existing injustices of the Genevese government, he brought up his son as if he were a patrician, to cherish the ideals of republican virtue that the city of Geneva was supposed to share with ancient Rome, and to be a patriot. Rousseau's education at his father's knee reached its peak in studying the heroic biographies of Plutarch, and Rousseau tells us in his *Confessions*, "I was a Roman before I was twelve."

In fact, by the time he was ten, the readings from Plutarch came to an end, because Isaac Rousseau had been forced to leave Geneva as a result

1

of challenging to a duel a person of higher rank than himself, not only making a "gentleman's" appeal to the sword, but, when he was told he was no gentleman, actually wielding the sword. With his father thus exiled from Geneva, Jean-Jacques became the ward of his mother's brother, Colonel Bernard, under whose care he was brought up for some years with his cousin, Abraham, as a boarder with a Calvinist pastor in a village outside the city walls.

All went well until the day came for the two boys to be prepared for a career. Abraham was set on the way to becoming an army officer like his father; Jean-Jacques was sent back to the proletarian quarter of St. Gervais to be a live-in apprentice with a coarse and brutish engraver: "Abraham was a boy of the fashionable quarters; I, wretched apprentice, was no more than a child of St. Gervais. There was no longer equality between us, in spite of our birth; it would have been beneath his dignity for him to continue our association."

Like his father, Jean-Jacques had come down in the world, and like his father, he found the situation so intolerable that he ended up by running away from Geneva. In the Duchy of Savoy on the city's borders, Catholic missionaries were on the lookout for potential converts among young people who ran away from the harsh austerity of the Calvinist regime, and Rousseau decided to take advantage of the opportunity. Savoy was still a more or less feudal type of society, and it was to the aristocracy of the duchy that Rousseau turned for help. He went first to the *curé* of Confignon because, as he explains in his *Confessions*, he knew that this was a person of noble blood. Then, wandering afterward from Confignon to Annecy, Rousseau made his way to the walls of every feudal chateau, dreaming of making friends with the lord and lady of the castle and winning the hand of the daughter. Rousseau says he never felt any sexual attraction to lower-class girls. He liked only those with fine clothes and well-dressed hair and delicate complexions. All the working girls he speaks of in the *Confessions* are described ungraciously, and even middle-class girls seem to have left him unmoved. It is the upper-class young ladies who figure in his fantasies, his memories, his reveries, even though he ended up with an illiterate laundry maid as his resident mistress.

ARISTOCRATIC SOCIETY

Rousseau's quest for aristocratic society in Savoy and Piedmont was not, however, unsuccessful. In Turin, where he was received into the Catholic Church, the Comte de Gouvon took Rousseau into his *palazzo* as a footman, and his son, the Abbé de Gouvon, promptly transformed Rousseau into his secretary and set about teaching him to appreciate literature. Back in Savoy, Rousseau settled down to a life of reading and conversation with his benefactress, his protectress, his "foster mother," Baroness de Warens. She was not very highly placed in the European aristocracy. Her title had been bought with an estate in the Swiss canton of Vaud for her husband at the time of her marriage; he sold it after she had deserted him and ruined him financially, and he ceased to call himself the Baron de Warens. But for Madame de Warens, being a baroness was an important part of the role she played in the Duchy of Savoy as an aristocratic Swiss convert helping the conversion of others, supported financially in this pious work by the king of Sardinia and the Catholic bishop of Annecy.

Madame de Warens always had a bad press. She was something of an adventuress, undoubtedly, and her sexual morals were not those of middle-class respectability, but she was a woman of great generosity and considerable culture. She educated Rousseau, providing the intellectual environment that enabled him to grow into the writer he eventually became. She did not, however, contribute much to his political education. Her own conception of politics was limited. She saw politics as intrigue, and characteristically she tried to win further favor with the king of Sardinia by engaging in espionage. In any case, so long as Rousseau lived with Madame de Warens in Savoy—a duchy that had declined into being a mere province of the Kingdom of Sardinia, governed by Italian bureaucrats and intendants—Rousseau was far removed from anything that deserved the name of politics.

However, at the age of twenty-seven, Rousseau went to spend a year in a more intellectually invigorating place, Lyons in France, where by good fortune he at once became acquainted with the leading figures of the Age of Enlightenment, whose proponents believed in natural law and universal order, taking a scientific approach to political and social problems. He became tutor to the family of Monsieur de Mably, whose two brothers were the Abbé de Condillac, the Lockean philosopher, and the Abbé de Mably, the pioneer socialist theorist. And when at the age of thirty, Rousseau went to Paris, he promptly became an intimate friend of Denis Diderot, philosopher and future editor of the *Encyclopaedia*.

Diderot (1713–1784) was another young man from the provinces seeking fame and fortune in the literary world of Paris. Together, Rousseau and Diderot were caught up in the flood of Enlightenment ideology and bourgeois aspiration. Diderot was content to stay in Paris, but Rousseau sought a wider experience of life. An important stage in his education was the year he spent, at the age of thirty-one, as secretary to the French ambassador in Venice. The Comte de Montaigu was a retired general with no qualifications or aptitude for diplomacy. Rousseau, who was efficient and quick and could speak Italian, performed the duties of embassy secretary. Ambitious, yearning for what he called "*gloire*" and "*fortune*," Rousseau bought himself expensive, elegant clothes in Paris and fancied himself as practicing an aristocratic profession in the service of the greatest king in Europe. This, however, is not how the ambassador regarded him. The comte saw Rousseau as his personal clerk, little better than a valet. His Excellency, who was never an easy man, became incensed when Rousseau put on the airs of a fellow diplomat, stretched himself languidly in the armchairs of the embassy, or demanded to have the embassy gondola at his personal disposal. There were often heated words on both sides, and within a year Rousseau was dismissed in the most humiliating manner possible. But at least he had been given time to learn how Venice was governed and to start writing a book on politics, which became *The Social Contract*. He also had time to acquire a taste for Italian opera.

Moreover, as soon as Rousseau returned to Paris, his luck changed. He found a pleasant job as secretary in the family of an immensely rich tax-farmer named Dupin and lived with them in the most beautiful of all French chateaux, at Chenonceaux. He published works about music, composed operas and ballets, wrote plays, and contributed articles to Diderot's prodigiously successful *Encyclopaedia*. He was indeed well on the way to achieving the "*gloire*" and "*fortune*" he hoped for as an intellectual of the Enlightenment, living in the context of the moneyed Paris bourgeois society that had opened its arms to him.

However, at the age of thirty-seven Rousseau had an "illumination" that led him to alter his way of life altogether. In his *Confessions* he tells of his walk to Vincennes to visit Diderot, who was imprisoned there, and his discovering on the way an advertisement for a prize essay at Dijon on the subject of whether the development of the arts and sciences had improved human morals, and his realization, in a blinding flash, that such progress had in fact corrupted morals. Hardly able to breathe, let alone walk, as he recalls, he sat down under a tree and wept.

THE FIRST DISCOURSE

The result of Rousseau's experience was the *Discourse on the Sciences and the Arts*, which won the Dijon prize in 1750 and earned the author immortality. Diderot encouraged Rousseau to compete, but the *Discourse* is in fact a sustained attack on everything that Diderot believed in and everything that the *Encyclopaedia* was intended to promote. Some of the things Rousseau says were being said by others, but not so eloquently, and besides, those others were reactionaries. As an *Encyclopaedist*, Rousseau was one of Diderot's most valued contributors. It was remarkable that someone in the radical camp should make such an attack on modern culture. For Rousseau claimed in his *Discourse* that science, far from saving us, was bringing ruin on humankind; progress was an illusion; the development of modernity had made people neither happier nor more virtuous. Virtue was possible, he argued, only in simple societies, where people lived austere and frugal lives. In modern sophisticated cultures, people were corrupt, and the greater the sophistication, the greater the corruption. Rousseau invoked the authority of Plato to support his case; for had not Plato said that all so-called scientific knowledge was not knowledge at all and proposed that poets and artists be banished from an ideal republic?

To Diderot, a cheerful and tolerant man, all these arguments were so many entertaining paradoxes, not to be taken too seriously. But clearly a man who did take them seriously could not remain in the position in which Rousseau had placed himself as an Encyclopaedist, a young intellectual of the Enlightenment seeking fame and fortune. A radical change in his way of life was inevitable, especially after he had won the prize at Dijon for his essay and his opinions became generally known. One of the first steps he took was to quit the job he had been given in the office of a rich friend named Dupin de Francueil, a job in which he had every possibility of making a great deal of money.

"In February 1751," Rousseau writes in the *Confessions*, "I renounced forever all ideas of fortune and fame." However ironically, he renounced all ideas of fortune only to acquire enormous fame. But it was not simply as the author of the *Discourse on the Sciences and the Arts* that Rousseau became a celebrity. He became even better known as a musicologist, or more precisely as a leading protagonist in the great controversy about music that excited Paris in the early 1750s. His adversary was Jean Philippe Rameau.

Rameau (1683–1764) was a disagreeable and boorish man, but his genius was such as to command universal respect. He was a fine composer and a successful one; he had as many as six operas performed in Paris within a period of twelve months until Madame de Pompadour, who disliked him, contrived to have productions of his operas limited to two a year. His works, of course, are still performed and enjoyed. Moreover, his writings on harmony and other aspects of musical theory placed him at the head of his profession in Europe. Rameau was the most highly educated, the most technically proficient musicologist of his time. Indeed, Rousseau himself in his contributions on musical subjects for the *Encyclopaedia* made the most deferential references to Rameau's work, as well he might, for Rousseau, when he was trying to teach himself the rudiments of musical theory, had done so with the help of the published works of the great French master. Respect, however, was not reciprocated. Rameau regarded Rousseau as a mountebank, a fraud, and a musical ignoramus, and since Rameau was a notoriously tactless man, he said so.

A REFORMER OF MUSIC

In Rousseau, Rameau had met a more formidable adversary than he realized. When Rousseau and Rameau became protagonists in a dispute about music, they might have seemed very unevenly matched, Rameau being the eminent scholar and Rousseau the self-taught amateur. But in truth the dispute was, at bottom, not simply musical but philosophical. Because of this Rousseau was able to stand up to Rameau so effectively, and in a certain sense to win.

Even as a musician Rousseau proved himself qualified to challenge Rameau. For when Rousseau wrote an opera, *Le Devin du village*, and saw it performed at Fontainebleau in October 1752 (despite all Rameau's efforts to sabotage it), it was an immediate favorite with the king and the court, and later became extremely popular at the Paris Opera House. The dispute between Rousseau and Rameau was part of what was called "*Le querelle des Bouffons*," a quarrel between two different schools of opera. Rameau was the leading exponent and defender of French opera, Rousseau the leading proponent of Italian opera. French opera, it must be noted, was not simply French; it was royalist, academic, cerebral, and sophisticated. Its complexity had everything to do with the Cartesian tradition of mathematical elaboration and rational order; its values were those of seventeenth-century French classicism. Harmony was its most intricate, difficult, and impressive characteristic. Furthermore, the *libretti* of French opera proclaimed the Bourbon ideals of *gloire*, the splendor of kings being represented in the image of gods. Superior beings were depicted on the stage and celebrated in music that appealed to superior minds, or that evoked patriotic sentiments with the sounds of trumpets and drums. French opera spoke to the ear in the same manner in which the architecture of Versailles spoke to the eye.

However, this was 1752, when the grand style of Versailles was beginning to lose its hold on public sympathies. Rameau himself was an innovator; he had given new life to the French opera in the 1730s by introducing lightness as well as intricacy into his compositions, by providing elements of dance absent from earlier French opera, and, in general, carrying French music from the seventeenth into the eighteenth century. Once having done all this, Rameau became the most impassioned defender of the French musical tradition he had so successfully modified. Rousseau, in becoming the champion of Italian opera against the French, had the advantage of a better acquaintance than had most French people with Italian music. He had first heard it as a boy of seventeen, wandering around Turin at a time when the king of Sardinia encouraged performances of the best Italian music as an ornament to his capital, and opened the doors of many concerts to the general public. And when Rousseau was working at the French Embassy in Venice, he had free access to all the opera houses and spent most of his evenings there.

How did Italian opera differ from the French? First of all, whereas French opera was pompous and highbrow, Italian opera had an unmistakably popular quality. Its music was melodic and simple; anyone could sing its tunes, as indeed in such places as Venice and Naples, everyone did sing them. Its themes, moreover, were domesticated. The persons depicted on the stage were less often gods than ordinary people. An example is *La Serva padrona* by Pergolesi, an opera that Rousseau himself prepared for publication in Paris. *La Serva padrona* is a charming *intermezzo* built around the story of a Neapolitan bachelor who is tricked into falling in love with his maidservant and ends up happily married to her. The moral of the story is that a maid is just as good as her mistress if only a man's eyes can be opened to the fact.

This egalitarian message made Pergolesi's opera all the more alarming to conservative opinion in Paris. And indeed the two sides in the *querelle des Bouffons* lined up from the start on a fairly obviously ideological basis. The party that supported the Italian opera included most of the liberal elements, among them the Encyclopaedists. These were the people disposed to welcome something new, something more "democratic," something that broke with the Cartesian metaphysics and the Bourbon cult of *gloire*, which the conservatives wished to defend.

THE BIRTH OF ROMANTICISM

It is ironical that Rousseau should seem to appear as a *chef de file* of the progressive party at just this moment in his life, when his *Discourse on the Sciences and the Arts* had proclaimed his repudiation of the whole progressive philosophy. But it must be remembered that even though Rousseau was opposing Rameau on ideological as well as purely musical grounds, the basis of his position was not liberalism but romanticism. Here we have to consider what Rousseau was actually saying, not what he was *thought* to be saying.

Rameau, in the Cartesian manner, argued that there are fixed rules that apply to all musical expression, whereas Rousseau claimed that the arrangement of music must vary with what had to be expressed. Rousseau was thus pleading for romantic liberty in art, against the rationalist insistence on rigid rules. Then again, whereas Rameau claimed that harmony was the central feature of music, reflecting the harmonic principles of nature itself, Rousseau asserted that melody was what mattered in music; harmony, he said, was an essentially artificial, even a "gothic" construction of the composer's intellect.

Here we are confronted by two different conceptions of nature. When Rameau spoke of nature, he thought of it as revealed in Newtonian as well as in Cartesian physics, the harmony of the spheres and the fixed order of the universe. Nature for Rousseau was what we see in the fields and forests—birds warbling and winds blowing, nature as opposed to culture, rather than nature (as it was for Rameau) as God's great design as under-

stood by the philosophical mind. It is against Rameau's rationalism that
Rousseau's argument is mainly directed. And if one speaks of this as an
ideological confrontation, it is because Cartesian rationalism had by this
time in French history taken on an ideological form, as a system of cultural
values used to prop up the authority of the church and king and the
systematic hierarchy of society.

Rousseau was acutely mindful of the political dimension of the quarrel. "I had come," he writes in the *Confessions*, "to see that everything
was intimately connected with politics, and whatever was done about it,
no nation would be other than what it was made by the system of its
government."

But just what political point is Rousseau trying to make? It is worth
comparing the libretto of the opera that brought him such a success in
Paris in 1752, *Le Devin du village*, with Pergolesi's *La Serva padrona*.
Rousseau's opera depicts a shepherdess, Colette, who is distressed because her betrothed, Colin, has gone off with an aristocratic lady. Colette
seeks the aid of the village soothsayer, who advises her how to win back
her lover, which she does, so that in the end shepherd and shepherdess
are happily united. Here we have a very different tale from that of the *La
Serva padrona*, where the servant is shown to be the right bride for the
master. In Rousseau's opera the argument is that people can best find love
among their own kind and that it is a mistake to try to trespass across the
barriers of class.

Can we be surprised that *Le Devin du village* became a favorite opera of
the king and of Madame de Pompadour? King Louis XV did not often
enjoy music, and Madame de Pompadour disliked Rameau's music because it was too highbrow. Somehow Rousseau's melodic style appealed
to them both. So here we have another curious situation. The conservatives want traditional opera because it is more "correct," while the king
and his intimates prefer the new Italianate opera because it is more enjoyable. Rousseau's situation is no less paradoxical. He provides in *le Devin du
village*, so to speak, liberal music with a conservative libretto—and so
conquers by his example a public he could not expect to persuade by his
argument. And yet that very conquest became an embarrassment to him.
He did not desire it; he was a republican; he did not approve of kings; he
had no wish to become a court musician in the service of a royal despot.

Rousseau's music had brought him fame, but it was fame of a kind he
did not want. He rejected the opportunity of winning more fame through
music under a king's patronage, just as a year or so earlier he had rejected
the opportunity of winning fortune under bourgeois patronage. Once
again he made a radical decision. He not only refused the offer of a royal
pension, he gave up writing music altogether.

Even so, he had written enough about music to propel European music
into new channels. After Rousseau come Gluck and Mozart, whose *Bastien*

und Bastienne was inspired by *Le Devin du village*; it all marks the first beginning of romantic music. Rameau, it turned out, was the last of a certain line of operatic composers; Rousseau was the theorist of a new line, a revolutionary in music.

THE SOLITARY LIFE

Rousseau's name is always associated with the idea of a social contract—that is, with the idea of human societies coming into being as a result of individuals pledging themselves to live together as members of one civil community. But two quite distinct types are in fact depicted in Rousseau's writings: the first is the social contract that "must have happened" generally at an early stage of human evolution; the second is one that would need to take place if people are to live together in freedom.

The idea of human societies being contractual in origin springs from a recognition that human beings are not social beings in the ways that ants and bees, for example, are social. Our instincts do not impel each of us to do unreflectively what is advantageous for the group or tribe. We may have, some of us more than others, altruistic feelings that drive us to do for the community as much or more than we do for ourselves, but even that entails a process of reasoning, thinking out what course of action would be best for society. There is no instinct directing each individual to perform an allotted social role, as there is in the social insects. Each human being has to decide what part he or she is to play, and where there is this freedom, there is controversy. People do not all agree on what is to be done for the good of all, even if all agree that the good of all should be promoted. Every human has a mind of his or her own; and every human being's instincts are self-protective. We are a race of individuals.

Rousseau believed more than most philosophers in the radical individualism of what he called "natural man"; yet he also believed that a person was, as Aristotle said, a political animal, a *zoon politikon*. How can we reconcile these beliefs? The answer may lie in the ambiguity of a word that figures prominently in all eighteenth-century thought: nature. For Rousseau, nature stood opposed to culture: natural man was original man, as he lived in the savage state under the rule of nature alone. But nature was also a force that demanded the attention of people in the civilized state. There its commands were of a different order and were often unheeded; unheeded to such an extent that Rousseau could even claim that modern individuals were alienated from nature and, as a result, that they had lost both their happiness and their freedom.

And yet Rousseau is in no sense a negative philosopher. He attempts to explain, first, how happiness and freedom have been lost, and next, how both can be recovered. Such is what he sets out to do in his two theories of the social contract. The first theory is expounded in his earlier writings, notably his *Discourse on the Origin of Inequality* and his *Essay on the Origin of Languages*. The second theory is expounded in *The Social Contract* published in 1762.

THE ORIGIN OF INEQUALITY

It was in the fall of 1753 that the Academy of Dijon announced an essay competition on the question "What is the origin of inequality among men, and is it authorized by Natural Law?" Rousseau answered promptly "If the Academy had the courage to raise such a question," he declared, "I would have the courage to respond." He returned to the theme of apparent progress concealing actual regression, which he had expounded in the *Discourse on the Sciences and the Arts* that had won the prize of 1749.

On this second occasion, Rousseau did not succeed at Dijon, but the work was altogether more original and remarkable. In less than one hundred pages of the *Discourse on the Origin of Inequality*, Rousseau outlined a theory of human evolution that prefigured the discoveries of Darwin. He revolutionized the study of anthropology and linguistics, and he made a seminal contribution to political thought.

Rousseau begins his inquiry by noting that there are two kinds of inequality among humans. The first kind constitutes natural inequalities arising from differences in strength and intelligence, agility, and so forth; the second are artificial inequalities, which derive from conventions that humans themselves have introduced into society. Rousseau claims that it is because of these artificial inequalities that some individuals are richer than others, some more honored than others, and some obeyed by others. He takes the object of his inquiry to be to discover the origins of such artificial inequalities, since there would be no point in asking why nature had come to bestow its gifts unequally. He therefore sees his first task as one of distinguishing what is properly and originally natural to humans from what they have made for themselves.

Rousseau does not claim to be the first to try to explain human society by contrasting it with a presocial state of nature; he simply argues that earlier writers failed in the attempt: "All these philosophers, talking ceaselessly of need, greed, oppression, desire and pride have transported into the state of nature concepts formed in society. They speak of savage man and they depict civilized man."

The philosopher Rousseau has most in mind here is Thomas Hobbes (1588–1679). In Hobbes the state of nature is represented as one of war of each individual against all individuals; human beings are seen as naturally aggressive, avaricious, proud, selfish, and afraid. Rousseau asserts, against Hobbes, that all the unpleasant characteristics of the human condition derive not from nature but from society and that if we look far enough back in our search for the origins of society and reach the true state of nature, we shall find a being who is admittedly solitary (as Hobbes says), but otherwise healthy, happy, free, and good.

In Rousseau's state of nature, there is no scarcity and no ill health. He notes that the "savages" who still exist in the modern world are reported by explorers to have robust constitutions, free from the diseases that afflict people in Europe, where the rich are overfed and the poor underfed, and everyone is harassed by the desires, anxieties, fatigues, excesses, passions, and sorrows that civilization generates. Domesticated humans, like domesticated animals, says Rousseau, grow soft, whereas in the state of nature they are fit, because they have to be in order to survive. "Nature treats them exactly as the law of Sparta treated the children of its citizens: it makes those who are well constituted strong and robust, and makes the others die."

The reference to Sparta is significant here, for Sparta, as Rousseau understood it, was an ideal model of a republic, and one of the reasons why it was ideal is that it enabled people to recover something of what they lost when they left the state of nature. Now, although Rousseau emphasizes the similarities between the life of original man and the life of a beast, he nevertheless depicts humans as being, from the beginning, radically different from other animals in possessing two characteristics, first, freedom, and second, the capacity for self-improvement.

THREE TYPES OF FREEDOM

The so-called natural man is free for Rousseau in three senses of the word *freedom*. One, he has free will. This form of freedom is for Rousseau a defining characteristic of human beings, and as such is possessed by all individuals in all conditions, whether of nature or society. But there are two other forms of freedom that he sees the natural man as having in the state of nature, but not necessarily having in society. One of these freedoms, which the individual could not possibly possess in civil society, is anarchic freedom—freedom from any kind of political rule. This would, of course, be absolute in the state of nature since by definition the state of nature is a condition in which there is no government and no positive law. The third freedom in Rousseau's state of nature is personal freedom, the independence of an individual who has no master, no employer, no superior, no one on whom he is in any way dependent.

Besides *liberté* in these three senses, Rousseau's natural man differs from the beasts in possessing *perfectibilité*. This word must not be translated—as it often is—as "perfectibility"; Rousseau did not assert in his *Discourse on Inequality*, or anywhere else, that man is perfectible; all he claimed was that humans have the capacity to better themselves by their own efforts. Rousseau never suggested that an individual would ever be perfect, or even that humans were on the road toward perfection. The French verb *perfecter*, as he used it, means simply "to improve," and the capacity for *perfectibilité*, which Rousseau attributed to human beings, was nothing more than a "capacity for self-improvement."

The story of human evolution as Rousseau unfolds it is in many ways a melancholy one, marked, in the first place, by the individual's loss of two of the three kinds of freedom that were enjoyed in the state of nature, and in the second place, by the misuse of the human capacity for self-improvement, doing things that have made the individual worse instead of better.

"Original man" was a simple being, with no language, very little capacity for thought, few needs, and, as a consequence, few passions. What we know as conceptual thinking, Rousseau suggests, developed only with speech, and in the early stages of life on earth, people needed no languages. "Having neither houses nor huts, nor any kind of property, everyone slept where he chanced to find himself, and often for one night only. Males and females united fortuitously, according to encounters, opportunities and desires. They required no speech to express what they had to say to one another, and they separated with the same ease."

The beginnings of human speech are studied by Rousseau, both in the *Discourse on the Origin of Inequality* and in the posthumously published *Essay on the Origin of Languages*. He argues in both that the first human words were natural cries. General ideas came into people's minds with the aid of abstract words, so that the development of language itself helped to create the difficulties with which civilized people torment themselves. The savage, living by instinct, has no moral experience, no concepts of right and wrong. In the state of nature, the individual is good, but there is no question of his being virtuous or vicious. The person is happy, free, innocent—and that is all.

Even so, human beings in the savage state have one sentiment or disposition that Rousseau speaks of as a "natural virtue," and that is compassion or pity. He suggests that this virtue can be witnessed even in animals, not only in the tenderness of mothers for their young, but in "the aversion of horses against trampling on any living body." He goes on to argue that this natural feeling of pity is the source of all the most important social virtues, such as kindness, generosity, mercy, and humanity. He adds a characteristic reflection on the corruption of this excellent sentiment among the men and women of today; because they are so removed from nature, they no longer feel pity. In the modern world, it is the least educated people, the ones in whom the power of reasoning is least developed, who exhibit toward their suffering fellow-humans the most lively and sincere commiseration.

FROM NATURE TO CULTURE

Rousseau depicts human evolution as taking place by a series of stages. The first really important transformation of the human condition was the creation of what Rousseau calls "nascent society." He locates as the central feature of this development the institution of settled domiciles or "huts." Once people made homes for themselves, the prolonged cohabitation of males and females led to the introduction of the family; and this marked—according to Rousseau's theory—the departure from the true state of nature, where the individual was solitary and sexually promiscuous, into a condition where people formed the habit of living under the same roof with a mate and were, therefore, no longer alone.

Rousseau speaks of this passage of the individual from the state of nature to nascent society as the "epoch of a first revolution which established and differentiated families" and which introduced "property of a sort." This "property of a sort" must, however, be distinguished from the full concept of property—that of lawful ownership—which emerges only after a further revolution. All that the individual has in nascent society is a feeling of possession for the hut he or she occupies.

Nascent society is the period of human evolution that Rousseau regards as almost ideal, the Garden of Eden in his vision of the past. Human beings had become gentler and more loving than they were in the savage state. No longer were men and women solitary and indifferent to the fate of others. Settled homes produced finer feelings. The habit of living together gave birth to the noblest sentiments known to man; for Rousseau these were conjugal love and paternal love. Nascent society was the golden mean between the "indolence" of the primitive state of nature and the "petulant activity" of modern pride. It was the best time the human race had ever known.

The reader is bound to ask why, if the simple condition of nascent society was so delightful, did people ever leave it. In the *Essay on the Origin of Languages*, Rousseau suggests that primitive peoples were driven to organize more developed societies as a result of "natural disasters, such as floods, eruptions of volcanoes, earthquakes, or great fires," as if only a miracle could explain their catastrophic passage to a condition of unhappiness. In the *Discourse on the Origin of Inequality*, he provides an alternative explanation for the development of organized society: economic shortage. As the number of persons on earth increased, the natural abundance of provisions diminished. Individuals could no longer feed themselves and their families on the herbs they could find, so they had to start eating meat and to unite with neighbors to hunt game in groups.

Thus associations larger than the family were formed, nascent society became "society"—although still an anarchic or prepolitical society. This development produced important moral and psychological changes in the individual. Ceasing in the context of the family to be a solitary person, the individual became in the context of society an egoistic person.

Even within the family, important changes took place. Individuals lost their independence. Women began to bear more children, and so became less capable of providing for their nourishment and protecting them. They had to rely on their mates. Women became weaker in the context of the family home. Males and females were no longer equal as they had been in the state of nature. Differences between the sexes increased as women became sedentary in the house, and men became even more active as they roamed around with male companions, looking for food and clothing and furnishings for their dwellings.

As ideas and sentiments were cultivated, the human race became sociable. People met in front of their huts or under a tree; singing and dancing became their amusements; and each looked at others, knowing that others looked back. Each wanted to excel in a neighbor's eyes: "He who sang or danced the best, he who was the most handsome, the strongest, the most adroit or the most eloquent became the most highly regarded; and this was the first step towards inequality, and at the same time towards vice." People began to base their conception of themselves on what other people thought of them. In society, says Rousseau, they became "denatured." Each one's *amour de soi-meme*, or self-love, an instinctive self-protective, self-regarding disposition derived from nature, is transformed into *amour-propre*, or pride, the desire to be superior to others and to be esteemed by them.

THE DESTRUCTIVE PASSION OF LOVE

Another important development took place in human experience at the stage of prepolitical association. Sex became a destructive factor. A trivial thing in the state of nature, sex has served from the earliest stages of civilization both to bring human beings together in love and to divide them in bitter rivalry. Romantic love has an evolutionary purpose, for whereas conjugal love keeps people within their own little family, romantic love carries them into a wider society. It is a motor of community, but at the same time it undermines sociability by the bitter conflicts it provokes as a consequence of competition between suitors for a particular person's favors.

Love grew even more important for women than for men as an instrument of their purposes. Rousseau says, "Love is extolled by women in order to establish their ascendance and to make dominant the sex that ought to obey." How does this come about? His argument is that women, weakened as they are domesticated and grown to be dependent on men to an extent that men are not dependent on women, have to use cunning to make a man stay attached to them. Each female must make some man (or men) love her enough to shelter, feed, and protect her, choose her as his cherished mate. In order for women to make men as dependent on them as they are dependent on men, they must dominate men, and dominate them by devious maneuvers and manipulations, since they cannot dominate them by force.

Rousseau maintains that in order to understand sexual relationships in society, it is necessary to stress the differences between male and female, and not to imagine that the sexual equality that prevailed in the state of nature can exist among the civilized.

There are however, some inequalities that Rousseau does deplore. The inequalities he sees as most inimical to freedom and to nature are those that arise from the division of labor. As Rousseau reconstructs the past, the division of labor began between smiths forging tools and farmers cultivating the land so as to produce food for both farmers and smiths. The cultivation of the land led to claims being made for rightful ownership of the piece of land a particular farmer had worked; in other words, it introduced what Rousseau calls the "fatal" concept of property. For once the institution of property was introduced, the differences between different individual capacities and circumstances produced even greater inequalities in individual possessions, which in turn led to a war between each and all.

At this point Rousseau's argument recalls that of Thomas Hobbes. And indeed, although Rousseau rejects Hobbes's claim that the state of nature is a state of war between all people, he gives a Hobbesian picture of the state of society as it was before the introduction, by a "social contract," of the institutions of government and law. The great difference between Rousseau and Hobbes is that Rousseau argues that a social condition, and not a state of nature, immediately preceded the introduction of government. Rousseau also claims that the state of nature was peaceful and innocent, and that it was only *after* the experience of living in society that people were led to introduce government—led to do so because conflicts over possessions arose with the division of labor. Nascent society "gave way to the most horrible state of war."

Both Hobbes and Rousseau envisage men finding the same remedy for the state of war between each and all, namely, by the institution, through common agreement, of a system of positive law, which all must obey. But whereas Hobbes's social contract is a rational and just solution equally advantageous to all, Rousseau's social contract, as it is described in the *Discourse on Inequality*, is a fraudulent contract imposed on the poor by the rich. In his later book, *The Social Contract*, Rousseau describes an altogether different sort of social contract—a just covenant that would ensure liberty under the law for everyone. But that is something people must enter in full knowledge of what they are doing. In the *Discourse on Inequal-*

ity, Rousseau describes a contract taking place in the remote past, when humans first emerged, most of them without much intelligence, from anarchic to political society.

THE FRAUDULENT CONTRACT

Rousseau imagines the first founder of civil government as a wily rich man saying to the poor: "Let us unite . . . let us institute rules of justice . . . Instead of directing our forces against each other, let us unite them in one supreme power which shall govern us according to wise laws." The poor, who can see that in setting up a system of positive law they are establishing peace, agree; they do not realize that they are transforming existing possessions into permanent legal property, and so perpetuating their own poverty as well as the wealth of the rich.

But even though the fraudulent social contract terminates the war of each against all to the advantage of the rich, in the end it does little good to anyone, however rich. It fails because the civilized individual cannot be happy. The savage, says Rousseau, has only to eat and he is at peace with nature "and the friend of all his fellow men." But the civil individual is never satisfied: "First of all it is a matter of providing necessities, then providing the extras; afterwards come the luxuries, then riches, then subjects, then slaves—he does not have a moment's respite."

The tragedy of modern man, as Rousseau sees it, is that it is no longer possible to find happiness in the only way it can be found, which is living according to nature. "Natural man" enjoys repose and freedom; "civilized man," on the contrary, is always active, always busy, always playing a part, sometimes bowing to greater individuals, whom he hates, or to richer ones, whom he scorns; always ready to do anything for honors, power, and reputation, and yet never having enough.

As an indictment of human civilization, Rousseau's *Discourse on the Origin of Inequality* would seem to offer no possibility of redemption, no prospect for the social human to recover freedom, happiness, or authenticity. But Rousseau's other writings are less discouraging; there we find indications of a way to salvation. The basis of hope is his belief that the individual is naturally good. If culture is responsible for all that has gone wrong, is not culture something that can be modified?

Rousseau's earlier work—*Discourse on the Science and the Arts*—had argued only that certain forms of culture were corrupting, not all forms of culture. And in the preface to his *Discourse on the Origin of Inequality*, there is a clear promise that a certain type of civil society can restore, even in the modern world, the freedom, happiness, and authenticity that the human race in general has lost in the course of its evolution.

The preface to the *Discourse on the Origin of Inequality* takes the form of a dedication to the Republic of Geneva, and in those pages, Rousseau holds up that republic as a model to the world: a civil society that has escaped the corruption of the rest. It is undoubtedly an idealized portrait of Geneva that he gives us. But the important thing is that it is there; it enables us to put down Rousseau's *Discourse* without a feeling of total despair.

Voltaire, however, who detested Rousseau, could find no redeeming feature in it: "I have received, Monsieur, your new book against the human race, and I thank you," he wrote after Rousseau had sent him a copy. "No one has employed so much intelligence to turn men into beasts. One starts wanting to walk on all fours after reading your book. However, in more than sixty years I have lost the habit."

Voltaire had not the patience to try to understand what Rousseau had been attempting to do—to provide a genuinely scientific account of the facts of the human condition before developing a speculative theory that might point the way to improvement. Rousseau's image of Geneva was a central feature of that theory. In dedicating his *Discourse on the Origin of Inequality* to his fellow citizens, he congratulates them on being "that people which, among all others, seems to me to possess the greatest advantages of society and to have guarded most successfully against the abuses of society."

GENEVA AS AN IDEAL CITY

The Republic of Geneva was undoubtedly a state unlike others. It had been an independent republic since the middle years of the sixteenth century, when its constitution was founded by a lawgiver of genius, Jean Calvin. But the circumstances of its institution were not simple. Before it acquired independence, sovereignty of the city was effectively divided between the bishop of Geneva and the dukes of Savoy, and the burghers had, by playing one ruler against the other, overthrown both. They had not intended, however, to proclaim themselves a republic; they aspired only to seek incorporation as a canton in the Swiss Confederation. This purpose was thwarted as a result of the Reformation, which divided the Swiss among themselves. When the Genevans chose to be Protestants, they alienated the Catholic Swiss cantons, which vetoed Geneva's entry into the Swiss Confederation until the nineteenth century (1815).

Calvin enabled the Genevans to make a virtue of a necessity; denied membership of a larger nation, they learned from him how to construct a successful little state of their own. They instituted an autonomous, independent city, where the people themselves were sovereign. Administration was placed in the hands of elected elders, and the guidance of the people entrusted to the clergy of the national Calvinist Church. The republican constitution was a skillful mixture of democratic, aristocratic, and theocratic elements. Almost by a miracle, Geneva survived as an independent city-state in an age of expanding kingdoms and empires.

In the dedication of his *Discourse on the Origin of Inequality*, Rousseau explains why he considers Geneva the nearest to an ideal state to be found on this earth. It is small; with a population of only several thousand, every citizen can be acquainted with every other citizen and everyone's life is open to the gaze of others. It is a state where everyone's private interests coincide with the public interest; where no one is subject to any law except the law the individual has made and imposed on himself; where the constitution has stood the test of time; where military virtues are cultivated but wars are not engaged in; where the magistrates are chosen by all, but then vested with undisputed authority; a city where democracy is wisely tempered.

This is not at all an accurate description of Geneva as it had become by the middle of the eighteenth century, but it is what Calvin had designed Geneva to be, what Geneva should have been, and what the rulers of Geneva in all their public pronouncements claimed that it was. To the author of the *Discourse on the Origin of Inequality*, the myth of Geneva was more important than the reality of Geneva. For it is that myth which holds out the possibility of what might be called the renegotiation of the social contract. The old fraudulent social contract, which had marked the intro- duction of government into human experience, could be re-enacted as a genuine social contract. A revolution could end all those centuries of servitude; and people could come together, as the Genevans had come together under the guidance of Calvin in the sixteenth century, and make a civil covenant that would not be a device by which the rich would cheat the poor, but a means of combining liberty and law.

The actual Geneva, which Rousseau visited for several months after he had written the *Discourse on the Origin of Inequality*, was a disappointment to him. He came to realize that it was far from being the "wisely tempered democracy" he had described in his dedication, but he did not forsake the idea of an authentic social contract as a means of reconciling liberty and law. He did not falter in his republicanism. This is what inspired his next most important essay in political theory, the book he called *The Social Contract*, which was published some seven years after the *Discourse on the Origin of Inequality*.

Thomas Hobbes was in Rousseau's mind when he wrote *The Social Contract* just as he had been when Rousseau wrote the earlier work. His knowledge of Hobbes was imperfect, but Hobbes, as Rousseau under- stood him, argued that people had to choose between law and liberty, between being governed and being free. For Hobbes freedom meant the absence of constraint: "the liberty of subjects is the silence of the law."

Freedom went with anarchy; law entailed the rule of an absolute and undivided sovereign. Human beings loved freedom, but the consequences of anarchy were so appalling that any sort of government was better than no government at all. Hobbes's social contract was a covenant made between people to surrender collectively their natural rights to a sovereign in return for the peace and security of a civil order, which that sovereign could impose by holding them all in awe.

LIBERTY RECONCILED WITH LAW

Rousseau did not agree that freedom stood thus opposed to government. Freedom was not the absence of constraint, but the exercise of ruling oneself. He believed it was possible to combine liberty and law, by instituting a regime that enabled people to rule themselves. It would entail, as Hobbes's system did, a covenant being made between individuals to surrender their natural rights to a sovereign; but that sovereign should be none other than the people themselves, united in one legislative corps.

Rousseau not only rejects Hobbes's idea that people must choose between being free and being ruled, he asserts that it is only through living in society that they can experience their fullest freedom. In the *Discourse on the Origin of Inequality*, Rousseau speaks of the three kinds of freedom humans enjoy in the state of nature, one, and perhaps two of which they lose on entering society. In *The Social Contract* he speaks of another kind of freedom, which they can experience only in a well-ordered society: political freedom. And this is something altogether superior to mere independence.

In the state of nature, an individual cannot, by definition, be a citizen. But once the individual has quit the state of nature and entered society, human nature can only be realized by becoming a citizen. In this sense Rousseau accepts Aristotle's definition of man as a *zoon politikon*. Here again we meet the two senses of "nature" in Rousseau's argument. Just as the family, unnatural in the state of nature, becomes natural in society, so does political freedom, totally alien to the savage, become natural for the civilized individual.

In a way, Rousseau's response to the challenge of Hobbes is wonderfully simple. Clearly, people can be at the same time ruled and free if they rule themselves. And this formula might plausibly be expressed as "democracy." But this is a word Rousseau seldom uses, and even then his use of it looks paradoxical. In the dedication of the *Discourse on the Origin of Inequality*, he praises the Republic of Geneva as a "democracy well tempered"; in *The Social Contract*, he writes: "If there were a nation of Gods, it would govern itself democratically. A government so perfect is not suited to men." There is in fact no contradiction here, in view of the particular use Rousseau makes of the word *government*. He carefully separates government as administration, from sovereignty as legislation. He maintains that legislation must be democratic, in the sense that every citizen should participate in it and participate in person. At the same time, Rousseau rejects—as unsuited to humans—democratic administration. The participation by all the citizens in the administration, or executive government of the state, Rousseau considers altogether too impractical and utopian an arrangement. Executive government, he argues, must be entrusted to duly elected magistrates or ministers.

The point Rousseau dwells on is that superiority in public office ought to correspond to superiority of capability and rectitude. Such a system he can call "aristocratic" in the true classical sense of that word: government by the best. This is clearly the sense he has in mind when he speaks in *The Social Contract* of an elective aristocracy as "the best form of government"; and in doing so he does not contradict the preference expressed in the *Discourse on the Origin of Inequality* for "democratic government, wisely tempered"—for what he means there is democratic legislation, wisely tempered by an aristocratic administration, democratically elected. He contrasts this sort of aristocracy with an aristocracy based on heredity, "the worst form of government."

THE PATRIOT CONDEMNED

By 1762, Geneva had come to be governed by a hereditary caste; therefore, we should not be surprised that *The Social Contract* was suppressed in Geneva. Rousseau could well protest that he had provided in his pages an advertisement for Geneva, but at the same time he showed how such a constitution came to be undermined. In fact, there was no hiding the implication that the constitution of Geneva had been undermined in just that way. And there were other features of Rousseau's argument that were bound to be offensive to people who proclaimed themselves not only good republicans but good Christians.

For although Rousseau distances himself from that universally detested atheist and materialist Thomas Hobbes, he does so only to align himself with a political philosopher of equally ill repute, Niccolò Machiavelli. Rousseau saw in Machiavelli not the supposed champion of monarchy who wrote *Il Principe*, but the ideologue of republicanism who wrote the *Discorsi*. Like Machiavelli, Rousseau was in love with the political systems of antiquity. He does not tell the whole truth when he says that in writing *The Social Contract*, "I took your constitution [of Geneva] as my model"; for his ideal constitution owes no less to Sparta, the republic he praises so highly in the *Discourse on the Sciences and the Arts*.

Sparta is in his mind when he tries to define political freedom. It is freedom expressed in participation in legislation—as distinct from the unimpeded enjoyment of rights. It is freedom as it was understood in Sparta: freedom experienced in active citizenship. And like the Spartans, Rousseau confines citizenship to adult males. There is only one kind of representation in his system: the head of the family represents the women and children.

The difference between male and female is an important feature of Rousseau's political theory. He had once worked as a research assistant to a pioneer of feminism, Madame Dupin, and he had no patience with her kind of argument for equal rights. Instead of equality between the sexes, Rousseau proclaims a sort of equilibrium between them: men should rule the world and women should rule men. One of Rousseau's criticisms of the modern world—of which France is his prime example (and from which Geneva is held to be an exception)—is that women have acquired an undue predominance. Rousseau believes it is right that women should rule men privately, but that it is men's task to rule the world publicly. This again is part of his republican ideology; it is as a republican that he attacks the sexual arrangements that prevail in the decadent kingdom of France. There he discerns a deplorable form of sexual uniformity in which men have come to resemble women by becoming equally effeminate; as a result they have been reduced to being the foppish slaves of women in society and of a despot in the state.

In Sparta things were different, and Rousseau is eager for Geneva to keep Sparta in mind. The women of Sparta claim that their duty was to rear citizens, not to aspire to be citizens themselves. Rousseau sees no place for women in legislative activity because his conception of the citizen is that of a citizen-soldier, and women cannot be asked to bear arms (they are too frail and too precious as mothers of future soldiers), nor can a mother be relied upon always to put the interests of the state before the interests of her own family, as a good citizen must. Women's skill is the use of hidden, personal, devious power; whereas public politics requires impersonal, rational legislation and open forthright utterance, for which men are suited by nature. The abilities of each sex, as Rousseau sees them, are distinct; man is the arm, and woman the eye of the partnership. If everything is in its place, there will be no confusion of roles; privately women will rule men and publicly men will rule the state.

THE GENERAL WILL

Rousseau's *Social Contract* begins with a sensational opening sentences: "Man was born free, but he is everywhere in chains." But the argument of the book is that men need not be in chains. When a state is based on a genuine social contract, people receive in exchange for their independence, a better kind of freedom, true political freedom or republican freedom. In entering this kind of social contract, the individual loses his "natural liberty and his unqualified right to lay hands on all that tempts him," but gains "civil liberty and the rightful ownership of what belongs to him."

In this formulation of Rousseau's argument, we confront a serious problem. It is easy to understand that an individual can be said to be free if he prescribes to himself the rules he obeys in his life; but how can a group of people be said to be free in prescribing for themselves the rules they obey? An individual is a person with a single will, but a group of people is a number of persons each with his or her own will. How can a group of persons have *a* will, in obedience to which all its members will be free? Yet it clearly must have such a single will, if any sense is to be made of Rousseau's proposition.

Rousseau's response to the problem is to define his civil society as an "artificial person" with a single will, which he calls '*la volonté générale*,' or "general will." The social contract that brings civil society into being is itself a form of pledge, and civil society remains in being as pledged group.

Rousseau sounds very much like Hobbes when he says that under the pact by which people enter into civil society, everyone makes a "total alienation of himself and all his rights to the whole community." However, it must be understood that Rousseau represents this alienation as a form of exchange—people give up natural rights in return for civil rights; the total alienation is followed by a total restitution, and the bargain is a good one because what people surrender are rights of dubious value, protected by nothing beyond an individual's own powers, rights without a moral basis; whereas what people receive in return are rights that are legitimate and enforced. The rights they lose are rights based on might; the rights they acquire are rights based on law.

There is no more haunting paragraph in *The Social Contract* than that in which Rousseau speaks of forcing a man to be free. But it would be wrong to put too much weight on these words, in the manner of those who consider Rousseau a forerunner of modern totalitarianism. He is "authoritarian" in the sense that he favors authority, but his authority is carefully distinguished from mere power and is offered as something wholly consistent with liberty—being based on the expressed assent and credence of those who follow it. Rousseau does not say that *men* may be forced to free, in the sense of a whole community being forced to be free; he says that *a* man may be forced to be free, and he is thinking here of the occasional individual who, as a result of being enslaved by his passions, disobeys the voice of law, or of the general will, within him. The general will is something inside each individual as well as in society generally, so that the person who is coerced by the community for a breach of that law is, in Rousseau's view of things, being brought back to an awareness of his own true will. Thus, in penalizing lawbreakers, society is literally correcting them, restoring them to their own true purposes. Legal penalties are a device for helping the individual in a struggle against his own passions as well as a device for protecting society against the antisocial depredations of lawbreakers. Political freedom and moral freedom come together in Rousseau; both consist of doing what one wants to do and doing what is right.

THE HEART LAID BARE

At the age of forty-four, Rousseau left Paris to live in the country on the edge of the forest of Montmorency. Diderot and his other Parisian friends warned him that he would die of boredom in such rustic solitude, but in fact the next five years proved to be the most productive in Rousseau's whole literary career, for it was at this time that he wrote not only the *Social Contract*, but also the *Letter to M. d'Alembert on the Theatre*, *Emile*, *Profession of Faith of a Savoyard Priest*, and *La Nouvelle Héloïse*.

His "solitude" was, in any case, far from complete. In his second year at Montmorency, he fell passionately in love with a neighbor, Countess Sophie d'Houdetot. Although the *affaire* was short-lived, and perhaps never consummated, it played a central part in the writing of *La Nouvelle Héloïse*. He began the novel soon after he left Paris as a sort of literary exercise on the model of the English author Richardson, allowing himself to develop a portrait of his ideal woman as the heroine, whom he named Julie. He was busily at work on this pleasing exercise when Madame d'Houdetot made a spectacular entry into his life, visiting him in his cottage in masculine riding clothes, all smiles and charm and flirtatious talk. Her Christian name was Sophie, and Rousseau quickly came to see in her the living embodiment of his Julie. As their relationship developed, he transformed the experience into material for his novel.

The plot of *La Nouvelle Héloïse* turns on the love of a middle-class tutor, Saint Preux, a character modeled on Rousseau himself, for his upper-class pupil, Julie. She returns his love; she even "yields" to his embraces, but she cannot marry him. The barriers of class are insurmountable. Her father insists that she marry a fellow nobleman he has chosen as her bridegroom. She obeys, and as a virtuous wife and mother, she purges the guilt of her lapse and forbidden love. Saint Preux goes away for several years, but then Julie's husband urges him to return and join their household. There is a moment of dramatic tension when it seems that Julie's love for Saint Preux is not dead after all, and their bodies almost touch again. Chastity triumphs on this occasion, but Julie dies by drowning soon afterward, so there remains the doubt as to how long her hidden love could have been denied if she had lived.

Rousseau's own love for Sophie d'Houdetot was thwarted in a similar way by the barriers of class, but thwarted also by the fact that Sophie was the settled mistress of the Marquis de Saint Lambert, a soldier absent on active service at the time that Rousseau and she were spending most of their days and some of their nights together. It was Saint Lambert's sudden return from the field that ended the *affaire* after less than three months. Faced with a similar choice to that of Julie in the novel, Sophie, like Julie, preferred the nobleman to the impoverished bourgeois intellectual; and she wrote Rousseau a *lettre de rupture*.

Thus rejected by his Sophie, Rousseau healed his wounds by throwing himself into intense literary activity. He went on to complete *La Nouvelle Héloïse* within a year, and it was to prove his most popular book with the reading public, especially the ladies. It was appreciated both as a tear-jerker and as a rather shocking novel. In a society that allowed a married woman as much sexual liberty as she allowed herself, but demanded that unmarried girls preserve their virginity, Rousseau's suggestion that a premarital lapse could be redeemed by marital virtue sounded distinctly immoral. Eighteenth-century France, however, was fairly tolerant of immorality. Besides, *La Nouvelle Héloïse* seemed to be suggesting that love itself could make a relationship innocent, even transform immorality into virtue. No other novelist before Rousseau had waxed so eloquent about the beauties of virtue, or fused the metaphysical and the sexual so powerfully, or given purity itself so erotic a character. In any case, *La Nouvelle Héloïse*, unlike Rousseau's later writings, met no problems with the censors.

AGAINST THE THEATRE

Rousseau himself took the side of the censors in another work he wrote at about the same time as *La Nouvelle Héloïse*, called *Letter to M. d'Alembert on the Theatre*. This essay was occasioned by an article that d'Alembert had written for Diderot's *Encyclopaedia* on the subject of Geneva, in which he had suggested that the introduction of a theatre to that city would have a civilizing and educational effect on the people. Rousseau attacked the proposal and defended the ban on theatrical entertainment that had existed in Geneva since Calvin had reformed its laws in the sixteenth century.

Rousseau argued, with his usual eloquence and remarkable critical acumen, that theatrical performances did not improve the morals of the spectators, but gave them vicarious excitement and cheap thrills, which diminished, rather than enhanced, their capacity for genuine emotional experience. He argued further that even the best of modern dramatists, such as Molière, made virtue look ridiculous and vice glamorous. Rousseau pleaded for Geneva to stick to its tradition of participatory cultural activities—dancing, games, and popular music, men's and women's clubs, places where people could meet and drink and socialize—rather than setting up theatres where people would sit mutely watching actors act.

Since Rousseau himself had written plays and had only a few years earlier been the leading champion of the Italian opera in Paris, this attack on the theatre startled many readers and increased the author's reputation as a "master of paradox." But Rousseau did not deny that the theatre could act as a brake on vice in sophisticated societies, or what he ventured to call corrupt societies, so that Paris, being one such society, could benefit from dramatic performances. Geneva, on the other hand, Rousseau maintained, was innocent. It was still a simple place with Puritan traditions, and he begged for it to be allowed to remain that way. Even so, he carried his arguments both against theatrical performances and against dramatic literature to a point where it is hard to see how he could allow either to serve a morally elevating purpose even in corrupt societies.

Rousseau had some qualms about the novel as well as plays, and he tried to persuade his publisher to forbid the sale of *La Nouvelle Héloïse* in Geneva. His publisher, a Dutchman of Swiss origins, protested that he could not afford to lose any market that was open to his book, and *La Nouvelle Héloïse* sold well in Geneva and seems to have pleased the Genevese no less than the French. Rousseau's *Letter to M. d'Alembert on the Theatre*, on the other hand, had a mixed welcome in that city. The clergy, and the more strictly Puritan lay citizens, received it eagerly, but the more fashionable people were angry at Rousseau's attempt to forbid Geneva to improve its cultural amenities. There was already a small theatre in the adjoining Savoyard town of Carouge, and Voltaire, installed in a rented villa nearby, was organizing performances of his own and other authors' plays for private audiences. A public theatre in the city seemed the logical next step. Rousseau's *Letter to M. d'Alembert* turned the tide of opinion. The majority of Genevese citizens rallied to the clergy, and the interdiction against theatricals was renewed and enforced more strictly than ever.

No one was more outraged by this than Voltaire. He had once been on friendly terms with Rousseau, but their relations cooled when Rousseau ventured to criticize a poem Voltaire wrote on the subject of providence. The earthquake of 1755 in Lisbon, where thousands of innocent lives were lost, had shaken Voltaire's faith in the goodness of the Deity, had convinced him that God had either gone to sleep or allowed some malicious fallen angel to take over the direction of the universe. Voltaire had never been an atheist, as were the younger *philosophes* of the Enlightenment such as Diderot, Holbach, and Grimm, who had alienated Rousseau with their extreme materialist views and their mockery of Christ. Voltaire was a Deist; or at any rate, he had been until the Lisbon earthquake, and he wrote the poem that called the goodness of the Deity into question.

A DEFENSE OF PROVIDENCE

Rousseau, having read Voltaire's poem questioning the Deity with considerable dismay, sent him a long letter (obviously intended for publication) defending his belief in an omnipotent and benevolent providence. Voltaire acknowledged Rousseau's letter politely, but he did not reply in detail. However, Rousseau took Voltaire's "real" answer to his letter to be the novel *Candide*, which makes brilliant mockery of the idea that our world is "the best of all possible worlds" and "all partial evil, good misunderstood."

Rousseau's most substantial reply, in turn, was the essay he called *The Profession of Faith of a Savoyard Priest*. Although the beliefs expounded in this text are ascribed to an unfrocked Catholic priest, they represent the mature religious thought of Rousseau himself. Born a Calvinist, converted at the age of sixteen to Catholicism, than re-converted at the age of forty-two to Calvinism, Rousseau finally settled on a religious doctrine of his own. In the *Profession of Faith* he set forth an impressive, and original, argument in support of it.

In his long letter to Voltaire he had declared: "All the subtleties of metaphysics will never make me doubt for an instant the immortality of the soul or the existence of a benevolent Providence: I feel it; I believe it; I wish and I hope for it to be true; I shall defend it to my last breath."

In the *Profession of Faith* he goes to some length in seeking to refute the materialism that had become so fashionable among the younger *philosophes* and that Voltaire himself appeared to have adopted. Rousseau claims that any reasonable consideration of the nature of the external world must persuade the observer that matter is more often than not in a state of movement. Since its natural state is not movement, but rest, it follows that some external agency must propel it into action. We know from experience how we ourselves can cause movement in particular objects; this enables us to recognize that all the multifarious moving bodies throughout the universe must have been set in motion by some supreme agent—a nonmaterial being, not wholly unlike the human being, possessing, as the human does, a will.

The movements we observe in nature are revealed by scientific study to follow certain regular patterns or laws; this harmony and order in the workings of nature proclaim the existence of an intelligent architect. The workings of natural law, moreover, can be shown to be purposive. The design and structure of natural beings are seen to serve an aim or end, and

Rousseau emphasizes "the unity of intention which is exhibited in the relations of all the parts of this great whole."

Rousseau goes on to suggest that the design of the universe also reveals the benevolence of its creator. He would not accept Voltaire's claim that the disaster of Lisbon was evidence of God's indifference to human suffering; he said it was due to human folly in building towns on volcanic soil. He defended the assertion of Alexander Pope that "partial evil" was "good misunderstood"—arguing that, whereas particular events in the world were bad, the whole universe, taken as a total system, was good, and that goodness was evidence of the goodness of its author.

Arguments of this kind, however, were not the most original or striking features of Rousseau's religious teaching. Rational arguments were less important to him that the compelling effect of faith itself. He needed to believe. He once wrote in a letter: "I have suffered too much to be able to live without faith." That faith, however, was simple. He believed in the existence and goodness of God and in the immortality of the soul. That was the sum total of his religious creed. There was no longer any question of his believing in the doctrines laid down by the church of Geneva or the church of Rome or any other external authority. He could not believe in anything contrary to reason, such as miracles.

He needed no church. Since nature revealed God to him, he chose to worship God in nature. And worship Rousseau undoubtedly did. He looked upon nature with different eyes from his contemporaries. He adored wild nature as much as he disliked the cultivated nature of gardens and conservatories. He saw God's majesty most clearly in the high mountains and dense forests; the Alps were his cathedral, where peaks and summits spoke more directly to his soul than all the Gothic spires of Christendom or the baroque domes of popery.

THE GOODNESS OF NATURE

Rousseau's religion was at one with his philosophy. Nature—differently defined, admittedly, in different contexts—was at the center of his system. What was natural, including what was natural in the individual—was good, and what was good was the work of a creator whose creatures owed reverence and adoration. Rousseau, moreover, could not only see God when he looked outside himself at the marvelous works of nature; he discerned God also inside himself and became aware of the presence of conscience, which was the voice of God within man. Conscience is the "infallible judge of good and evil" placed within each one of us—an immortal, celestial voice that makes us worthy of our creator. But Rousseau also speaks of conscience as the "sacred voice of nature," for indeed, in the end, there is no dichotomy between God and nature, which is divine creation.

Thus, Rousseau's religious theory is also a moral theory: conscience is the guide to good conduct, and it is also a natural impulse, a feeling rather than a set of principles, which means that morals cannot be formalized. One consequence of this ethical theory was that it enabled Rousseau to sustain a large measure of ambiguity in his own moral judgments. His critics saw it as a ruinous defect. Indeed his religious writings caused scandal in France in a way that his political writings had never done. He alienated the Church and Christian believers by repudiating miracles and all other doctrines that did not conform to reason. At the same time he alienated the rationalists and religious skeptics by proclaiming the supremacy of faith over reason as a source of knowledge of God and morality.

The book that caused the greatest offense was *Emile, a Treatise on Education*. This is perhaps not altogether surprising since it was directed to forming the minds of those about whom any society is generally most solicitous—the young. In it Rousseau recommends a wholly revolutionary approach to the upbringing of a son. His whole technique of education, as he writes at the outset, is based on the principle that the child is naturally good.

"Everything is good that comes from the Author of nature; everything degenerates in the hands of man."

His fundamental principle being that the child's nature is good, it follows that the first aim of education should be to avoid corruption rather than to impose conventional rules of conduct or traditional learning on the pupil. Rousseau did not, however, suggest that today's natural child was yesterday's natural man or savage. Evolution had modified the human person even as it was formed in the womb. This meant, among other things, that today's boys were different from girls even though males and females in the state of nature had been almost identical. Therefore, Rousseau argued that boys and girls should be given a different sort of upbringing.

The "Emile" of *Emile* is a boy, and most of the book is about his education, but the later chapters deal with the education of a girl, Sophie, who is destined to be Emile's mate. There is nothing particularly novel in Rousseau's proposals for the education of Sophie; not surprisingly, it is enough that she be a good country girl unsullied by the influence of the city. The radicalism is in Rousseau's plan for Emile. What is particularly novel is his insistence that the education of the senses be given priority over the education of the mind. Whether a boy ever learns Latin, for example, is a matter of indifference to Rousseau; it may be useful in cultivating logical thinking, but that is far less important that moral judgment, less important even than acquiring a healthy body. The formation of character is the first aim of education, a sound physique is second, and the improvement of the intellect third.

But Rousseau warns his tutor that he must work with nature, and not against it. The boy must not be made to feel that his freedom is being infringed. The tutor must control him by the way he arranges the circumstances that surround the child and govern his life, so that the boy will do what the tutor wants him to do without feeling that he is obeying an external will. The child should never be given a command, never be allowed to suspect that the tutor claims authority over him. The boy's awareness of his own weakness and of the tutor's strength will prompt him freely to look to the tutor for guidance. Even so, Rousseau recommends a good many stratagems for the tutor's use in order that the child may come to do what the tutor wants him to want. Despite all his pleas for honesty and transparence, Rousseau does not see much room for plain dealing in the relations between tutor and pupil—not at any rate until the child reaches adolescence, and it becomes possible for the tutor to reason with him.

PROGRESSIVE EDUCATION

In *Emile*, Rousseau stresses the need for a progressive education, which follows the different stages of the boy's development. "Nature wants children to be children before being men." The child's mind cannot handle abstractions, so it must be trained by means of contact with things. Books are discouraged. The only book Rousseau will authorize a child to read is *Robinson Crusoe*, because that at least teaches one the possibility of solving the problems of living without any aid beyond one's own resources. Rousseau wants his pupil to learn how to live, as Robinson Crusoe learned, by his own efforts, his own experience, and his own experiments. Like a savage, the child must know that he is dependent on *things*, but he must be trained not to be dependent on *people* and kept as free as possible from acquiring habits of submission.

The child's reason must be exercised in solving the practical problems of living as distinct from the acquisition of abstract knowledge, since "childhood," as he expresses it, "is the sleep of reason." Rousseau wanted also to harden his pupil, have him learn to swim, face the cold lightly clad, and remove all fear of night and darkness from his imagination. He would never punish the boy, but rather have him learn from the natural consequences of bad actions to understand his error himself.

Emile is taught no catechism. No religion is imposed on him, or even introduced to him until he reaches the age of sixteen. Rousseau wanted to avoid having "stunted images of Divinity" engraved on the minds of children. In the fullness of time, the child would learn to see God everywhere, in the works of nature.

THE BITTERNESS OF EXILE

The publication of *Emile* in 1762 marked the end of Rousseau's life of relative peace and literary activity in the valley of Montmorency. The Paris *parlement* ordered the book to be burned and the author arrested, and Rousseau was advised by his friends to leave the country. Although he had protectors in the royal court at Versailles—Malesherbes, the minister in charge of publications, and the duke of Luxembourg, captain of the King's guard—the Paris *parlement* was a legal court with sovereign powers of its own, and its members, dominated by the Jansenist, or more fanatically Puritan tendency in the Catholic Church, were determined to stamp out heresy. Friends at Versailles could not save Rousseau, and he prudently accepted the offer of the duke of Luxembourg to use his coach to take him to Switzerland, to Berne and to Neuchâtel, that is, and not the city of Geneva, for the authorities there had gone one step beyond those in Paris. They had burned *The Social Contract* as well as *Emile* and issued an order for the philosopher's arrest.

In Neuchâtel he came again under royal protection, for that canton was then subject to the monarchy of Frederick II of Prussia, a noted champion of religious toleration. However, the parishioners of the village where Rousseau lodged, egged on by a Calvinist pastor, stoned the author of *Emile*, and he hurried from Neuchâtel to begin a life of wandering and mental disturbance, which lasted until his death sixteen years later, in 1778, at the age of 66.

During those last, unsettled years of his life, Rousseau wrote very little on philosophical, ethical, or religious subjects, but he did publish several works on politics. The first, *Letters Written from the Mountains*, was a reply to a pamphlet by Robert Tronchin entitled *Letters Written from the Country*, in which the procureur-général of the Republic of Geneva sought to justify the suppression of *Emile* and *The Social Contract*. Rousseau produced a stinging indictment of the whole political system of his city state; and the republic he had described as recently as 1755 in the dedication to *Discourse on the Origin of Inequality* as an ideal "well-tempered democracy," he castigated in 1763 as one of the worst tyrannies in history. "Geneva," he wrote, "is ruled by twenty-five despots. Athens, at least, had thirty."

In reality, perhaps, Geneva had not greatly changed in those eight years, but the suppression of his own books had awoken Rousseau to facts that he failed to recognize at earlier stages in his own experience. It had taken him a long time to rid himself of the romanticized image of Geneva he had received from his father and cherished in exile.

Two other political works of Rousseau that he wrote in his later years were *Constitution for Corsica* and *Considerations on the Government of Poland*. In the 1760s it seemed as if the island of Corsica, having ended its subjection to the Italian republic of Genoa, might perpetuate itself as an independent state, and a group of Corsican nationalists, impressed by Rousseau's argument in *The Social Contract*, invited him to draft a constitution for their island. However, Corsica was annexed by France in 1769, so Rousseau's constitution was never submitted for actual enactment.

Rousseau did not suggest to his Corsican friends that they model their state on the Calvinist-Spartan principles of *The Social Contract*. He had always said that different peoples need different sorts of governments, and for Corsica he recommended a representative government, with frequent elections, so that public opinion could make itself felt. At the same time he urged the Corsicans to cherish their frugality, because riches destroy all possibility of democracy. So long as they remain an agricultural society, Rousseau thought, and preserve their simple, primitive traditions, they may keep their freedom. They should have as little money in circulation as possible and use barter as often as they can: "All men must live, and none must get rich at the expense of others." In this way, there would be no great inequalities of fortunes, and Corsica would remain a nation of simple people, living close to nature. Above all, he stressed the need for a national spirit, an austere patriotism and devotion to the public good.

A CONSERVATIVE MESSAGE

Rousseau's recommendations to the Polish people were different from those to the Corsicans, as we should expect them to be, since Poland was a very different country from Corsica—a large, land-locked kingdom with a long tradition of feudal government and politics. Republican constitutions, he had always said, were suited only to small states, so there was no question of his advising the Polish people to set up a republic. The best he could suggest for them was to modify their constitutional monarchy, at that time one of the most confused in Europe, with a king elected by a diet whose members each had a right of veto. Freedom was simply not a realistic option for the Poles. On one hand, there was the "self-interest and prejudice" of noblemen; on the other, the "vice and laziness" of the serfs. Such people would not even know the price of liberty, let alone be able to pay it. "Liberty is a food easy to eat, but hard to digest; it takes very strong stomachs to digest it."

Considerations on the Government of Poland reveals the deeply conservative element in Rousseau's political thinking. He believed that people could never have good government unless they already had some experience of good government, and a civic spirit inbred in the people. He did not believe in revolution. All popular revolutions, he wrote, bring terrible discussions and infinite disorders. Once the dismemberment of common life begins, greater slavery is inevitable, and greater evils are introduced on the pretext of improving things. Reforms, he urged the Poles to remember, must be piecemeal and judicious "without any preceptible revolution."

Ironically, the author of these words has gone down in the history books as the great ideologue of the French Revolution of 1789. But presumably the makers of the French Revolution who venerated Rousseau had read only his earlier writings—*Discourse on Inequality* and *The Social Contract*—and themselves transformed an innovative political philosophy into a program of radical political action. They interpreted Rousseau's message to the sovereign citizens of Geneva as a message to the oppressed subjects of the king of France, which is something he had expressly discouraged.

Indeed, in his later years, Rousseau kept discreetly silent on the subject of France. After a visit to England—a visit overshadowed by his quarrel with David Hume, whom he falsely suspected of making fun of him behind his back—Rousseau remained on French soil until his death, sometimes calling himself Monsieur Renou, moving from place to place, and generally avoiding publicity. He undoubtedly developed persecution mania, but the truth is that he *was* persecuted by a number of persons, especially by former friends such as Voltaire and Diderot.

His last writings were mostly literary and autobiographical. In *Rousseau Juge de Jean-Jacques*, he set out to confront and answer his adversaries in dialogue form. In *Reveries of a Solitary Walker*, he looked back, in the last year of his life, on certain experiences he had, beliefs he had held, and places he had visited in a rumintative mood. It is a moving, beautifully written series of "walks" or essays, and in one he makes this curious observation:

> The several short intervals of prosperity in my life have left me
> with virtually no pleasant memory of the way in which they af-
> fected me. Conversely, during all the most miserable moments of
> my life, I always felt myself filled with tender, sweet and delight-
> ful sentiments which, in pouring a healing balm over the wounds
> of my broken heart, seemed to transform suffering into pleasure.

The most substantial work of Rousseau's later years was, however, his *Confessions*. In this he set out not only to unburden his conscience, but to make a wholly original contribution to literature by describing with absolute candor one man's experience of life on this earth. He realized that whereas it might be easy to own up to terrible crimes or outrageous vices, it would be difficult for any individual to admit to the petty, mean, shameful, ugly little deeds one did one's best to forget. Rousseau had the courage to do what he intended—he admitted his little thefts, his cowardly lies, his cruelties, and also his unheroic sexual experiences, the *fiascos*, the masturbation, the undeclared masochistic yearnings. He expected no absolution, but he hoped for understanding from his readers.

What he received has been, in large part, reproaches and blame for the sins he admitted or scorn for his indiscretion in admitting them. He is widely—and unjustly—assumed to have been a thoroughly unpleasant person, but his works have never ceased to command the attention of readers, and his influence has exceeded that of any other modern writer, with the solitary exception of Marx.

The Confessions
1749

On my return to Paris, I received the agreeable news that Diderot had been released from the donjon, and confined to the château and park of Vincennes on parole, with permission to see his friends. How painful it was to me not to be able to run to him on the spot! But I was detained for two or three days at Madame Dupin's by duties which I could not neglect, and, after what seemed three or four centuries of impatience, I flew into my friend's arms. O indescribable moment! He was not alone; D'Alembert and the treasurer of the Sainte-Chapelle were with him. When I entered, I saw no one except him. I made a single bound; I uttered a single cry; I pressed my face to his; I embraced him closely without an utterance, except that of my tears and sighs; I was choked with tenderness and joy. The first thing he did, after leaving my arms, was to turn towards the ecclesiastic and say to him: "You see, sir, how my friends love me!" Completely overcome by my emotion, I did not at that time think of this manner of turning it to advantage; but, when occasionally reflecting upon it afterwards, I have always thought that this would not have been the first idea that would have occurred to me had I been in Diderot's place.

I found him greatly affected by his imprisonment. The donjon had made a terrible impression upon him, and, although he was comfortable at the castle and allowed to walk where he pleased in a park that was not even surrounded by walls, he needed the society of his friends, to avoid giving way to melancholy. As I was certainly the one who had most sympathy with his sufferings, I believed that I should also be the one whose presence would be most consoling to him, and, in spite of very pressing engagements, I went at least every other day, alone or with his wife, to spend the afternoon with him.

The summer of 1749 was excessively hot. Vincennes is reckoned to be two leagues distant from Paris. Being unable to afford a conveyance, I set out at two o'clock in the afternoon on foot, when I was alone, and walked fast, in order to get there sooner. The trees on the road—always lopped after the fashion of the country—hardly afforded any shade, and often, exhausted by heat and fatigue, I threw myself on the ground, being unable to walk any further. In order to moderate my pace, I bethought myself of taking a book with me. One day I took the *Mercure de France,* and, while reading as I walked, I came upon the subject proposed by the Academy of Dijon as a prize essay for the following year: "Has the progress of the arts and sciences contributed more to the corruption or purification of morals?"

From the moment I read these words, I beheld another world and became another man. Although I have a lively recollection of the impression which they produced upon me, the details have escaped me since I committed them to paper in one of my four letters to M. de Malesherbes. This is one of the peculiarities of my memory which deserves to be mentioned. It only serves me so long as I am dependent upon it. As soon as I commit its contents to paper it forsakes me, and when I have once written a thing down, I completely forget it. This peculiarity follows me even into music. Before I learned it, I knew a number of songs by heart. As soon as I was able to sing from notes, I could not retain a single one in my memory, and I doubt whether I should now be able to repeat, from beginning to end, a single one of those which were my greatest favorites.

What I distinctly remember on this occasion is, that on my arrival at Vincennes I was in a state of agitation bordering upon madness. Diderot perceived it. I told him the reason, and read to him the Prosopopoea of Fabricius,* written in pencil under an oak-tree. He encouraged me to allow my ideas to have full play, and to compete for the prize. I did so, and from that moment I was lost. The misfortunes of the remainder of my life were the inevitable result of this moment of madness.

With inconceivable rapidity, my feelings became elevated to the tone of my ideas. All my petty passions were stifled by the enthusiasm of truth, liberty and virtue; and the most astonishing thing is, that this fervor continued in my heart for more than four or five years, in a higher degree, perhaps, than has ever been the case with the heart of any other man.

I worked at this Discourse in a very curious manner, which I have adopted in almost all my other works. I devoted to it the hours of the night when I was unable to sleep. I meditated in bed with my eyes shut, and turned and re-turned my periods in my head with incredible labor. Then, when I was finally satisfied with them, I stored them up in my memory until I was able to commit them to paper; but the time spent in getting up and dressing myself made me forget everything, and when I sat down in front of my paper I could recall scarcely anything of what I had composed. I conceived the idea of making Madame le Vasseur my

---

Prosopopée de Fabricius: a soliloquy of the famous Roman general, introduced by Rousseau in his essay.

secretary. I had taken lodgings for her, her husband and her daughter, nearer to my own; and she, in order to save me the expense of a servant, came every morning to light my fire and attend to my little wants. When she came, I dictated to her from my bed the result of my labors of the preceding night; and this plan, to which I have long adhered, has saved me from forgetting much.

When the Discourse was finished, I showed it to Diderot, who was pleased with it, and suggested a few corrections. This production, however, although full of warmth and vigor, is altogether destitute of logic and arrangement. Of all the works that have proceeded from my pen, it is the weakest in argument and the poorest in harmony and proportion; but, however great a man's natural talents may be, the art of writing cannot be learnt all at once.

I sent off the work without mentioning it to anyone, with the exception, I fancy, of Grimm, with whom I began to be on most intimate terms after he went to live with the Comte de Frièse. He had a piano, which formed our meeting-place, and at which I spent in his company all my spare moments, singing Italian airs and *barcarolles*, without break or intermission from morning till evening, or, rather, from evening till morning; and whenever I was not to be found at Madame Dupin's I was sure to be found at Grimm's, or, at least, in his company, either on the promenade or at the theatre. I gave up going to the Comédie Italienne, where I had a free pass, but which he did not care for, and paid to go the Comédie Française, of which he was passionately fond. At length I became so powerfully attracted to this young man, and so inseparable from him, that even poor "aunt" was neglected—that is to say, I saw less of her, for my attachment to her has never once wavered during the whole course of my life.

This impossibility of dividing the little spare time I had in accordance with my inclinations, renewed more strongly than ever the desire, which I had long since entertained, of having only one establishment for Thérèse and myself; but the obstacle presented by her numerous family and, above all, want of money to buy furniture, had hitherto prevented me. The opportunity of making an effort to provide a home presented itself, and I seized it. M. de Francueil and Madame Dupin, feeling that 800 or 900 *francs* a year could not be sufficient for me, of their own accord raised my salary to fifty *louis;* and, in addition, Madame Dupin, when she heard that I wanted to furnish my own rooms, gave me some assistance. With the furniture, which Thérèse already had, we put all together, and, having rented some small rooms in the Hôtel de Languedoc, in the Rue de Grenelle-Saint-Honoré, kept by very respectable people, we settled there as comfortably as we could, and we lived there quietly and agreeably for seven years, until I removed to the Hermitage.

Thérèse's father was a good old man, of a very peaceful disposition and terribly afraid of his wife, upon whom he had bestowed the name of

"Criminal Lieutenant,"* which Grimm afterwards jestingly transferred to
the daughter. Madame le Vasseur was not lacking in intelligence, that is to
say, in address; she even prided herself on her politeness and distinguished manners; but she had a confidential, wheedling tone, which was
unendurable to me. She gave her daughter bad advice, tried to make her
dissemble with me, and cajoled my friends separately, at the expense of
one another, and at my own; in other respects, she was a fairly good
mother, because she found it worth her while to be, and she concealed her
daughter's faults, because she profited by them. This woman, whom I
loaded with care, attention, and little presents, and whose affection I was
exceedingly anxious to gain, by reason of my utter inability to succeed,
was the only cause of trouble in my little establishment; for the rest, I can
say that, during these six or seven years, I enjoyed the most perfect
domestic happiness that human weakness can permit. My Thérèse's heart
was that of an angel; intimacy increased our attachment, and we daily felt
more and more how perfectly we were made for each other. If our pleasures could be described, their simplicity would appear ridiculous; our
walks, *tête-à-tête*, outside the city, where I spent my eight or ten *sous*
magnificently in some tavern; our little suppers at the open window, at
which we sat opposite each other on two low chairs placed upon a trunk,
which filled up the breadth of the window-niche. In this position, the
window served us as a table, we breathed the fresh air, we could see the
surrounding country and the passers-by, and, although we were on the
fourth storey, we could look down upon the street while we ate. Who
could describe, who could feel the charm of these meals, at which the
dishes consisted of nothing more than a quartern loaf of coarse bread, a
few cherries, a morsel of cheese, and half a pint of wine, which we shared
between us? Friendship, confidence, intimacy, tranquillity of mind, how
delicious are your seasonings! Sometimes we remained there till mid-
night, without thinking of it or suspecting how late it was, until the old
lady informed us. But let us leave these details, which must appear insipid
or ridiculous. I have always felt and declared, that it is impossible to
describe true enjoyment.

At the same time I indulged in a somewhat coarser enjoyment, the last
of the kind with which I have to reproach myself. I have mentioned that
Klüpfel, the minister, was of an amiable disposition; my relations with
him were nearly as intimate as with Grimm, and became equally confidential. They sometimes shared my table. These meals, somewhat more than
simple, were enlivened by the witty and broad jokes of Klüpfel and the
humorous Germanisms of Grimm, who had not yet become a purist.

Sensuality did not preside at our little orgies; its place was supplied by

---

*Lieutenant Criminel: a former magistrate of the Châtel (the name of two old courts, civil
and criminal) of Paris.

gaiety, and we were so well satisfied with each other that we were unable to separate. Klüpfel had furnished a room for a young girl, who, notwith-standing, was at everybody's disposal, since he was unable to keep her by himself. One evening, as we were entering the *café*, we met him coming out to go and sup with her. We rallied him; he revenged himself gallantly by taking us to share the supper, and then rallied us in turn. The poor creature appeared to me to be of a fairly good disposition, very gentle, and little adapted for her profession, for which an old hag, whom she had with her, dressed her as well as she was able. The conversation and the wine enlivened us to such a degree that we forgot ourselves. The worthy Klüpfel did not desire to do the honors of his table by halves, and all three of us, in turn, went into the adjoining room with the girl, who did not know whether she ought to laugh or cry. Grimm has always declared that he never touched her, and that he remained so long with her simply in order to amuse himself at our impatience. If he really did not touch her, it is not likely that he was prevented by any scruples, since, before going to live with the Comte de Frièse, he lived with some girl in the same quarter of Saint-Roch.

I left the Rue des Moineaux, where this girl lived, feeling as ashamed as Saint-Preux, when he left the house where he had been made drunk, and I had a vivid remembrance of my own story when writing his. Thérèse perceived, from certain indications, and, above all, from my confused air, that I had something to reproach myself with; I relieved my conscience of the burden by making a prompt and frank confession. In this I did well; for, the next morning, Grimm came in triumph to her, to give her an exaggerated account of my offense, and since that time he has never failed spitefully to remind her of it. This was the more inexcusable in him, since I had freely and voluntarily taken him into my confidence and had the right to expect from him that he would not give me cause to repent it. I never felt so much as on this occasion the goodness of my Thérèse's heart, for she was more indignant at Grimm's conduct than offended at my unfaithfulness, and I only had to submit to tender and touching re-proaches on her part, in which I did not detect the slightest trace of anger.

This excellent girl's good-heartedness was equalled by her simplicity of mind. Nothing more need be said; however, I may be permitted to men-tion an example of it, which I recollect. I had told her that Klüpfel was preacher and chaplain to the Prince of Saxe-Gotha. In her estimation a preacher was so extraordinary a person that, oddly confounding two most dissimilar ideas, she got it into her head to take Klüpfel for the Pope. I thought she was mad when she told me, for the first time, on my return home, that the Pope had called to see me. I made her explain herself, and made all haste to go and tell the story to Grimm and Klüpfel, whom we ever afterwards called Pope, and gave the name of Pope Joan to the girl in the Rue des Moineaux. Our laughter was inextinguishable, and almost choked us. Those who have made me say, in a letter which they have been pleased to attribute to me, that I have only laughed twice in my life, were not acquainted with me at that time or in my youthful days; otherwise, this idea would certainly never have occurred to them.

In the following year (1750) I heard that my Discourse, of which I had not thought any more, had gained the prize at Dijon. This news awoke again all the ideas which had suggested it to me, animated them with fresh vigor, and stirred up in my heart the first leavening of virtue and heroism, which my father, my country, and Plutarch had deposited there in my infancy. I considered that nothing could be grander or finer than to be free and virtuous, above considerations of fortune and the opinion of mankind, and completely independent. Although false shame and fear of public disapproval at first prevented me from living in accordance with my principles, and from openly insulting the maxims of my age, from that moment my mind was made up, and I delayed carrying out my intention no longer than was necessary for contradiction to irritate it and render it victorious.

While philosophizing upon the duties of man, an event occurred which made me reflect more seriously upon my own. Thérèse became pregnant for the third time. Too honest towards myself, too proud in my heart to desire to belie my principles by my actions, I began to consider the destination of my children and my connection with their mother, in the light of the laws of nature, justice, and reason, and of that religion—pure, holy and eternal, like its author—which men have polluted, while pretending to be anxious to purify it, and which they have converted, by their formulas, into a mere religion of words, seeing that it costs men little to prescribe what is impossible, when they dispense with carrying it out in practice.

If I was wrong in my conclusions, nothing can be more remarkable than the calmness with which I abandoned myself to them. If I had been one of those low-born men, who are deaf to the gentle voice of Nature, in whose heart no real sentiment of justice or humanity ever springs up, this hardening of my heart would have been quite easy to understand. But is it possible that my warm-heartedness, lively sensibility, readiness to form attachments, the powerful hold which they exercise over me, the cruel heartbreakings I experience when forced to break them off, my natural goodwill towards all my fellow-creatures, my ardent love of the great, the true, the beautiful, and the just; my horror of evil of every kind, my utter inability to hate or injure, or even to think of it; the sweet and lively emotion which I feel at the sight of all that is virtuous, generous, and amiable; is it possible, I ask, that all these can ever agree in the same heart with the depravity which, without the least scruple, tramples underfoot the sweetest of obligations? No! I feel and loudly assert—it is impossible. Never, for a single moment in his life, could Jean-Jacques have been a man without feeling, without compassion, or an unnatural father. I may have been mistaken, never hardened. If I were to state my reasons, I should say too much. Since they were strong enough to mislead me, they might mislead many others, and I do not desire to expose young people, who may read my works, to the danger of allowing themselves to be misled by the same error. I will content myself with observing, that my error was such that, in handing over my children to the State to educate, for want of means to bring them up myself, in deciding to fit them for becoming workmen and peasants rather than adventurers and fortune-hunters, I thought that I was behaving like a citizen and a father, and considered myself a member of Plato's Republic. More than once since then, the regrets of my heart have told me that I was wrong; but, far from my reason having given me the same information, I have often blessed Heaven for having preserved them from their father's lot, and from the lot which threatened them as soon as I should have been obliged to abandon them. If I had left them with Madame d'Epinay or Madame de Luxembourg, who, from friendship, generosity, or some other motive, expressed themselves willing to take charge of them, would they have been happier, would they have been brought up at least as honest men? I do not know; but I do know that they would have been brought up to hate, perhaps to betray, their parents; it is a hundred times better that they have never known them.

My third child was accordingly taken to the Foundling Hospital, like the other two. The two next were disposed of in the same manner, for I had five altogether. This arrangement appeared to me so admirable, so rational, and so legitimate, that, if I did not openly boast of it, this was solely out of regard for the mother; but I told all who were acquainted with our relations. I told Grimm and Diderot. I afterwards informed Madame d'Epinay, and, later, Madame de Luxembourg, freely and voluntarily, without being in any way obliged to do so, and when I might easily have kept it a secret from everybody; for Gouin was an honourable woman, very discreet, and a person upon whom I could implicitly rely. The only one of my friends to whom I had any interest in unbosoming myself was M. Thierry, the physician who attended my poor "aunt" in a dangerous confinement. In a word, I made no mystery of what I did, not only because I have never known how to keep a secret from my friends, but because I really saw no harm in it. All things considered, I chose for my children what was best, or, at least, what I believed to be best for them. I could have wished, and still wish, that I had been reared and brought up as they have been.

While I was thus making my confessions, Madame le Vasseur on her part did the same, but with less disinterested views. I had introduced her and her daughter to Madame Dupin, who, out of friendship for me, did them a thousand kindnesses. The mother confided her daughter's secret to her. Madame Dupin, who is good-hearted and generous, whom she never told how attentive I was to provide for everything, in spite of my moderate means, herself made provision for her with a generosity which, by her mother's instructions, the daugher always kept a secret from me during my stay in Paris, and only confessed to me at the Hermitage, after several other confidences. I did not know that Madame Dupin, who never gave me the least hint of it, was so well informed. Whether Madame de Chenonceaux, her daughter-in-law, was equally well informed, I do not know; but Madame de Francueil, her step-daughter, was, and was unable to hold her tongue. She spoke to me about it the following year, after I had left their house. This induced me to address a letter to her on this subject, which will be found in my collections, in which I have set forth those reasons for my conduct, which I was able to give without compromising Madame le Vasseur and her family, for the most decisive of them came from that quarter, and upon them I kept silence.

I can rely upon the discretion of Madame Dupin and the friendship of Madame de Chenonceaux; I felt equally sure in regard to Madame de Francueil, who, besides, died long before my secret was noised abroad. It could only have been disclosed by those very people to whom I had confided it, and, in fact, it was not until after I had broken with them, that it was so disclosed. By this single fact they are judged. Without desiring to acquit myself of the blame which I deserve, I would rather have it upon my shoulders than that which their malice deserves. My fault is great, but it was due to error; I have neglected my duties, but the desire of doing an injury never entered my heart, and the feelings of a father cannot speak very eloquently on behalf of children whom he has never seen; but, to betray the confidence of friendship, to violate the most sacred of all agreements, to disclose secrets poured into our bosoms, deliberately to dishonor the friend whom one has deceived, and who still alone with her, solemnly teaching her arithmetic, and wearying her with my everlasting figures, without ever uttering a single word of gallantry or casting a glance of admiration upon her. Five or six years later, I should have been neither so wise nor so foolish; but it was destined that I should only love truly once in my life, and that the first and last sighs of my heart should be given to another than her.

Since I had lived at Madame Dupin's, I had always been satisfied with my lot, without showing any desire to see it improved. The increase in my salary, due to her and M. de Francueil together, was quite voluntary on their part. This year, M. de Francueil, whose friendship for me increased daily, wanted to make my position somewhat more comfortable and less precarious. He was Receiver-General of Finance. M. Dudoyer, his cashier, was old, well to do, and anxious to retire. M. de Francueil offered me his place; and, in order to make myself fit to take it, I went for a few weeks to M. Dudoyer's house, to receive the necessary instructions. But, whether it was that I had little talent for this occupation, or that Dudoyer, who seemed to me to have someone else in his eye as his successor, did not instruct me in good faith, my acquisition of the knowledge required was slow and unsatisfactory, and I was never able to get into my head the state of accounts, which perhaps had been purposely muddled. However, without having grasped the intricacies of the business, I soon acquired sufficient knowledge of its ordinary routine to undertake the general management. I even commenced its duties. I kept the ledgers and the cash; I paid and received money, and gave receipts; and although I had as little inclination as ability for such employment, advancing years made me more sensible: I determined to overcome my dislike, and to devote myself entirely to my duties. Unfortunately, just as I was beginning to get used to them, M. de Francueil went away on a short journey, during which I remained in charge of his cash, which at that time, however, did not amount to more than 25,000 or 30,000 francs. The care and anxiety which this deposit caused me convinced me that I was not made for a cashier, and I have no doubt that the impatience with which I awaited his return contributed to the illness which subsequently attacked me.

I have already mentioned, in the first part of this work, that I was almost dead when I was born. A defective formation of the bladder caused, during my childhood, an almost continual retention of urine; and my aunt Suzon, who took care of me, had the greatest difficulty in keeping me alive. However, she at length succeeded: my robust constitution at length gained the upper hand, and my health improved so much during my youth that, with the exception of the attack of langor which I have described, and the frequent necessity of making water, which the least heating of the blood always rendered a matter of difficulty, I reached the age of thirty without feeling my early infirmity at all. The first touch of it which I had was on my arrival at Venice. The fatigue of the journey, and the fearful heat which I had suffered, brought on a constant desire to make water and an affection of the kidneys, which lasted till the beginning of the winter. After my visit to the *padoana*, I looked upon myself as a dead man, and yet I never suffered the slightest inconvenience from it. After having exhausted myself more in imagination than in reality for my Zulietta, I was in better health than ever. It was only after Diderot's imprisonment that the overheating, caused by my journeys to Vincennes during the fearful heat, brought on a violent pain in the kidneys, and since that time I have never recovered my health completely.

At the time of which I am speaking, having perhaps overtired myself with my distasteful work at the confounded office, I became worse than before, and was confined to my bed for five or six weeks in the most melancholy condition that can be imagined. Madame Dupin sent the celebrated Morand to see me, who, in spite of his cleverness and delicacy of touch, caused me incredible suffering, and could never get to probe me. He advised me to consult Daran, who managed to introduce his bougies, which were more flexible, and afforded me some relief; but, when giving Madame Dupin an account of my condition, he declared that I had less than six months to live.

This verdict, which I afterwards heard, caused me to reflect seriously upon my condition, and upon the folly of sacrificing the repose and comfort of my few remaining days to the slavery of an employment for which I felt nothing but aversion. Besides, how could I reconcile the strict principles which I had just adopted with a situation which harmonized so ill with them? Would it not have been very bad taste in me, cashier of a Receiver-General of Finance, to preach disinterestedness and poverty? These ideas fermented so strongly in my head together with the fever, and combined so powerfully, that from that time nothing could uproot them, and, during the period of my recovery, I quietly determined to carry out the resolutions which I had made during my delirium. I renounced for ever all plans of fortune and promotion. Resolved to pass my few remaining days in poverty and independence, I employed all my strength of mind in breaking away from the bonds of the opinion of the world, and in courageously carrying out everything which appeared to me to be right, without troubling myself about what the world might think of it. The obstacles which I had to overcome, the efforts which I made to triumph over them, are incredible. I succeeded as much as was possible, and more than I had myself hoped. If I had been as successful in shaking off the yoke of friendship as that of public opinion, I should have accomplished my purpose, perhaps the greatest, or, at any rate, the most conducive to virtue, that a mortal has ever conceived; but, while I trampled underfoot the senseless judgments of the common herd of the so-called great and wise, I suffered myself to be subjugated and led like a child by so-called friends, who, jealous of seeing me strike out a new path by myself, thought of nothing but how to make me appear ridiculous, and began by doing their utmost to degrade me, in order to raise on outcry against me. It was the change in my character, dating from this period, rather than my literary celebrity, that drew their jealousy upon me; they would perhaps have forgiven me for distinguishing myself in the art of writing; but they could not forgive me for setting an example, in my change of life, which seemed likely to cause them inconvenience. I was born for friendship; my easy and gentle disposition found no difficulty in cherishing it. As long as I was unknown to the world, I was loved by all who knew me, and had not a single enemy; but, as soon as I became known, I had not a single friend. This was a great misfortune; it was a still greater one that I was surrounded by people who called themselves my friends, and who only made use of the privileges which this name allowed them to drag me to my ruin. The sequel of these memoirs will reveal this odious intrigue; at present I only point out its origin; my readers will soon see the first link forged.

In the state of independence in which I intended to live, it was necessary, however, to find means of subsistence. I bethought myself of a very simple plan: copying music at so much a page. If a more solid employment would have fulfilled the same end, I should have adopted it; but as I had taste and ability for this, and as it was the only occupation which would provide my daily bread without personal dependence, I was satisfied with it. Believing that I no longer had need of foresight, and silencing the voice of vanity, from cashier to a financier I became a copyist of music. I thought I had gained greatly by the choice, and I have so little regretted it, that I have never abandoned this employment except under compulsion, and then only to resume it as soon as I was able.

The success of my first Discourse made it easier for me to carry out this resolution. After it had gained the prize, Diderot undertook to get it printed. While I was in bed he wrote me a note, informing me of its publication and the effect it had produced. "It has gone up like a rocket," he told me; "such a success has never been seen before." This voluntary approval of the public, in the case of an unknown author, gave me the first real assurance of my ability, as to which, in spite of my inner feelings, I had until then always been doubtful. I saw the great advantage I might derive from it in view of the resolution which I was on the point of carrying out, and I judged that a copyist of some literary celebrity would not be likely to suffer from want of work.

As soon as my resolution was taken and confirmed, I wrote a note to M. de Francueil to inform him of it, thanking him and Madame Dupin for all their kindness, and asking for their custom. Francueil, quite unable to understand the note, and believing that I was still delirious, came to me in all haste, but he found my mind so firmly made up that he was unable to shake my resolution. He went and told Madame Dupin and everyone else that I had gone mad. I let him do so, and went my way. I began my reformation with my dress. I gave up my gold lace and white stockings, and put on a round wig. I took off my sword and sold my watch, saying to myself with incredible delight, "Thank Heaven, I shall not want to know the time again!"

On the Sciences and the Arts
A Discourse on the Question Posed by the Academy of Dijon

"Has the revival of the sciences and the arts contributed to the improvement or the corruption of morals?"

It was by this species of cultivation which is all the more captivating as it seems less affected, that Athens and Rome were so distinguished in the ages of their splendor and magnificence: and it is doubtless by the same means that our own age and nation will distinguish itself above all those of antiquity. A philosophical precision without pedantry; a culture free from affectation, equally distant from the rusticity of the Germans and the buffoonery of the Italians; these are the effects in France today of a taste acquired by liberal studies, and improved by conversation with the world. How happy would it be to live among us, if our external appearances were always a picture of the inward disposition of our hearts; if decorum were virtue; if the principles we professed were the rules of our conduct; and if real philosophy were inseparable from the title of a philosopher! But so many good qualities seldom go together; virtue delights not in so much pomp. A superb dress may denote opulence; elegance a man of taste; but the truly healthy and robust are known by different indications. It is under the rustic habit of a laborer, and not beneath the lace or embroidery of a courtier, that we should look for bodily strength and activity. Exterior ornaments are no less foreign to virtue, which is the strength and activity of the soul. The man of probity is an athlete who loves to combat his adversary naked; he despises those paltry trappings which prevent the exertion of his strength, and were for the most part invented only to conceal some deformity.

It is a noble and beautiful prospect to see man, rising by his own efforts out of nothing, and dissipating by the light of reason that darkness with which nature enveloped him; to see him raise himself in imagination beyond his native sphere; penetrating the celestial regions, and, like the sun, encompassing, with giant strides the vast extent of the universe: To behold him again descending to himself—a task still more noble and difficult—there to investigate his own nature and faculties, and so discover the design of his creation and his duty to his fellow creatures. The operation of all these marvels has been renewed within a few generations.

Europe had relapsed into the barbarism of primitive times. The inhabitants of that part of the world which is at present so greatly enlightened, long lived in a state even worse than that of ignorance. A scientific jargon, more despicable than ignorance, had usurped the name of learning, and formed an almost invincible obstacle to its restoration.

Things had arrived at such a pass, that it required a total revolution in men's ideas, to bring them back again to commonsense. This was at length brought about by those from which it was least expected. It was the ignorant Moslem, that perpetual scourge of letters, who was the immediate cause of their revival among us. The fall of the throne of Constantine carried into Italy the ruins of ancient Greece, with which precious spoils France in her turn was enriched.

Man is subject to intellectual as well as to corporeal needs. The latter constitute the fabric of society, and the former the ornaments of it. So long as government and the laws provide for the security and happiness of a people, the arts and sciences, less despotic though perhaps more powerful, conceal the iron chains of slavery under a garland of flowers. They stifle in the breasts of men that sense of liberty for the enjoyment of which they seem to have been born; and, by making them love their slavery, form what is called a cultured people.

Before art had polished our manners, and taught our passions to speak the language of affectation, our manners were rude but natural; a difference in behavior proclaimed at first sight a difference of character. Human nature was not in itself better; but men found their security in the ease of knowing each other's character: and this advantage, of which we know not the value, saved them from many vices.

At present, more subtle researches and a more refined taste, have reduced the art of pleasing to a common system. Hence it is that a servile and fallacious conformity prevails in modern manners; so that one would think our minds were all cast in the same mold. Politeness requires this thing, decorum that; ceremony has its forms, and fashion its laws, by which we are constantly prevented from following the dictates of our own spirit or understanding. We no longer dare to appear what we really are, but live under a perpetual constraint; in this throng of mankind, which we call the world, all act under the same circumstances exactly alike, unless some very particular and powerful motives prevent them. For this reason, we are ever at a loss to know a man's true character; and, even to know one's friend, one must wait for some crisis to prove his friendship; that is, until it is too late; as it is just on those occasions that such knowledge is of any use to us.

What a train of vices must necessarily attend this uncertainty! Sincere friendship, real esteem, and perfect confidence are banished from among men: while umbrage, suspicion, fear, coldness, reserve, hatred, and betrayal lie constantly concealed under that uniform and deceitful veil of politeness, that false candor and urbanity, which we owe to the superior culture of this enlightened age. Oaths and imprecations have become vulgar, and the name of our Creator is no longer profaned in polite company, whose delicate ears are nevertheless not in the least offended by the worst blasphemy. We are grown too modest to boast our own merit, but scruple not to enhance it by derogating from that of others. We do not rudely attack even our enemies, but artfully calumniate them. Our prejudices against other nations diminish, but so at the same time does our love for our own country. A despicable ignorance has given way to a dangerous skepticism. Some vices indeed are condemned, and others grown unfashionable; but we still have many that are honored with the name of virtues, and it has become necessary that we should either have, or at least affect to have them.

Such is the purity which our morals have acquired; thus it is that we have become virtuous. Let the arts and sciences reclaim the share they have had in this salutary work. To this I shall add but one reflection more; which is this, that if an inhabitant of some distant country should endeavor to form an idea of European morals from the state of our sciences, the perfection of our arts, the decorum of our public entertainments, the politeness of our behavior, the affability of our speech, our constant professions of benevolence, and from those tumultuous assemblies of people of all ranks that appear from morning till night eager to oblige each other; such a stranger, I say, would believe our system of morals to be totally contrary to what it really is.

Where there is no apparent effect, it is idle to look for a cause: but here the effect is certain: depravity is manifest and our minds have been corrupted· in the same proportion as our arts and sciences have been improved. Will it be said, that this is a misfortune peculiar to the present age? No, the evils resulting from our vain curiosity have developed with our world. The daily ebbing and flowing of the tides are not more regularly influenced by the moon than are the morals of a people by the progress of the arts and sciences. Virtue has disappeared in proportion as their light has been displayed above the horizon, and the same phenomenon has been observed in all times and in all places.

Turn your eyes to Egypt, the first school of mankind; that ancient country, famous for its fertility under a burning sky; the place from which Sesostris set out in his expedition to conquer the world. Egypt became the mother of philosophy and the fine arts; soon after which it was conquered by Cambyses, and then successively by the Greeks, the Romans, the Arabs, and finally the Turks.

Let us next look at Greece, once peopled by heroes who twice made themselves masters of Asia. Education, as yet in its infancy, had not corrupted the character of its inhabitants; but the progress of the sciences led to a dissoluteness of manners and then to the imposition of the Macedonian yoke: from which time Greece, at once learned, voluptuous and enslaved, experienced nothing better than a change of masters in any of its revolutions. Even the eloquence of Demosthenes himself could not revive a body enervated by luxury and the arts.

It was not till the days of Ennius and Terence that Rome, founded by a shepherd and rendered illustrious by farmers, began to degenerate. But after the appearance of an Ovid, a Catullus, a Martial, and the rest of those numerous obscene authors, whose very names are sufficient to put modesty to the blush, Rome, which had been the temple of virtue, became the theatre of vice, the disgrace among nations, and the toy of barbarians. Thus the capital of the world at length submitted to the yoke of the slavery it had once imposed on others; the day of its fall was the eve of the day when it conferred on one of its citizens the title of umpire in subjects of taste.

But why should we look to past ages, for proofs of a truth of which the present affords us ample evidence? There is a vast empire in Asia, in which the paths of literature lead to the first and most honorable employments in the state. If the sciences improved our morals, if they inspired us with courage and taught us to lay down our lives for the good of our country, the Chinese would be a wise, free, and invincible people. But, if there is hardly a vice which they do not practice, if there is hardly a crime with which they are not familiar, if neither the sagacity of their ministers, the pretended wisdom of their laws, nor the multitude of inhabitants who people that vast empire, could preserve them from the subjection to the yoke of the rude and ignorant Tartars, of what use were all their men of science and literature?

Let us consider, by way of contrast the morals of those few nations who, being preserved from the contagion of useless knowledge, have by their virtues become happy in themselves and afford a shining example to others. Such were the first inhabitants of Persia, a nation so singular that virtue was taught them in the same manner as the sciences are taught us. They subdued Asia with great ease, and they achieved the singular glory of having the history of their political institutions read by posterity as a philosophical romance. Such were the Scythians, of whom are transmitted from antiquity such high praises. Such were the early Germanic peoples, whose simplicity, innocence, and virtue, delighted the historian Tacitus, when he was wearied with describing the crimes and villanies of an enlightened, opulent, and voluptuous people. Such had been even Rome itself in the days of its poverty and ignorance.

It is not through stupidity that rustic peoples have preferred other exercises to those of the intellect. They were not unaware that in other countries there were idle men who spent their time disputing about the sovereign good, and about vice and virtue. They knew also that these proud reasoners, so lavish in praising themselves, indiscriminately stigmatized other nations with the contemptuous name of Barbarians. But they studied the morals of of those cultured people, and came to disdain their learning.

Can it be forgotten that in the very heart of Greece there arose a city as famous for the happy ignorance of its inhabitants, as for the wisdom of its laws; a republic of demi-gods rather than of men, so greatly superior seemed their virtues to those of mere humanity! O Sparta, you put to shame the vanity of science; and while the vices, which accompany the fine arts, were introduced with them into Athens, even as its tyrant was carefully collecting the works of the prince of poets, you banished from your walls at once the artists and the arts, the learned and their learning.

This difference of policy produced its effects. Athens became the seat of politeness and taste, the country of orators and philosophers. The elegance of its buildings was equal to that of its language; and on every side could be seen marble and canvas worked by the hands of the most skilful artists. It is from Athens that we derive those astonishing works which will serve as models to all succeeding corrupted ages. The picture of Lacedaemonia is not so brilliant.

Of Sparta, the neighboring nations observed, that "men were born virtuous, the air itself seeming to inspire them with virtue." But all its inhabitants have left us is the memory of their heroic actions; things that should be esteemed more valuable than the most remarkable relics of Athenian art.

It is true that among the Athenians there were some few wise men who withstood the general torrent, and preserved their integrity even in the company of the muses. But let us listen to the judgment which the first, and most unhappy of them, passed on the artists and scholars of his time:

"I have examined the poets," says he, "and I look upon them as people whose talents deceive both themselves and others: they give themselves out for wise men, and are taken for such; but in reality they are fools."

"From poets," continues Socrates, "I turned to the artists. Nobody was more ignorant of the arts than I; and nobody was more fully persuaded that the artists possessed amazing knowledge. I soon discovered, however, that their situation was no better than that of the poets; both the one and the other had the same illusion of their own wisdom.

"We know none of us, neither the sophists, the poets, the orators, the artists, nor myself, in what consists the true, the good, or the beautiful. But there is this difference between us; that, though none of these people know anything, they all believe they know something, whereas for my part, if I know nothing, I do not doubt my own ignorance. So all the superiority of wisdom once imputed to me by the oracle, is reduced merely to my being fully convinced that I am ignorant of what I do not know."

Thus we find Socrates, the wisest of men in the opinion of an oracle, and the most learned of all the Athenians in the opinion of all Greece, praising ignorance. Were he now alive also, there is little reason to think that our modern scholars and artists would induce him to change his mind. No, that honest philosopher would still persist in despising our vain sciences. He would not help to swell the tide of books that flows in upon us from all quarters; he would leave us only, as he did to his disciples, the example and the memory of his virtues; the noblest method of instructing mankind.

Socrates began at Athens, and the elder Cato continued in Rome, to inveigh against those seductive and subtle Greeks who corrupted the virtue and diminished the courage of their fellow-citizens. The arts and sciences and disputation, however, again prevailed. Rome abounded with philosophers and orators, while its military discipline was neglected, agriculture was held in contempt, and patriotism gave place to the formation of factions. The sacred names of liberty, self-sacrifice, and obedience to the laws gave way to the names of the founders of particular sects, such as Epicurus, Zeno, and Arcesilas. It was even a saying among their own philosophers, that "their men of learning had eclipsed their men of honour." Before that time the Romans were satisfied with the practice of virtue; they were undone when they began to study its theory.

What would the great soul of Fabricius have felt, if to his misfortune he had been called back to life, on seeing the pomp and magnificence of that Rome, which his arm had saved from ruin, and his great name rendered more illustrious than all its conquests. Ye gods! (he would have said) what has become of those thatched roofs and rustic hearths which were formerly the dwelling place of temperance and virtue? What fatal splendor has succeeded the ancient Roman simplicity? What is this strange language, this effeminacy of manners? What is the use of these statues, paintings, and fine buildings? Foolish people, what have you done? You, who are lords and masters of the earth, have made yourselves slaves to the frivolous nations you have subdued. Are you content to be governed by talkers and rhetoricians? Has it been only to enrich architects, painters, sculptors and actors, that you have shed so much blood in the conquest of Greece and Asia? Are the spoils of Carthage the wages of a flute-player? Romans! Romans! hasten to demolish those amphitheatres; break to pieces those marble statues; burn those paintings; drive from among you those slaves who keep you in subjection, and whose fatal arts have corrupted your morals. Let others render themselves illustrious by such vain talents; the only talent worthy of Rome is that of conquering the world, and extending the empire of virtue.

But let us leap across the distance of time and place, and examine what has happened in our own experience and country; or rather let us turn aside from those odious scenes that may offend our delicacy, and spare ourselves the pain of repeating the same things under different names. It was not in vain that I invoked the shade of Fabricius, for what have I put into his mouth that might not have come with as much propriety from Louis XII or Henri IV of France? It is true, that in France, Socrates would not have been compelled to drink hemlock; but he would have swallowed a potion infinitely more bitter, the most insulting ridicule and contempt a hundred times worse than death.

Thus it is that luxury, profligacy and slavery have been, in all ages the penalty for our ambitious endeavors to quit that happy state of ignorance in which the wisdom of Providence had placed us. That thick veil with which Providence covered all its operations ought to be a sufficient warning that it never designed us to search for knowledge.

These reflections are undoubtedly mortifying to the pride of human nature. What! will it be said, is probity the child of ignorance? Is virtue incompatible with science? How fatal are the conclusions that flow from such propositions? And yet to reconcile these apparent contradictions, we need only examine the emptiness and vanity of those pompous titles which impress us and are so liberally bestowed on human knowledge. Let us consider, therefore, the arts and sciences in themselves. Let us see what must result from their progress.

An ancient tradition passed from Egypt into Greece, according to which a god who was an enemy of the repose of mankind was the inventor of the sciences. What must have been the opinion of the Egyptians, then, with whom the sciences first took life; they who beheld, at a shorter distance, the sources from whence they sprung? In fact, whether we turn to the annals of the world, or substitute philosophical investigations for the uncertain chronicles of history, we shall not find the origin of human knowledge corresponding to the idea we are fond of entertaining of it. Astronomy was born of superstition; eloquence of ambition, hatred, falsehood, and flattery; geometry of avarice; physics of an idle curiosity; and moral philosophy, like all the rest, of human pride. Thus the arts and sciences owe their birth to our vices; we should be less doubtful of their advantages, if they had sprung from our virtues.

The defect of their origin is, indeed, all too plainly seen in their objects. What would become of the arts if they were not cherished by luxury? If men were not unjust, what would be the use of jurisprudence? What would become of history, if there were no tyrants, wars, or conspiracies? In a word, who would want to pass his life in barren speculations, if everybody, attentive only to the duties of humanity and the needs of nature, employed themselves solely in serving their country, obliging their friends, and relieving the unfortunate? Are we then destined, it may be asked, to live and die on the brink of that well where truth lies hidden at the bottom? This reflection alone is, in my opinion, enough to discourage, from the start, any man who seriously seeks to instruct himself by the study of philosophy.

What a variety of dangers surround us! What a number of false paths present themselves in the investigation of the sciences! Through how many errors, more perilous than truth is useful, must we not pass to reach the truth! The disadvantages we lie under are evident, for the false is capable of an infinite variety of combinations; while the truth has only one simple way of being such. Besides, where is the man who sincerely desires to find it? Or even admitting his good will, by what characteristic marks is he sure to know it? Amidst that infinite diversity of opinions which prevail in the world, where is the criterion by which he may certainly judge of it? Again, what is still more difficult, if we should even be fortunate enough to discover the truth, which of us knows how to make a proper use of it?

If our sciences are futile in the objects they propose, they are no less dangerous in the effects they produce. Being themselves the effect of indolence, they generate idleness in turn, and an irreparable loss of time is the first harm they do to society. To fail to do good is a great evil in the political as well as in the moral world; and a useless citizen should be regarded as a pernicious member of society.

We cannot reflect on the morals of mankind, without contemplating with pleasure the simplicity which prevailed in primitive ages. This picture may be justly compared to that of a beautiful coast, adorned by the hands of nature alone towards which our eyes are constantly turned, but from which we perceive ourselves to moving with reluctance. When men were innocent and virtuous, they loved to have the gods as witnesses of their actions, and they dwelt with their gods in the same crude habitations; but when they became vicious, they grew tired of such inconvenient spectators, and banished the gods to magnificent temples. At length, indeed, they expelled their deities even from these; at any rate the temples of the gods ceased to be more magnificent than the palaces of the citizens. This was the height of depravity; nor could vices ever be carried a greater length than when they were seen supported, as it were, on columns of marble and engraven on Corinthian capitals at the doors of great men's houses.

As the conveniences of life increase, the arts are brought to perfection, and luxury prevails; true courage flags; military virtues disappear; and this again is the effect of the sciences, and of those arts which are exercised in the obscurity of the study. When the Goths ravaged Greece, the libraries escaped the flames merely from an opinion propagated among them, that it was foolish to divest the enemy of those means which diverted their attention from military exercises, and kept them engaged in indolent and sedentary occupations.

The Romans confessed that military virtue diminished among them in proportion as they began to be connoisseurs in painting, sculpture, and the rest of the fine arts. And as if this celebrated country was to be for ever an example to other nations, the revival of letters in Florence once again demolished, perhaps for ever, the martial reputation which Italy seemed a few centuries ago to have recovered.

Again, if the cultivation of the sciences is prejudicial to military achievement, it is still more so to moral qualities. Hence an absurd method of education serves, even from our infancy, to improve our wit and corrupt our understanding. We see today, on every side, great schools where the young are educated at a great expense, and taught everything except their duty. Your sons are kept ignorant of their own language, while they are taught to speak others that are nowhere in use. In like manner they learn to make verses which they can hardly understand; and, without being capable of distinguishing truth from error, they are taught the art of disguising both to others by dialectical sophistry. But as for magnanimity, equity, temperance, humanity, courage, these are words of which they know not the meaning. The pleasing name of patriot never reaches their ears; and if they ever hear of God it is to hear Him represented as an object of terror rather than of reverence. I well know that children ought to be occupied, and that idleness is for them of a danger to be feared. But what should they be employed about? What should they be taught? This is undoubtedly an important question. Let them be taught what they are to practice when they come to be men; not what they are to forget before they come to man's estate.

Our gardens are embellished with statues and our galleries with pictures. What do you imagine these masterpieces of art, thus exhibited to public admiration, represent? The great men who have defended our country, or the still greater men who have enriched it by their virtues? No, they present extravagant images of loose desires and perverted understandings, carefully selected from ancient mythology, and shown to the early curiosity of our children, doubtless in order that they may see models of vicious actions before they have learned to read the history of them.

The question is no longer: 'Is he a man of honesty?' but, 'Is he a man of ingenuity?' We ask not of a book, whether it is useful, but whether it is well written? Prizes are lavished on wit and cleverness, while virtue is left to its own reward. Numerous are the honors awarded for fine writing, none for good actions.

A wise man does not run after the gifts of fortune; but he is by no means indifferent to glory, and when he sees it so ill distributed in the world, his virtue, which might have been animated by a little emulation, and rendered advantageous to society, droops and dies away in obscurity and indigence. This comes about when the pleasing arts are preferred to the useful, something which has been all too well confirmed since the revival of the arts and sciences. We have natural philosophers, geometricians, chemists, astronomers, poets, musicians, and painters in plenty: but we have no longer a true patriot amongst us; or if there be found a few dispersed up and down the country, they are left to perish in their rustic poverty unnoticed and neglected. Such is the situation to which we are reduced: and such are our sentiments with regard to those who give us our daily bread and afford us nourishment for our children.

But if the progress of the arts and sciences has added nothing to our real happiness; if, on the contrary, it has corrupted our morals, and if that corruption has vitiated our taste; what are we to think of the herd of those popular authors who have removed those impediments which nature purposely laid in the way to the temple of the muses, in order to test the strength of those who might be tempted to seek knowledge? What shall we think also of those compilers of books who have indiscreetly opened a door to the sciences, and have introduced into their sanctuary a populace unworthy to approach it, when it was greatly to be wished that all who should be found incapable of making progress in the sciences should be repulsed at the outset, and thereby induced to apply themselves to employments more beneficial to society? A man who remains all his life-time a poor versifier, or a second-rate geometrician, might have made nevertheless an excellent clothier. Those whom nature intended to be scholars, have no need of a master. Francis Bacon, Descartes and Newton, those preceptors of mankind, had no preceptors themselves. What guide could indeed have conducted them so far as their sublime genius directed? Ordinary masters would only have cramped their abilities, by confining them within the narrow limits of their own. It was from the obstacles they met with at first that they learned to exert themselves, and thence to traverse the vast space they covered. If it be proper for some men to study the arts and sciences, it is only for those who perceive themselves strong enough to go forward alone on their own resources. It belongs only to these happy few, to erect monuments of glory to the human understanding. But if we wish nothing to be above their genius, nothing should be beyond their hopes. This is the only encouragement they require. The soul insensibly adapts itself to the objects on which it is employed, and thus it is that great occasions have always produced great men. Cicero, the greatest orator in the world was Consul of Rome, and Francis Bacon perhaps the greatest philosopher, was Lord Chancellor of England. Can it be imagined, that if the former had been a professor at a university, and the latter a pensioner of an academy; can it be imagined, I say, that in such circumstances their works would not have suffered from their situation? Let princes not disdain to admit into their councils those who are the most capable of advising them well. Let them renounce that antiquated prejudice, originally arising from the ambition of the great, that the art of governing mankind is more difficult than that of instructing them, as if it were easier to induce men to do good voluntarily than to compel them to do it by force. Let the learned of the first rank in merit find an honorable place in their courts; let them there enjoy the only recompense they deserve, that of promoting by their influence the happiness of a people whom they have enlightened by their wisdom. Only then are we likely to see what virtue, science and power can do, when animated by the noblest emulation, and working for the happiness of mankind.

As for us, ordinary men, on whom heaven has not been pleased to bestow great talents; since we are not destined to reap such glory, let us be content to remain in obscurity. Let us not covet a reputation we shall never attain; and which, in the present state of things, would never make up to us for the trouble it would cost, even if we were qualified to obtain it. Why should we build our happiness on the opinions of others, when we possess a solid foundation for it in our own breasts? Let us leave to others the task of instructing mankind in their duty, and confine ourselves to the doing of our own. We need no greater knowledge than this.

Discourse on the Origin of Inequality

The first man who, having enclosed a piece of land, thought of saying "This is mine" and found people simple enough to believe him, was the true founder of civil society. How many crimes, wars, murders; how much misery and horror the human race would have been spared if someone had pulled up the stakes and filled in the ditch and cried out to his fellow men: "Beware of listening to this impostor. You are lost if you forget that the fruits of the earth belong to everyone and that the earth itself belongs to no one!" But it is highly probable that by this time things had reached a point beyond which they could not go on as they were; for the idea of property, depending on many prior ideas which could only have arisen in successive stages, was not formed all at once in the human mind. It was necessary for men to make much progress, to acquire much industry and knowledge, to transmit and increase it from age to age, before arriving at this final stage of the state of nature. Let us therefore look farther back, and try to review from a single perspective the slow succession of events and discoveries in their most natural order.

Man's first feeling was that of his existence, his first concern was that of his preservation. The products of the earth furnished all the necessary aids; instinct prompted him to make use of them. While hunger and other appetites made him experience in turn different modes of existence, there was one appetite which urged him to perpetuate his own species: and this blind impulse, devoid of any sentiment of the heart, produced only a purely animal act. The need satisfied, the two sexes recognized each other no longer, and even the child meant nothing to the mother, as soon as he could do without her.

Such was the condition of nascent man; such was the life of an animal limited at first to mere sensation; and scarcely profiting from the gifts bestowed on him by nature, let alone was he dreaming of wresting anything from her. But difficulties soon presented themselves and man had to learn to overcome them. The height of trees, which prevented him from reaching their fruits; the competition of animals seeking to nourish themselves on the same fruits; the ferocity of animals who threatened his life—all this obliged man to apply himself to bodily exercises; he had to make himself agile, fleet of foot, and vigorous in combat. Natural weapons—branches of trees and stones—were soon found to be at hand. He learned to overcome the obstacles of nature, to fight when necessary against other animals, to struggle for his subsistence even against other men, or to indemnify himself for what he was forced to yield to the stronger.

To the extent that the human race spread, men's difficulties multiplied with their numbers. Differences between soils, climates, and seasons would have forced men to adopt different ways of life. Barren years, long hard winters, scorching summers consuming everything, demanded new industry from men. Along the sea coast and river banks they invented the hook and line to become fishermen and fish eaters. In the forests they made bows and arrows, and became hunters and warriors. In cold countries they covered themselves with the skins of the beasts they killed. Lightning, a volcano, or some happy accident introduced them to fire—a fresh resource against the rigor of winter. They learned to conserve this element, then to reproduce it, and finally to use it to cook the meats they had previously eaten raw.

This repeated employment of entities distinct from himself and distinct from each other must naturally have engendered in men's minds the perception of certain relationships. Those relationships which we express by the words "large," "small," "strong," "weak," "fast," "slow," "fearful," "bold," and other similar ideas, compared when necessary and almost unthinkingly, finally produced in him some kind of reflection, or rather a mechanical prudence which would indicate to him the precautions most necessary for his safety.

The new knowledge which resulted from this development increased his superiority over other animals by making him conscious of it. He practiced setting snares for them; he outwitted them in a thousand ways, and though many animals might surpass him in strength of combat or in speed of running, he became in time the master of those that might serve him and the scourge of those that might hurt him. Thus the first look he directed into himself provoked his first stirring of pride; and while hardly as yet knowing how to distinguish between ranks, he asserted the priority of his species, and so prepared himself from afar to claim priority for himself as an individual.

Although his fellow men were not to him what they are to us, and although he had hardly any more dealings with them than he had with other animals, they were not forgotten in his observations. The resemblances which he learned with time to discern between them, his female and himself, led him to think of others which he did not actually perceive; and seeing that they all behaved as he himself would behave in similar circumstances, he concluded that their manner of thinking and feeling entirely matched his own; and this important truth, once well rooted in his mind, made him follow, by an intuition as sure as logic and more prompt, the best rules of conduct it was suitable to observe towards them for the sake of his own advantage and safety.

Instructed by experience that love of one's own wellbeing is the sole motive of human action, he found himself in a position to distinguish the rare occasions when common interest justified his relying on the aid of his fellows, and those even rarer occasions when competition should make him distrust them. In the first case, he united with them in a herd, or at most in a sort of free association that committed no one and which lasted only as long as the passing need which had brought it into being. In the second case, each sought to grasp his own advantage, either by sheer force, if he believed he had the strength, or by cunning and subtlety if he felt himself to be the weaker.

In this way men could have gradually acquired some crude idea of mutual commitments, and of the advantages of fulfilling them; but only so far as present and perceptible interests might demand, for men had no forsight whatever, and far from troubling about a distant future, they did not even think of the next day. If it was a matter of hunting a deer, everyone well realized that he must remain faithfully at his post; but if a hare happened to pass within the reach of one of them, we cannot doubt that he would have gone off in pursuit of it without scruple and, having caught his own prey, he would have cared very little about having caused his companions to lose theirs.

It is easy to understand that such intercourse between them would not demand a language much more sophisticated than that of crows or monkeys, which group together in much the same way. Inarticulate cries, many gestures and some imitative noises must have been for long the universal human language; the addition to this in each country of certain articulated and conventional sounds (the institution of which, I have already said, is none too easy to explain) produced particular languages, crude and imperfect, rather like those we find today among various savage nations. I pass in a flash over many centuries, pressed by the brevity of time, the abundance of the things I have to say, and by the almost imperceptible progress of the first stages—for the more slowly the events unfolded, the more speedily they can be described.

Those first slow developments finally enabled men to make more rapid ones. The more the mind became enlightened, the more industry improved. Soon, ceasing to doze under the first tree, or to withdraw into caves, men discovered that various sorts of hard sharp stones could serve as hatchets to cut wood, dig the soil, and make huts out of branches, which they learned to cover with clay and mud. This was the epoch of a first revolution, which established and differentiated families, and which introduced property of a sort from which perhaps even then many quarrels and fights were born. However, as the strongest men were probably the first to build themselves huts which they felt themselves able to defend, it is reasonable to believe that the weak found it quicker and safer to imitate them rather than try to dislodge them; and as for those who already possessed huts, no one would readily venture to appropriate his neighbor's, not so much because it did not belong to him as because it would be no use to him and because he could not seize it without exposing himself to a very lively fight with the family which occupied it.

The first movements of the heart were the effect of this new situation, which united in a common dwelling husbands and wives, fathers and children; the habit of living together generated the sweetest sentiments known to man, conjugal love and paternal love. Each family became a little society, all the better united because mutual affection and liberty were its only bonds; at this stage also the first differences were established in the ways of life of the two sexes which had hitherto been identical. Women became more sedentary and accustomed themselves to looking after the hut and the children while men went out to seek their common subsistence. The two sexes began, in living a rather softer life, to lose something of their ferocity and their strength; but if each individual became separately less able to fight wild beasts, all, on the other hand, found it easier to group together to resist them jointly.

This new condition, with its solitary and simple life, very limited in its needs, and very few instruments invented to supply them, left men to enjoy a great deal of leisure, which they used to produce many sorts of commodities unknown to their fathers; and this was the first yoke they imposed on themselves, without thinking about it, and the first source of the evils they prepared for their descendants. For not only did such commodities continue to soften both body and mind, they almost lost through habitual use their power to please, and as they had at the same time degenerated into actual needs, being deprived of them became much more cruel than the possession of them was sweet; and people were unhappy in losing them without being happy in possessing them.

Here one can see a little more clearly how the use of speech became established and improved imperceptibly in the bosom of each family, and one might again speculate as to how particular causes could have extended and accelerated the progress of language by making language more necessary. Great floods or earthquakes surrounded inhabited districts with seas or precipices; revolutions of the globe broke off portions of continents into islands. One imagines that among men thus brought together, and forced to live together, a common tongue must have developed sooner than it would among those who still wandered freely through the forests of the mainland. Thus it is very possible that islanders, after their first attempts at navigation, brought the use of speech to us; and it is at least very probable that society and languages were born on islands and perfected there before they came to the continent.

Everything begins to change its aspect. Men who had previously been wandering around the woods, having once adopted a fixed settlement, come gradually together, unite in different groups, and form in each country a particular nation, united by customs and character—not by rules and laws, but through having a common way of living and eating and through the common influence of the same climate. A permanent proximity cannot fail to engender in the end some relationships between different families. Young people of opposite sexes live in neighboring huts; and the transient intercourse demanded by nature soon leads, through mutual frequentation, to another kind of relationship, no less sweet and more permanent. People become accustomed to judging different objects and to making comparisons; gradually they acquire ideas of merit and of beauty, which in turn produce feelings of preference. As a result of seeing each other, people cannot do without seeing more of each other. A tender and sweet sentiment insinuates itself into the soul, and at the least obstacle becomes an inflamed fury; jealousy awakens with love; discord triumphs, and the gentlest of passions receives the sacrifice of human blood.

To the extent that ideas and feelings succeeded one another, and the heart and mind were exercised, the human race became more sociable, relationships became more extensive and bonds tightened. People grew used to gathering together in front of their huts or around a large tree; singing and dancing, true progeny of love and leisure, became the amusement, or rather the occupation, of idle men and women thus assembled. Each began to look at the others and to want to be looked at himself; and public esteem came to be prized. He who sang or danced the best; he who was the most handsome, the strongest, the most adroit or the most eloquent became the most highly regarded, and this was the first step towards inequality and at the same time towards vice. From those first preferences there arose, on the one side, vanity and scorn, on the other, shame and envy, and the fermentation produced by these new leavens finally produced compounds fatal to happiness and innocence.

As soon as men learned to value one another and the idea of consideration was formed in their minds, everyone claimed a right to it, and it was no longer possible for anyone to be refused consideration without affront. This gave rise to the first duties of civility, even among savages: and henceforth every intentional wrong became an outrage, because together with the hurt which might result from the injury, the offended party saw an insult to person which was often more unbearable than the hurt itself. Thus, as everyone punished the contempt shown him by another in a manner proportionate to the esteem he accorded himself, revenge became terrible, and men grew bloodthirsty and cruel. This is precisely the stage

reached by most of the savage peoples known to us; and it is for lack of
having sufficiently distinguished between different ideas and seen how far
those peoples already are from the first state of nature that so many
authors have hastened to conclude that man is naturally cruel and needs
civil institutions to make him peaceable, whereas in truth nothing is more
peaceable than man in his primitive state; placed by nature at an equal
distance from the stupidity of brutes and the fatal enlightenment of civilized man, limited equally by reason and instinct to defending himself
against evils which threaten him, he is restrained by natural pity from
doing harm to anyone, even after receiving harm himself: for according to
the wise Locke; 'Where there is no property, there is no injury.'

But it must be noted that society's having come into existence and
relations among individuals having been already established meant that
men were required to have qualities different from those they possessed
from their primitive constitution; morality began to be introduced into
human actions, and each man, prior to laws, was the sole judge and
avenger of the offences he had received, so that the goodness suitable to
the pure state of nature was no longer that which suited nascent society; it
was necessary for punishments to be more severe to the extent that opportunities for offense became more frequent; and the terror of revenge had
to serve in place of the restraint of laws. Thus although men had come to
have less fortitude, and their natural pity had suffered some dilution, this
period of the development of human faculties, the golden mean between
the indolence of the primitive state and the petulant activity of our own
pride, must have been the happiest epoch and the most lasting. The more
we reflect on it, the more we realize that this state was the least subject to
revolutions, and the best for man (P); and that man can have left it only as
the result of some fatal accident, which, for the common good, ought
never to have happened. The example of savages, who have almost always been found at this point of development, appears to confirm that the
human race was made to remain there always; to confirm that this state
was the true youth of the world, and that all subsequent progress has been
so many steps in appearance towards the improvement of the individual,
but so many steps in reality towards the decrepitude of the species.

As long as men were content with their rustic huts, as long as they
confined themselves to sewing their garments of skin with thorns or fish-
bones, and adorning themselves with feathers or shells, to painting their
bodies with various colors, to improving or decorating their bows and
arrows; and to using sharp stones to make a few fishing canoes or crude
musical instruments; in a word, so long as they applied themselves only to
work that one person could accomplish alone and to arts that did not
require the collaboration of several hands, they lived as free, healthy,
good and happy men so far as they could be according to their nature, and
they continued to enjoy among themselves the sweetness of independent

intercourse; but from the instant one man needed the help of another, and it was found to be useful for one man to have provisions enough for two, equality disappeared, property was introduced, work became necessary, and vast forests were transformed into pleasant fields which had to be watered with the sweat of men, and where slavery and misery were soon seen to germinate and flourish with the crops.

Metallurgy and agriculture were the two arts whose invention produced this great revolution. For the poet it is gold and silver, but for the philosopher it is iron and wheat which first civilized men and ruined the human race. Both metallurgy and agriculture were unknown to the savages of America, who have always therefore remained savages; other peoples seem to have remained barbarians, practicing one of these arts and not the other; and one of the best reasons why Europe, if not the earliest to be civilized, has been at least more continuously and better civilized than other parts of the world, is perhaps that it is at once the richest in iron and the most fertile in wheat.

It is very difficult to suggest how men came first to know and to use iron; for it is impossible to believe they would think on their own of drawing ore from the mine and undertaking the necessary preparations for smelting before they knew what the outcome would be. On the other hand, we can even less easily attribute this discovery to some accidental fire, since mines are formed only in barren places, denuded of trees and plants, so that one might say that nature had taken pains to hide this deadly secret from us. There remains, therefore, only the faint possibility of some volcano, by pouring out metallic substances in fusion giving those who witnessed it the idea of imitating this operation of nature. What is more, we would have to assume those men having enough courage to undertake such arduous labor and enough foresight to envisage from afar the advantages they might derive from it—an assumption hardly to be made even of minds more developed than theirs.

As for agriculture, the principle of it was known long before the practice of it was established, and it is indeed hardly conceivable that men who were ceaselessly occupied drawing their subsistence from trees and plants did not fairly promptly acquire an idea of the means used by nature to propagate plants. Even so men's industry probably turned in that direction only very late—possibly because trees, which together with hunting and fishing provided their food, needed no husbandry, or because men had no knowledge of the use of wheat, or because they had no implements for cultivating it, or for lack of foresight into future needs, or, finally, for lack of the means of preventing others taking possession of the fruits of their labor. As soon as they became more skilled, we can believe that men began, with sharp stones and pointed sticks, to cultivate a few vegetables or roots around their huts; although it was long before they knew how to process wheat or had the implements necessary for large-scale cultivation; they had also to learn that in order to devote oneself to that activity and sow seeds in the soil, one must resign oneself to an immediate loss for the sake of a greater gain in the future—a forethought very alien to the turn of mind of the savage man, who, as I have said, is hard pressed to imagine in the morning the needs he will have in the evening.

The invention of other arts must therefore have been necessary to compel the human race to apply itself to agriculture. As soon as some men were needed to smelt and forge iron, other men were needed to supply them with food. The more the number of industrial workers multiplied, the fewer hands were engaged in providing the common subsistence, without there being any fewer mouths to consume it; and as some men needed commodities in exchange for their iron, others finally learned the secret of using iron for the multiplication of commodities. From this arose, on the one hand, ploughing and agriculture, and, on the other, the art of working metals and of multiplying their uses.

From the cultivation of the land, its division necessarily followed, and from property once recognized arose the first rules of justice: for in order to render each his own, each must be able to have something; moreover, as men began to direct their eyes towards the future and all saw that they had some goods to lose, there was no one who did not fear reprisals against himself for the injuries he might do to another. This origin is all the more natural, in that it is impossible to conceive of the idea of property arising from anything other than manual labor, for one cannot see what besides his own labor a man can add to things he has not actually made in order to appropriate them. It is his labor alone which, in giving the cultivator the right to the product of the land he has tilled, gives him in consequence the right to the land itself, at least until the harvest, which, being repeated from year to year, brings about a continued occupation, easily transformed into property. Grotius says that when the ancients gave Ceres the title of Legislatrix, and the festival celebrated in her honor the name of Thesmophoria, they implied that the division of the earth had produced a new sort of right: that is to say, the right to property different from the one derived from natural law.

Things in this state might have remained equal if talents had been equal, and if, for example, the use of iron and the consumption of foodstuffs had always exactly balanced each other, but this equilibrium, which nothing maintained, was soon broken: the stronger did more productive work, the more adroit did better work, the more ingenious devised ways of abridging his labor: the first farmer had greater need of iron or the smith greater need of wheat, and with both working equally, the one earned plenty while the other had hardly enough to live on. It is thus that natural inequality merges imperceptibly with inequality of ranks, and the differences between men, increased by differences of circumstance, make themselves more visible and more permanent in their effects, and begin to exercise a correspondingly large influence over the destiny of individuals.

Things having once arrived at this point, it is easy to imagine the rest. I shall not pause to describe the successive invention of the other arts, the progress of language, the testing and employment of talents, the inequality of fortunes, the use and abuse of riches, and all the details which follow from this and which anyone can easily supply. I shall simply limit myself to casting a glance over the human race as it is placed in this new order of things.

Behold, then, all our faculties developed, memory and imagination brought into play, pride stimulated, reason made active and the mind almost at the point of the perfection of which it is capable. Behold all the natural qualities called into action, the rank and destiny of each man established, not only as to the quantity of his possessions and his power to serve or to injure, but as to intelligence, beauty, strength, skill, merit or talents; and since these qualities were the only ones that could attract consideration it soon became necessary either to have them or to feign them. It was necessary in one's own interest to seem to be other than one was in reality. Being and appearance became two entirely different things, and from this distinction arose insolent ostentation, deceitful cunning and all the vices that follow in their train. From another point of view, behold man, who was formerly free and independent, diminished as a consequence of a multitude of new wants into subjection, one might say, to the whole of nature and especially to his fellow men, men of whom he has become the slave, in a sense, even in becoming their master; for if he is rich he needs their services; if he is poor he needs their aid; and even a middling condition does not enable him to do without them. He must therefore seek constantly to interest others in his lot and make them see an advantage, either real or apparent, for themselves in working for his benefit; all of which makes him devious and artful with some, imperious and hard towards others, and compels him to treat badly the people he needs if he cannot make them fear him and does not judge it in his interest to be of service to them. Finally, a devouring ambition, the burning passion to enlarge one's relative fortune, not so much from real need as to put oneself ahead of others, inspires in all men a dark propensity to injure one another, a secret jealousy which is all the more dangerous in that it often assumes the mask of benevolence in order to do its deeds in greater safety; in a word, there is competition and rivalry on the one hand, conflicts of interest on the other, and always the hidden desire to gain an advantage at the expense of other people. All these evils are the main effects of property and the inseparable consequences of nascent inequality.

Before the invention of symbols to represent it, wealth could hardly consist of anything except land and livestock, the only real goods that men could possess. But when estates became so multiplied in number and extent as to cover the whole of the land and every state to border on another one, no estate could be enlarged except at the expense of its neighbor; and the landless supernumeraries, whom weakness or indolence had prevented from acquiring an estate for themselves, became poor without having lost anything, because, while everything around them changed they alone remained unchanged, and so they were obliged to receive their subsistence—or to steal it—from the rich; and out of this situation there was born, according to the different characters of the rich and the poor, either dominion and servitude, or violence and robbery. The rich, for their part, had hardly learned the pleasure of dominating before they disdained all other pleasures, and using their old slaves to subdue new ones, they dreamed only of subjugating and enslaving their neighbors; like those ravenous wolves, which, having once tasted human flesh, refuse all other nourishment and desire thenceforth only to devour men.

Hence, as the strongest regarded their might, and the most wretched regarded their need as giving them a kind of right to the possessions of others, equivalent, according to them, to the right of property, the elimination of equality was followed by the most terrible disorder. The usurpations of the rich, the brigandage of the poor and the unbridled passions of everyone, stifling natural pity and the as yet feeble voice of justice, made men greedy, ambitious and bad. There arose between the right of the stronger and the right of the first occupant a perpetual conflict which ended only in fights and murders (Q). Nascent society gave place to the most horrible state of war; the human race, debased and desolate, could not now retrace its path, nor renounce the unfortunate acquistions it had made, but laboring only towards its shame by misusing those faculties which should be its honor, brought itself to the brink of ruin.

> *Shocked at a new-found evil, at once rich and wretched,*
> *He wants to flee from his wealth, and hates what he once prayed for.*
> [OVID, *Metamorphosis*. XI. 127]

It is impossible that men should not eventually have reflected on so melancholy a situation, and on the calamity which had overwhelmed them. The rich above all must have perceived how disadvantageous to them was a perpetual state of war in which they bore all the costs, and in which the risk of life was universal but the risk of property theirs alone. Furthermore, whatever disguises they might put upon their usurpations, they knew well enough that they were founded on precarious and bogus rights and that force could take away from them what force alone had acquired without their having any reason for complaint. Even those who had been enriched by their own industry could not base their right to property on much better titles. In vain would one say: "I built this wall; I earned the right to this field by my own labor." For "Who gave you its extent and boundaries?" might be the answer. "And in virtue of what do you claim payment from us for work we never instructed you to do? Do you not know that a multitude of your brethren perish or suffer from need of what you have to excess, and that you required the express and unanimous consent of the whole human race in order to appropriate from the common subsistence anything beyond that required for your own subsistence?" Destitute of valid reasons to justify himself and of forces adequate to defend himself; easily crushing an individual but crushed himself by troups of bandits; alone against all, and unable because of mutual jealousies to form alliances with his equals against enemies united by the common hope of plunder, the rich man under pressure of necessity conceived in the end the most cunning project that ever entered the human mind: to employ in his favor the very forces of those who attacked him, to make his adversaries his defenders, to inspire them with new maxims and give them new institutions as advantageous to him as natural right was disadvantageous.

To this end, having demonstrated to his neighbors the horror of a situation which set each against all, made men's possessions as burdensome to them as their needs, and afforded no security either in poverty or in riches, he invents specious reasons to lead his listeners to his goal.

"Let us unite," he says, "to protect the weak from oppression, to restrain the ambitious, and ensure for each the possession of what belongs to him; let us institute rules of justice and peace to which all shall be obliged to conform, without exception, rules which compensate in a way for the caprice of fortune by subjecting equally the powerful and the weak to reciprocal duties. In a word, instead of directing our forces against each other, let us unite them together in one supreme power which shall govern us all according to wise laws, protect and defend all the members of the association, repulse common enemies, and maintain us in everlasting concord."

It needed much less than the equivalent of this speech to win round men so uncultivated and so easily seduced, especially as they had too many disputes to settle among themselves to be able to do without umpires, and too much avarice and ambition to be able to do for long without masters. All ran towards their chains believing that they were securing their liberty; for although they had reason enough to discern the advantages of a civil order, they did not have experience enough to foresee the dangers. Those most capable of predicting the abuses were precisely those who expected to profit from them; and even the wisest saw that men must resolve to sacrifice one part of their freedom in order to preserve the other, even as a wounded man has his arm cut off to save the rest of his body.

Such was, or must have been, the origin of society and of laws, which put new fetters on the weak and gave new powers to the rich, which irretrievably destroyed natural liberty, established for all time the law of property and inequality, transformed adroit usurpation into irrevocable right, and for the benefit of a few ambitious men subjected the human race thenceforth to labor, servitude and misery. It is easy to see how the foundation of one society made the establishment of all the rest unavoidable, and how, being faced with united forces, it was necessary for others to unite in turn. Societies, as they multiplied and spread, soon came to cover the whole surface of the earth, and it was no longer possible to find a single corner of the universe where one might free oneself from the yoke and withdraw one's head from beneath the sword, often precariously held, which every man saw perpetually hanging over him. Positive law having thus become the common rule over citizens, there was room for natural law only as between the various societies where, under the name of international law, it was moderated by certain tacit conventions designed to make intercourse possible and to supplement natural compassion, which having lost as between society and society nearly all the force it had as between man and man, no longer dwells in any but a few great cosmopolitan souls, who, breaking through the imaginary barriers that separate peoples, and following the example of the Sovereign Being who created them, include the whole human race in their benevolence.

The bodies politic, thus remaining in the state of nature in their relationship to each other, soon experienced the same disadvantages that had forced individuals to quit it; the state of nature proved indeed even more harmful to these large bodies than it had previously been for the individuals of whom they were composed. From this there arose wars between nations, battles, murders, reprisals which make nature tremble and offend reason, and all those horrible prejudices which count the honor of shedding human blood a virtue. The most decent men learned to regard the killing of their fellows as one of their duties; and in time men came to massacre one another by thousands without knowing why, committing more murders in a single day's battle and more atrocities in the sack of a single city than were committed in the state of nature throughout entire centuries over the whole face of the earth. Such are the first effects we note of the division of the human race into different societies. But let us return to their foundation.

I know that many have suggested other origins for political societies, such as conquest by the most powerful or the union of the weak; and the choice between these causes makes no difference to what I wish to establish. However, the one I have just outlined seems to me the most natural for the following reasons:

(1) In the first place, the right of conquest, being no true right in itself, cannot be the basis of any other right; the victor and the vanquished always remain towards each in the state of war, unless the conquered nation, with its freedom fully restored, voluntarily chooses its conqueror for its chief. Up to that point, whatever capitulations may have been

made, the fact that they have no basis but violence and are therefore *ipso facto* null and void means that there cannot be on this hypothesis any authentic society or true body politic, nor any law but the law of the strongest.

(2) The words "strong" and "weak" are, in the second case, ambiguous; for during the interval between the establishment of the right to property or the right of the first occupant and the establishment of political government, the sense of these terms is better expressed by the words "poor" and "rich," since before the institution of laws a man can have had in effect no means of subjecting his equals other than by attacking their goods or making them a part of his own.

(3) The poor, having nothing to lose but their freedom, it would have been the utmost folly on their part to strip themselves voluntarily of the only good they still possessed without gaining anything in exchange. The rich, on the contrary, being vulnerable, so to speak, in every part of their possessions, it was much easier to injure them; and it was necessary in consequence for them to take more precautions for their own protection; and finally it is reasonable to suppose a thing to have been invented by those to whom it was useful rather than by those to whom it was injurious.

Nascent government did not have a constant and regular form. The lack of wisdom and experience allowed only present inconveniences to be seen, and men thought of remedies for others only when they presented themselves. In spite of the endeavors of the wisest lawgivers, the political state always remained imperfect because it was almost entirely the product of chance; and since it began badly, time, while revealing the defects and suggesting remedies, could never repair the vices of the constitution. Constitutions were continually being patched up, when it was really necessary to begin by clearing the ground and removing the old materials, as Lycurgus did in Sparta in order to build a stable and lasting edifice. At first, society consisted only of a few general conventions which all the individuals committed themselves to observe, conventions of which the community made itself the guarantor towards each individual. Experience had to show how weak was such a constitution, how easy it was for lawbreakers to avoid conviction or punishment for crimes of which the public alone was witness and judge. The laws had to be evaded in a thousand ways, inconveniences and disorders had to multiply constantly for men to be brought finally to think of entrusting the dangerous responsibility of public authority to certain individuals and committing to the magistrates the duty of securing obedience to the deliberations of the people. For to say that the chiefs were chosen before the union was instituted, and that ministers of laws existed before the laws themselves is to suggest something that does not deserve serious consideration.

It would be no more reasonable to believe that men threw themselves straightway into the arms of an absolute master, unconditionally and irrevocably, and that the first idea which proud and unconquered men conceived for their common security was to rush headlong into slavery. Why, in fact, did they give themselves a superior if it was not for him to defend themselves against oppression, and to protect their possessions, their liberties and their lives, which are, so to speak, the constituent elements of their being? Now, since the worst thing that can happen to one in the relations between man and man is to find oneself at the mercy of another, would it not be contrary to common sense for men to surrender into the hands of a chief the only things they needed his help in order to preserve? What equivalent benefit could he offer them in return for the concession of so great a right? And if he had dared to demand it on the pretext of defending them, would he not promptly have received the reply recorded in the fable: "What worse would the enemy do to us?" It is therefore incontestable—and indeed the fundamental principle of all political right—that people have given themselves chiefs in order to defend their liberty and not to enslave them. "If we have a prince," said Pliny to Trajan, "it is in order that he may preserve us from having a master."

Politicians utter the same sophisms about love of liberty that philosophers utter about the state of nature; on the strength of things that they see, they make judgments about very different things that they have not seen, and they attribute to men a natural propensity to slavery because they witness the patience with which slaves bear their servitude, failing to remember that liberty is like innocence and virtue: the value of it is appreciated only so long as one possesses it oneself, and the taste for it is lost as soon as one loses it. "I know the delights of your country," said Brasidas to a satrap, who was comparing the life of Sparta with that of Persepolis, "but you cannot know the pleasures of mine."

Even as an unbroken horse erects its mane, paws the ground with its hoof, and rears impetuously at the very approach of the bit, while a trained horse suffers patiently even the whip and spur, savage man will not bend his neck to the yoke which civilized man wears without a murmur; he prefers the most turbulent freedom to the most tranquil subjection. We must not, therefore, look to the degradation of enslaved peoples as a basis for judging man's natural disposition for or against servitude, but look rather to the prodigious achievements of all free peoples who have striven to protect themselves from oppression. I know that enslaved peoples do nothing but boast of the peace and repose they enjoy in their chains, and *miserrimam servitutem pacem appellant.** But when I see free peoples sacrificing pleasure, repose, wealth, power, even life itself for the sake of preserving that one good which is so disdained by those who have lost it; when I see animals, born free and hating captivity, breaking their heads against the bars of their prison; when I see multitudes of naked savages scorn

*"They call a state of wretched servitude a state of peace," Tacitus, *Histories*, IV. xvu.

European pleasures and brave hunger, fire, the sword and death simply to preserve their independence, I feel that it is not for slaves to argue about liberty.

As for paternal authority, from which several writers have derived absolute government and all society, it is enough, without invoking the refutations of Locke and Sidney, to notice that nothing on earth can be farther from the ferocious spirit of despotism than the gentleness of that authority which looks more to the advantage of he who obeys than to the interest of he who commands; to notice that by the law of nature the father is the master of the child only for such time as his help is necessary to him and that beyond this stage the two are equals, the son, becoming perfectly independent of his father, owing him only respect and not obedience, for gratitude is manifestly a duty which ought to be observed and not a right which can be claimed. Instead of saying that civil society derives from paternal power, we ought to say, on the contrary, that the latter derives its main force from the former. No individual was recognized as the father of several children until such time as they lived in families together and settled around him. The goods of the father, of which he is truly the master, are the ties which keep his children dependent on him, and he may choose to give them a share of his estate only to the extent that they have deserved it from him by constant deference to his will. But subjects are far from having some similar favor to expect from their despot, for in belonging, with all they possess, to him as his personal property—or at least being claimed by him as such—they are reduced to receiving from him as a favor whatever he leaves them of their own goods. He bestows justice when he robs them, and grace when he lets them live.

If we go on thus to examine facts in the light of right, we shall find no more substance than truth in the so-called voluntary establishment of tyranny, and it would be difficult to prove the validity of any contract which bound only one of the parties, which gave everything to one and nothing to the other, and which could only be prejudicial to one contractant. This odious system is very far from being, even today, that of wise and good monarchs, especially of the kings of France, as we may see from several statements in their edicts, and particularly in the following passage from a celebrated statement published in 1667 in the name, and by order, of Louis XIV:

> Let it not therefore be said that the Sovereign is not subject to
> the laws of his State, since the contrary proposition is a truth of the
> law of nations, which flattery has sometimes denied but which true
> princes have defended as divine protectors of their states. How
> much more legitimate is it to say with the wise Plato that the per-
> fect felicity of a kingdom consists in a prince being obeyed by his
> subjects, the prince obeying the law, and the law being just and
> always directed to the public good.

I shall not pause to consider whether since freedom is the noblest of man's faculties, it is not to degrade our nature, to put ourselves on the level of beasts enslaved by instinct, even to offend the Author of our being, to renounce without reserve the most precious of all His gifts and subject ourselves to committing all the crimes He has forbidden in order to please a cruel or impassioned master, nor whether that sublime Artisan would be more angered at seeing His finest work destroyed than at seeing it dishonored. I shall only ask by what right those who do not fear debasing themselves in this way have been able to subject succeeding generations to the same ignominy, and to renounce on behalf of their posterity things which were not derived from their generosity and without which life itself is a burden to all who are worthy of life?

Pufendorf says that just as one transfers property to another by agreements and contracts, one can divest oneself of one's freedom in favor of another. This, it seems to me, is a very bad argument, for, first of all, the goods I alienate become something wholly foreign to me, and an abuse of them is a matter of indifference to me; while it is very important to me that my freedom is not abused, and I cannot lay myself open to becoming an instrument of crime without incurring the guilt for whatever crime I am forced to commit. Besides, since the right to property is only conventional and of human institution, everyone may dispose at will of what he possesses; but this is not the case with the essential gifts of nature, such as life and liberty, which everyone is allowed to enjoy and of which it is at least doubtful whether anyone has the right to divest himself. By giving up liberty, a man degrades his being: by giving up life, he does his best to annihilate it, and since no temporal goods could compensate for the loss of either life or liberty, it would be an offense against both nature and reason to renounce them at any price whatever. But even if one could alienate one's liberty like one's goods, the difference would be very great in the case of one's children, who enjoy their father's goods only by transmission of his right to them, whereas their freedom is a gift they receive as men from nature, so that their parents had never had a right to divest them of it. Thus, just as it was necessary to do violence to nature to establish slavery, nature had to be altered to perpetuate that right, and jurists who have solemnly affirmed that the child of a slave will be born a slave have decided, in other words, that a man will not be born a man.

It therefore seems to me certain that governments did not originate in arbitrary power, which is only the final stage of the corruption of governments, and which brings them back in the end to that very law of the strongest which they were first introduced to remedy; even if they had begun in this way, such power, being in its nature illegitimate, could not serve as the basis for rights in society, nor consequently for the inequality instituted in society.

Without entering here into the research that needs yet to be undertaken into the nature of the fundamental pact of all government, I shall limit myself, following common opinion, to considering here the establishment of the body politic as a true contract between a people and the chiefs that people chooses, a contract whereby both parties commit themselves to observe the laws which are stipulated in its articles and which form the bonds of their union. The people having, on the subject of social relations, united all their wills into a single will, all the articles on which that will pronounces become so many fundamental laws obligatory on every member of the state without exception; and one of these laws regulates the choice and powers of the magistrates charged to watch over the execution of the other laws. This power extends to everything that can maintain the constitution without going so far as to change it. Added to this are honors, which make the laws and their ministers command respect, and prerogatives, which compensate the ministers personally for the hard work which good administration entails. The magistrate, on his side, binds himself to use the power entrusted to him only in accordance with the intentions of the constituents, to maintain each in the peaceful enjoyment of what belongs to him and at all times to prefer the public interest to his own advantage.

Before experience had demonstrated, or knowledge of the human heart had made men foresee the inevitable abuses of such a constitution, it must have appeared all the better insofar as those charged with watching over its preservation were those who had the greatest stake in it. For the magistrature and its rights being established solely upon the fundamental laws, the magistrates would cease to be legitimate as soon as the laws were destroyed; the people would no longer owe them obedience; and because it is not the magistrate but the law which constitutes the essence of the state, each individual would return by right to his natural liberty.

Given the least careful thought, one could find new reasons to confirm this point and to see from the very nature of the contract that it cannot be irrevocable, for if there were no superior power to secure the fidelity of the contracting parties, nor compel them to fulfill their reciprocal engagements, each party would remain sole judge of his own cause, and each would always have the right to renounce the contract as soon as he considered that the other had violated its conditions, or as soon as those conditions ceased to suit his pleasure. It would seem that the right of abdication can be founded on this principle. Now to consider only, as we do here, what is of human institution, if the magistrate, who has all the power in his hands and who appropriates all the advantages of the contract, enjoys nonetheless the right to renounce his authority, all the more reason is there for the people, who pay for all the faults of their chiefs, to have the right to renounce their dependence. However, the frightful dissensions and infinite disorders that this dangerous power would necessarily bring about show us better than anything else how much human governments needed a basis more solid than reason alone, and how necessary it was to the public repose that divine will should intervene to give the sovereign authority a sacred and inviolable character which stripped subjects of the fatal right of disposing of it. If religion had done men only this service it would be enough to impose on them the duty of adopting and cherishing religion, despite its abuses, since it saves men from even more bloodshed than fanaticism causes. But let us follow the thread of our hypothesis.

The different forms of government owe their origin to the greater or lesser differences which exist between individuals at the moment a government is instituted. Was one man eminent in power, virtue, riches, or influence? Then he alone was elected magistrate, and the state became monarchic. If several men, more or less equal among themselves, were superior to all the others, they were elected jointly, and formed an aristocracy. Where those whose fortunes and talents were less disproportionate, and who were less far removed from the state of nature, kept the supreme administration in common they formed a democracy. Time showed which of these forms was the most advantageous for men. Some remained subject to laws alone; others were soon obeying masters. Citizens wished to keep their liberty; subjects thought only of taking it away from their neighbors, unable to endure the prospect of others enjoying a thing they had ceased to enjoy themselves. In a word, on one side were riches and conquests; on the other, happiness and virtue.

In these various governments, all magistrates were originally elective; and where wealth did not conquer, preference was accorded to merit, which gives a natural authority, and to age, which gives experience in business and gravity in deliberations. The elders of the Hebrews, the Gerontes of Sparta, the Senate of Rome, and the very etymology of our word *seigneur*, show how old age was respected in the past. But the more often the choice fell on men advanced in age, the more often elections had to take place and the more the troublesome aspects of election made themselves felt; intrigues began, factions were formed, parties became embittered, civil wars broke out; in the end the blood of citizens was sacrificed for what was claimed to be the happiness of the state, and men were on the verge of relapsing into the anarchy of earlier times. Ambitious leaders took advantage of this situation to perpetuate their offices in their own families; at the same time, the people, accustomed to dependence, to repose and to the conveniences of life, and already incapable of breaking the chains it bore, agreed to allow its servitude to be increased for the sake of assuring its tranquillity. Thus, the chiefs in becoming hereditary accustomed themselves to thinking of their magistrates as a family possession, and to regarding themselves as proprietors of the state of which they were originally only the officers, to calling their co-citizens their slaves, and numbering them, like cattle, among their belongings, and to calling themselves the equals of the gods and the king of kings.

If we follow the progress of inequality in these different revolutions, we shall find that the establishment of law and the right of property was the first stage, the institution of magistrates the second, and the transformation of legitimate into arbitrary power the third and last stage. Thus, the status of rich and poor was authorized by the first epoch, that of strong and weak by the second, and by the third that of master and slave, which is the last degree of inequality, and the stage to which all the others finally lead until new revolutions dissolve the government altogether or bring it back to legitimacy.

To understand the necessity of this progress, we must consider less the motives for the establishment of the body politic than the way in which that body performs in action and the disadvantages it introduces, for the vices which make social institutions necessary are the same vices which make the abuse of those institutions inevitable. Leaving aside the unique case of Sparta, where the laws concerned mainly the education of children and where Lycurgus established morals so well that it was almost unnecessary to add laws, laws, being in general less strong than passions, restrain men without changing them; so that it would be easy to prove that any government which, without being corrupted or degenerate, worked perfectly according to the ends of its institution, would have been instituted unnecessarily, and that a country where nobody evaded the laws or exploited the magistracy would need neither laws nor magistrates.

Political distinctions necessarily introduce civil distinctions. The growing inequality between the people and its chiefs is soon reproduced between individuals, and is modified there in a thousand ways according to passions, talents and circumstances. The magistrate cannot usurp illegitimate power without enrolling clients to whom he is forced to yield some part of it. Besides, citizens allow themselves to be oppressed only so far as they are impelled by a blind ambition; and fixing their eyes below rather than above themselves, come to love domination more than independence, and agree to wear chains for the sake of imposing chains on others in turn. It is difficult to reduce to obedience a man who has no wish to command, and the most adroit politician could not enslave men whose only wish was to be free; on the other hand, inequality extends easily among ambitious and cowardly souls, who are always ready to run the risks of fortune and almost indifferent as to whether they command or obey, according to fortune's favor. Thus there must have come a time when the eyes of the people were so dazzled that their leaders had only to say to the least of men: "Be great, with all your posterity," and at once that man appeared great in the eyes of all the world as well as in his own eyes and his descendants exalted themselves all the more in proportion to their distance from him; the more remote and uncertain the cause, the greater the effect; the more idlers who could be counted in a family, the more illustrious it became.

If this were the place to go in details, I would explain how inequality of influence and authority becomes inevitable among individuals as soon as, being united in the same society, they are forced to compare themselves with one another and to take into account the differences they discover in the continual dealings they have with one another. These differences are of several kinds, but since wealth, nobility or rank, power and personal merit are generally the four principal qualities by which one is measured in society, I would prove that harmony or conflict between these several sorts of distinction is the surest indication of the good or bad constitution of a state. I would show that as between these four kinds of inequality, personal qualities are the origin of all the others, and wealth is the last to which they are all reduced because wealth, being the most immediately useful to wellbeing and the easiest to communicate, can be readily used to buy all the rest—an observation which enables us to judge fairly exactly how far each people has distanced itself from its primitive institution, and the progress it has made towards the extreme stage of corruption. I would observe to what extent this universal desire for reputation, honors and promotion, which devours us all, exercises and compares talents and strengths; I would show how it excites and multiplies passions, and how, in turning all men into competitors, rivals or rather enemies, it causes every day failures and successes and catastrophies of every sort by making so many contenders run the same course; I would show that this burning desire to be talked about, this yearning for distinction which keeps us almost always in a restless state is responsible for what is best and what is worst among men, for our virtues and our vices, for our sciences and our mistakes, for our conquerors and our philosophers—that is to say, for a multitude of bad things and very few good things. Finally, I would prove that if one sees a handful of powerful and rich men on the pinnacle of grandeur and fortune, while the crowd grovels below in obscurity and wretchedness, it is because the former value the things they enjoy only to the extent that the others are deprived of them and because, even without changing their condition, they would cease to be happy if the people ceased to be miserable.

However, these details alone would provide the material for a substantial work, in which the advantages and disadvantages of any government would be weighed in relation to the rights of the state of nature, and where one would strip all the different masks behind which inequality has hidden itself up to the present time and may do so in centuries to come, according to the nature of governments and the revolutions which time will necessarily produce in them. One would see the multitude oppressed inside society as a consequence of the very precautions taken against threats from outside; one would see oppression increase continually without the oppressed ever being able to know where it would end, nor what legitimate means remained for them to halt it. One would see the rights of citizens and the freedom of nations extinguished little by little, and the protests of the weak treated as seditious noises. One would see politics confer on a mercenary section of the people the honor of defending the common cause; one would see arising from this the necessity of taxation, and the disheartened farmer quitting his fields even in peacetime, abandoning his plough to buckle on the sword. One would see the birth of fatal and bizarre codes of honor. One would see the defenders of the fatherland become sooner or later its enemies, holding for ever a drawn dagger over their fellow citizens, soldiers who in time would be heard to say to the oppressor of their country:

> If you command me to sink my sword into my brother's breast, or in my father's throat, or even into the womb of my pregnant wife, I shall do it all, despite my repugnance, with my own right hand.
>
> Lucan, *Pharsalia*, I

From the extreme inequality of conditions and fortunes, from the diversity of passions and talents, from useless arts, pernicious arts and foolish sciences would arise a mass of prejudices, equally contrary to reason, happiness and virtue; one would see chiefs fomenting everything that might weaken assemblies of men by disuniting them, stirring up everything that might give society an appearance of concord while sowing the seeds of real dissension, everything that might inspire defiance and mutual hatred in different social orders through conflict between their rights and their interests, and by these means strengthen the power which subdues them all.

It is from the bosom of this disorder and these revolutions that despotism, by degrees raising up its hideous head and devouring everything that it had seen to be good and sound in any part of the state, would finally succeed in trampling on both the laws and the people and establishing itself on the ruins of the republic. The times leading up to these final changes would be times of troubles and calamities; but in the end all would be consumed by the monster, and the people would no longer have chiefs and laws, but only tyrants. After this moment also there would be no morals or virtue, for despotism, "in which there is no hope to be derived from an honorable deed," admits, wherever it prevails, no other master; and as soon as it speaks, there is neither probity nor duty to consult, and the blindest obedience is the solitary virtue which remains for slaves.

This is the last stage of inequality, and the extreme term which closes the circle and meets the point from which we started. It is here that all individuals become equal again because they are nothing, here where subjects have no longer any law but the will of the master, nor the master any other rule but that of his passions, here that notions of the good and principles of justice vanish once more. Here everything is restored to the sole law of the strongest, and consequently to a new state of nature different from the one with which we began only that that one was the state of nature in its pure form and this one is the fruit of an excess of corruption. There is so little difference, moreover, between the two states, and the contract of government is so fully dissolved by despotism that the despot is only master for as long as he is the strongest; as soon as he can be expelled, he has no right to protest against violence. The insurrection which ends with the strangling or dethronement of a sultan is just as lawful an act as those by which he disposed the day before of the lives and property of his subjects. Force alone maintained him; force alone overthrows him; all things happen according to the natural order; and whatever the result of these short and freqeunt revolutions, no man can complain of the injustice of another, but only of his own imprudence or his misfortune.

In thus discovering and tracing the lost and forgotten paths which must have led men from the natural state to the civil state, in reconstructing together with the intermediate situations which I have just noted, those which lack of time has made me omit or which imagination has not suggested to me, no attentive reader can fail to be impressed by the immense space which separates these two states. It is in this slow succession of things that he will see the solution to an infinity of moral and political problems which philosophers cannot solve. He will understand that since the human race of one age is not the human race of another age, the reason why Diogenes could not find a man is that he searched among his contemporaries for a man of a time that no longer existed; Cato, he will say, perished with Rome and liberty because he was out of place in his century, and the greatest of men could astound the world that he would have ruled five centuries earlier. In a word, the attentive reader will explain how the soul and the human passions through imperceptible degeneration change, so to speak, their nature; explain why our needs and our pleasures change their objects in the long run; and why since original man has disappeared by degrees, society no longer offers to the eyes of philosophers anything more than an assemblage of artificial men and factitious passions which are the product of all men's new relations and which have no true foundation in nature. What reflection teaches on this subject is perfectly confirmed by observation; savage man and civilized man differ so much in the bottom of their hearts and inclinations that that which constitutes the supreme happiness of the one would reduce the other to despair. The savage man breathes only peace and freedom; he desires only to live and stay idle, and even the *ataraxia* of the Stoic does not approach his profound indifference towards every other object. Civil man, on the contrary, being always active, sweating and restless, torments himself endlessly in search of ever more laborious occupations; he works himself to death, he even runs towards the grave to put himself into shape to live, or renounces life in order to acquire immortality. He pays court to great men he loathes and to rich men he despises; he spares nothing to secure the honor of serving them; he boasts vaingloriously of his own baseness and of their patronage, and being proud of his slavery he speaks with disdain of those who have not the honor of sharing it. What a spectacle for a Carib would be the arduous and envied labors of a European minister! How many cruel deaths would not that indolent savage prefer to the horrors of such a life, which often is not even sweetened by the satisfaction of doing good? In order for him to understand the motives of anyone assuming so many cares, it would be necessary for the words "power" and "reputation" to have a meaning for his mind; he would have to know that there is a class of men who attach importance to the gaze of the rest of the world, and who know how to be happy and satisfied with themselves on the testimony of others rather than on their own. Such is, in fact, the true cause of all these differences: the savage lives within himself; social man lives always outside himself; he knows how to live only in the opinion of others, it is, so to speak, from their judgment alone that he derives the sense of his own existence. It is not my subject here to show how such a disposition gives birth to so much indifference to good and evil coupled with such beautiful talk about morality; or how, as everything is reduced to appearances, everything comes to be false and warped, honor, friendship, virtue, and often even vices themselves, since in the end men discover the secret of boasting about vices; or show how, as a result of always asking others what we are and never daring to put the question to ourselves in the midst of so much philosophy, humanity, civility and so many sublime maxims, we have only façades, deceptive and frivolous, honor without virtue, reason without wisdom, and pleasure without happiness. It is enough for me to have proved that this is not at all the original state of men, and that it is only the spirit of society together with the inequality that society engenders which changes and corrupts in this way all our natural inclinations.

I have tried to set out the origin and progress of inequality, the establishment and the abuse of political societies, to the extent that these things can be deduced from the nature of man by the light of reason alone, independently of the sacred dogmas which give to sovereign authority the sanction of divine right. It follows from this exposition that inequality, being almost non-existent in the state of nature, derives its force and its growth from the development of our faculties and the progress of the human mind, and finally becomes fixed and legitimate through the institution of property and laws. It follows furthermore that that moral inequality, authorized by positive law alone, is contrary to natural right, whenever it is not matched in exact proportion with physical inequality—a distinction which sufficiently determines what we ought to think of that form of inequality which prevails among all civilized peoples; for it is manifestly contrary to the law of nature, however defined, that a child should govern an old man, that an imbecile should lead a wise man, and that a handful of people should gorge themselves with superfluities while the hungry multitude goes in want of necessities.

Essay on the Origin of Languages

THE FORMATION OF SOUTHERN LANGUAGES

In the first times[1] men, scattered over the face of the earth, had no society other than that of the family, no laws other than those of nature, no language other than gesture and a few inarticulate sounds.[2] They were not bound by any idea of common brotherhood and, since they had no arbiter other than force, they believed themselves to be one another's enemies. Their weakness and ignorance gave them that opinion. Since they knew nothing, they feared everything; they attacked in self-defense. A man abandoned alone on the face of the earth at the mercy of mankind, had to be a ferocious animal. He was ready to inflict on others all the harm he feared from them. Fear and weakness are the sources of cruelty.

Social attachments develop in us only with our knowledge. Pity, although natural to man's heart, would remain eternally inactive without imagination to set it in motion. How do we let ourselves be moved to pity? By transporting ourselves outside ourselves; by identifying with the suffering being. We suffer only to the extent that we judge him to suffer; it is not in ourselves but in him that we suffer. Think how much acquired knowledge this transport presupposes! How could I imagine evils of which I have no idea? How could I suffer when I see another suffer, if I do not even know that he suffers, if I do not know what he and I have in common? Someone who has never reflected cannot be clement, or just, or pitying; any more than he can be wicked and vindictive. He who imagines nothing feels only himself; in the midst of mankind he is alone.

Reflection is born of the comparison of ideas, and it is their variety that leads us to compare them. Whoever sees only a single object has no occasion to make comparisons. Whoever sees only a small number, and

---

[1] I call first the times of men's dispersion, regardless of the age one chooses to assign to mankind at that period.

[2] Genuine languages have not a domestic origin; only a more comprehensive and lasting convention can establish them. The savages of America almost never speak except when away from home; in his hut everyone remains silent and speaks to his family by means of signs; and such signs are infrequent because a savage is less restless, less impatient than a European, has fewer needs, and takes care to attend to them himself.

always the same ones from childhood on, still does not compare them, because the habit of seeing them deprives him of the attention required to examine them; but as a new object strikes us, we want to know it, and we look for relations between it and the objects we do know; that is how we learn to observe what we see before us, and how what is foreign to us leads us to examine what touches us.

Apply these ideas to the first men, and you will see the reason for their barbarism. Since they had never seen anything other than what was around them, they did not know even that; they did not know themselves. They had the idea of a Father, a son, a brother, but not of a man. Their hut held all those who were like themselves; a stranger, an animal, a monster were all the same to them: outside of themselves and their family, the whole universe was naught to them.

Hence the apparent contradictions one sees in the fathers of nations: so much naturalness and so much inhumanity, such ferocious ways [*moeurs*] and such tender hearts, so much love for their family and aversion toward their species. All their sentiments, focused on those close to them, were therefore the more vigorous. Everything they knew, they held dear. Hostile to the rest of the world, which they neither saw nor knew, they hated only what they could not know.

These times of barbarism were the golden age, not because men were united but because they were separated. Everyone, it is said, considered himself to be master of everything; that may be so; but no one knew or desired more than was ready to hand; his needs, far from drawing him closer to those like himself, drew him away from them. Men may have attacked one another upon meeting, but they rarely met. Everywhere the state of war prevailed, yet the whole earth was at peace.

The first men were hunters or shepherds, and not tillers of the soil; the first goods were herds, not fields. Before ownership of the earth was divided, no one thought of cultivating it. Agriculture is an art that requires tools; to sow in order to reap is a measure requiring foresight. Man in society seeks to expand; isolated man contracts. Beyond where his eye can see or his arm reach there no longer is either right or property for him. Once the Cyclops has rolled the stone in front of the entrance to his cave, his herds and he are safe. But who would protect the harvest of a man whom the laws do not protect?

I will be told that Cain was a tiller of the ground and that Noah planted a vineyard. Why not? They were alone; what did they have to fear? Besides, that does nothing to counter my point; I have stated above how I conceive of the first times. When Cain became a fugitive, he was, after all, compelled to give up agriculture; the wandering life of Noah's descendants must have made them forget it also. The earth had to be populated before it could be cultivated; the two cannot readily be done together. During the first dispersion of mankind, until the family was stabilized and man had a fixed dwelling, there was no more agriculture. Peoples that do not settle cannot possibly cultivate the soil. Such formerly were the Nomads, such were the Arabs living in their tents, the Scythians in their wagons, such are still the wandering Tartars and the savages of America in our time.

As a rule, of all the peoples whose origin we know, the first barbarians are found to be voracious and carnivorous rather than agricultural and granivorous. The Greeks [refer by] name [to] the person who first taught them to till the soil, and they would seem not to have learned this art until comparatively late. But when they add that until the time of Triptolemus they lived solely off acorns, they make an implausible claim and one which their own history belies; for they had been eating meat prior to Triptolemus, since he forbade them to eat it. Besides, it would seem that they did not take this prohibition very seriously.

At Homer's feasts an ox is slaughtered to regale one's guests, as one might nowadays slaughter a suckling pig. On reading that Abraham served a calf to three people, that Eumaeus had two kids roasted for Ulysses's dinner, and that Rebecca did the same for her husband's, one may gather what tremendous devourers of meat men were in those times. To get a notion of the meals of the ancients one need only consider the meals of present-day savages; I almost said those of Englishmen.

The first cake that was eaten was the communion of mankind. When men began to settle, they cleared a bit of land around their hut; it was a garden rather than a field. The little grain they gathered was ground between two stones, made into a few cakes baked in ashes, or over embers, or on a hot stone, and eaten only at feasts. This ancient practice, consecrated among the Jews by Passover, is preserved to this day in Persia and in the [East] Indies. There they eat only unleavened breads, and these breads, made up of thin sheets, are baked and eaten at every meal. Only when more bread came to be needed did it occur to people to leaven it, for small quantities do not readily lend themselves to leavening.

I know that large-scale agriculture already prevailed at the time of the patriarchs. It must have been introduced into Palestine quite early, since Egypt is so close. The book of Job, perhaps the oldest of all extant books, refers to cultivation of the fields; it lists five hundred pairs of oxen as part of Job's wealth. The reference to pairs indicates that these oxen were yoked for work; it is explicitly stated that these oxen were ploughing when the Sabeans carried them off, and one can readily gather what an expanse of land five hundred teams of oxen must have ploughed.

All this is true; but let us not confuse different times. What we call the age of the patriarchs is very remote from the first age. Scripture lists ten generations between them in those centuries when men lived to a very advanced age. What did they do during those ten generations? We know nothing about it. Since they lived scattered and almost without society, they scarcely spoke: how could they have written and, given the regularity of their isolated life, what events would they have transmitted to us?

Adam spoke; Noah spoke; granted. Adam had been taught by God himself. When they separated, the children of Noah gave up agriculture, and the common language perished together with the first society. This would have happened even if there had never been a tower of babel. Solitaries living on desert islands have been known to forget their own language. After several generations away from their country men rarely preserve their original language, even when they work together and live in society with one another.

Scattered throughout this vast desert of a world, men relapsed into the dull barbarism they would have been in if they had been born of the earth. By following [the thread of] these entirely natural ideas the authority of Scripture can easily be reconciled with ancient records, and there is no need to treat as fables traditions that are as old as are the peoples that have handed them down to us.

In that brutish state, they had to live. The more active, the more robust, those who were always on the move, could only live off fruit and the hunt: so they became hunters, violent, bloodthirsty and, in time, they became warriors, conquerors, usurpers. History has stained its records with the crimes of these first Kings; war and conquests are nothing but manhunts. Once they had conquered, it only remained for them to devour men. That is what their successors learned to do.

The greater number, less active and more peaceable, stopped as soon as they could, gathered cattle, tamed them, taught them to heed man's voice, learned to tend them and increase their number so as to have them for food; and that is how pastoral life began.

Human industry expands with the needs that give it rise. Of the three ways of life available to man, hunting, herding, and agriculture, the first develops strength, skill, speed of body, courage and cunning of soul; it hardens man and makes him ferocious. The land of the hunters does not long remain that of the hunt.[3] Game has to be pursued over great distances; hence horsemanship. Game that flees has to be caught; hence light weapons—the sling, the arrow, the javelin. The pastoral art, father of repose and of the indolent passions, is the most self-sufficient art; it almost effortlessly provides man with food and clothing; it even provides him with his dwelling. The tents of the first shepherds were made of animal skins; so were the roofs of the ark and the tabernacle of Moses. As

---

[3] The practice of hunting is not at all favorable to population [growth]. This was noted at the time that the islands of Santo Domingo and Tortuga were inhabited by buccaneers, and it is confirmed by the state of northern America. None of the fathers of large nations were hunters by [e]state; all of them were farmers or shepherds. Hunting must, then, in their case, be viewed less as a primary means of subsistence than as a supplement to the pastoral state.

for agriculture, it arises later and involves all the arts; it introduces property, government, laws, and gradually wretchedness and crimes, which for our species are inseparable from the knowledge of good and evil. Hence the Greeks did not view Triptolemus merely as the inventor of a useful art, but as a founder and a wise man to whom they owed their first regulations and their first laws. Moses, on the other hand, appears to have disapproved of agriculture in attributing its invention to a wicked man and making God reject his offerings. The first tiller of the ground would seem to have proclaimed by his character the bad effects of his art. The author of Genesis had seen farther than had Herodotus.

The preceding division corresponds to the three states of man considered in relation to society. The savage is a hunter, the barbarian a herdsman, civil man a tiller of the ground.

So that regardless of whether one inquires into the origin of the arts or studies the earliest morals [or ways of life, *moeurs*], everything is seen to be related in its principle to the means by which men provide for their subsistence; and of these, the means that unite men are a function of climate and of the nature of the soil. Hence the diversity of languages and their contrasting characteristics must also be explained by the same causes.

Mild climates, lush and fertile lands were the first to be populated and the last where nations were formed, because there men could more easily do without one another, and the needs that cause society to be born made themselves felt later.

Assume perpetual spring on earth; assume water, cattle, pastures everywhere; assume men issuing from the hands of nature and dispersed throughout all this: I cannot imagine how they would ever have renounced their primitive liberty and left the isolated and pastoral existence that so well suits their natural indolence,[4] in order to impose on themselves without any necessity the slavery, the labors, and the miseries that are inseparable from the state of society.

He who willed man to be sociable inclined the globe's axis at an angle to the axis of the universe by a touch of the finger. With this slight motion I see the face of the earth change and the vocation of mankind settled; I hear, far off, the joyous cries of a heedless multitude; I see Palaces and Cities raised; I see the birth of the arts, laws, commerce; I see peoples forming, expanding, dissolving, succeeding one another like the waves of the sea; I see men

---

[4] The extent to which man is naturally lazy, is simply inconceivable. It would seem that he lives solely in order to sleep, to vegetate, to remain motionless; he can scarcely decide to go through the motions required to keep from dying of hunger. Nothing sustains the savages' love of their state as much as this delicious indolence. The passions that cause man to be restless, provident, active, are born only in society. To do nothing is man's primary and strongest passion after that of self-preservation. Upon looking at it more closely, it would be found that, even among us, people work only in order to get to rest, that it is still laziness that makes us industrious.

clustered in a few points of their habitation in order there to devour one another, and turn the remainder of the world into a frightful desert, a worthy monument to social union and the usefulness of the arts.

The earth nourishes men; but after the first needs have dispersed them, other needs unite them, and it is only then that they speak and cause others to speak about them. I must be allowed time to explain my meaning, so that I am not found to be in contradiction with myself.

When one inquires into where the fathers of mankind were born, whence the first colonies came, the first emigrations originated, you will not name the happy climes of Asia Minor or of Sicily or Africa, or even Egypt; you will name the sands of Chaldea, the rocks of Phoenicia. You will find that it is so at all times. Regardless of how many Chinese live in China, Tartars also go to live there; the Scythians inundated Europe and Asia; the mountains of Switzerland are currently pouring into our fertile regions a continuous stream of colonists that gives no indication whatsoever of drying up.

It is said to be natural for the inhabitants of a barren land to leave it for a better. Very well; but why does this better land make room for others, instead of swarming with its own inhabitants? To leave a barren land, one has to be there in the first place; why then are so many men born there rather than elsewhere? Harsh lands might be expected to be populated only with the excess from fertile lands, and yet we see the opposite to be the case. Most Latin peoples called themselves aboriginal,[5] whereas Magna Graecia, which is more fertile, was populated exclusively by foreigners. All Greek peoples acknowledged that they originally grew out of various colonies, except the one whose soil was the worst, namely the Attic people, who called themselves Autochthonous or self-born. Finally, without piercing the night of time, modern centuries provide one conclusive piece of evidence: indeed, where on earth is the climate drearier than in what has been called the factory of mankind?

Human associations are in large measure the work of accidents of nature: local floods, overflowing seas, volcanic eruptions, major earthquakes, fires started by lightning and destroying forests, everything that must have frightened and dispersed the savage inhabitants of a land, must afterwards have brought them together to restore in common their common losses. The frequent ancient traditions about natural disasters show what instruments providence used to force humans to come together. Ever since societies have been established, these great accidents have ceased and become increasingly rare; it would seem that this too has to be so; the same calamities that brought together men who were scattered, would disperse those who are united.

[5] The terms *Autochthons* and *Aborigines* merely mean that the first inhabitants of the land were savage, without societies, without laws, without traditions, and that they populated it before they spoke.

The revolutions of the seasons are another more general and more permanent cause, one that must have produced the same effect in the climates that are subject to it. Forced to make provisions for winter, people have to help one another and are thus compelled to establish some kind of convention amongst themselves. When expeditions become impossible and they can no longer get about because of the extreme cold, boredom unites them as much as [did] need: the Lapps, buried in their ice, the Eskimos, the most savage of all peoples, come together in their caverns in winter, and in summer they act as if they had never known one another. Increase their development and their enlightenment by one degree, and they will be united forever.

Neither man's stomach nor his intestines are made to digest raw meat, and he generally cannot stand its taste. With the possible single exception of the Eskimos whom I just mentioned, even savages grill their meats. Fire, in addition to being necessary for cooking meats, also delights the eye, and its warmth is pleasing to the body. The sight of the flame, which causes animals to flee, attracts men.[6] Around a common hearth people gather, feast, dance; the sweet bonds of familiarity imperceptibly draw man to his kind, and on this rustic hearth burns the sacred fire that introduces the first sentiments of humanity into men's hearts.

In warm lands, unevenly scattered springs and rivers are further meeting places, all the more necessary inasmuch as men can do without water even less than they can do without fire. Barbarians who live off their herds are especially in need of common watering places, and we learn from the history of the most remote ages that that is indeed where their treaties as well as their quarrels began.[7] Easy access to water can delay the emergence of society among those who live where it is plentiful. In arid places, on the other hand, people had to cooperate in sinking wells and digging ditches to provide water for their cattle. Associations of men are found there almost from time immemorial, for the land had either to remain desert or to be made inhabitable by man's labor. But our tendency to refer everything to our own practices calls for a few reflections on this subject.

The first state of the earth differed greatly from its present state, when it is seen embellished or disfigured by men's hand. The chaos which the

---

[6] Fire gives much pleasure to animals as well as to man, once they have become accustomed to its sight and felt its gentle warmth. Often it would even prove no less useful to them than to us, if only to warm their young. Yet no one has ever heard of any animal, wild or domestic, which, even by imitating us, has acquired the skills required to make fire. And these are the reasoning beings that are said to form an evanescent prehuman society, although their intelligence could not rise to the level of drawing sparks from a stone and catching them [on tinder], or at least of keeping some abandoned fire going! Upon my word, the philosophers quite openly mock us. Their writings clearly show that they indeed take us for beasts.

[7] See the instance of the one as well as of the other between Abraham and Abimelech in connection with the well of the Oath, in chapter 21 of *Genesis*.

Poets feigned among the elements did prevail among its productions. In those remote times when revolutions were frequent, when numberless accidents altered the nature of the soil and the features of the terrain, everything grew in a jumble, trees, vegetables, shrubs, grasses: no species had time to seize for its own the terrain that best suited it, and to choke out the others there; they would separate slowly, gradually, and then a sudden upheaval would jumble everything.

The relation between man's needs and the productions of the earth is such that, as long as it is populated, everything subsists; but before men united had, by their common labors, introduced a balance among its productions, they could all subsist only if nature alone attended to the equilibrium which the hand of man preserves today; nature maintained or restored this equilibrium by revolutions, just as men maintain or restore it by their inconstancy. Men were not yet at war with one another, but the elements seemed to be; men did not burn cities, dig mines, fell trees; but nature sparked volcanoes, aroused earthquakes, the fire of heaven devoured forests. A bolt of lightning, a flood, a volcanic eruption did then in a few hours what a hundred thousand human arms now do in a century. I see no other way in which the system could have subsisted and the equilibrium maintained itself. In the two realms of organic beings, the larger species would in the long run have absorbed the smaller:[8] the entire earth would soon have been covered with nothing but trees and ferocious beasts; eventually everything would have perished.

The water cycle which nourishes the earth would, little by little, have broken down. Mountains get worn down and smaller, rivers silt up, the sea rises and spreads, everything imperceptibly tends toward the same level; men's hand slows this drift and delays this progress; without them it would proceed faster, and the earth might perhaps already be under water. Springs are poorly distributed and, prior to human labor, they flowed less evenly, fertilized the earth less [adequately], made its inhabitants' supply of drinking water more difficult. Rivers were often inaccessible, and their banks steep or marshy: since human art did not retain them in their beds, they often overflowed, flooded one bank or the other, changed directions and course, divided into various branches; sometimes they

---

[8] It is claimed that by a kind of natural action and reaction, the various species of the animal kingdom would of themselves remain in a perpetual balancing [or seesaw] which would be tantamount to their being in equilibrium. Once the devouring species has increased too much at the expense of the devoured species, the first, so the argument goes, finding no more food, will have to decrease and allow the other time to replenish its numbers; until it again provides ample food for the first and once more decreases while the devouring species is replenished anew. But such an oscillation seems quite implausible to me: for according to this system there has to be a period during which the preyed-upon species increases and the predator species decreases; which seems to me to be altogether contrary to reason.

would dry up, sometimes quicksands blocked access to them; it was as if they did not exist, and men died of thirst surrounded by water.

How many arid lands there are that are inhabitable only thanks to men's draining or chaneling of rivers. Almost the whole of Persia subsists only by means of this artifice; China abounds in People because of its many canals; without their canals, the Low Countries would be flooded by rivers, as they would be flooded by the sea without their dikes; Egypt, the most fertile country on earth, is inhabitable only as a result of human labor. On the great plains where there are no rivers and where the grade is not sufficiently steep, there is no alternative to wells. So that the reason why the first peoples mentioned in history did not live in lush lands or easily accessible shores is not that these happy climes were deserted, but that their numerous inhabitants could do without one another and there-fore lived isolated in their families with no outside communication for a longer time. But in arid regions, where water could only be had from wells, people had no alternative but to get together to dig them, or at least to agree about their use. Such must have been the origin of societies and of languages in warm lands.

Here the first ties between families were established; here the first meetings between the sexes took place. Young girls came to fetch water for the household, young men came to water their herds. Here eyes accustomed from childhood to [see] always the same objects began to see sweeter ones. The heart was moved by them and, swayed by an unfamil-iar attraction, it grew less savage and felt the pleasure of not being alone. Imperceptibly water came to be more needed, the cattle were thirsty more often; one arrived in haste, and left with reluctance. In this happy age when nothing recorded the hours, nothing required them to be counted; the only measure of time was enjoyment and boredom. Beneath old oaks, conquerors of years, spirited young people gradually forgot their ferocious-ness; little by little they tamed one another; in striving to make them-selves understood, they learned to make themselves intelligible. Here the first festivals took place; feet skipped with joy, an eager gesture no longer proved adequate, the voice accompanied it with passionate accents, plea-sure and desire merged into one and made themselves felt together. Here, finally, was the true cradle of peoples, and from the pure crystal of the fountains sprang the first fires of love.

What! were men born of the earth before that time? Did generation succeed upon generation without union between the sexes and without any mutual understanding? No, there were families, but there were no Nations; there were domestic languages, but there were no popular lan-guages; there were marriages, but there was no love. Each family was self-sufficient and propagated itself from its own stock alone: children of the same parents grew up together and gradually found ways to make themselves intelligible to one another; the distinction between the sexes appeared with age, natural inclinations sufficed to unite them, instinct served in lieu of passion, habit in lieu of predilection, people became man and wife without having ceased to be brother and sister.[9] None of this was sufficiently lively to untie tongues, none of it such as to draw forth the accents of the ardent passions sufficiently frequently to establish them as institutions; and the same may be said of the occasional, not very pressing needs that may have led some men to collaborate on common labors; one started the basin of the fountain, another later finished it, often without their having had the slightest need of any agreements, and sometimes without even having seen one another. In a word, in mild climates, in fertile regions, it took all the liveliness of the agreeable passions to start men speaking. The first languages, daughters of pleasure rather than of need, long remained under the aegis of their father; their seductive accent faded only with the sentiments that had given them birth, when new needs introduced among men, forced everyone to think only of himself and to withdraw his heart within himself.

THE FORMATION OF THE LANGUAGES OF THE NORTH

Eventually all men become alike, but the order of their progress differs. In southern climates, where nature is prodigal, needs are born of the passions; in cold countries, where nature is miserly, the passions are born of the needs, and the languages, sad daughters of necessity, reflect their harsh origin.

Although man can become accustomed to inclement weather, to cold, discomfort, even to hunger, there is a point beyond which nature succumbs. Whatever is weak perishes, the victim of these cruel ordeals; whatever remains is strengthened, and there is no middle ground between vigor and death. That is why northern peoples are so sturdy; they did not, initially, grow sturdy because of the climate; rather, only those who were sturdy survived in that climate; and it is not surprising that the children preserve their fathers' good constitution.

It is immediately evident that men who are more sturdy must have a less delicate vocal apparatus, their voices must be rougher and stronger. Besides, what a difference there is between the touching inflections that

[9] The first men had to marry their sisters. In view of the simplicity of the first morals, this practice continued without prejudice as long as families remained isolated and even after the most ancient peoples had come together; but the law that abolished it is no less sacred for being by human institution. Those who view it solely in terms of the bond it established between families fail to see its most important aspect. In view of the intimacy between the sexes that inevitably attends upon domestic life, the moment such a sacred law ceased to speak to the heart and to awe the senses, men would cease to be upright, and the most frightful morals would soon cause the destruction of mankind.

issue from movements of the soul, and the cries wrested by physical needs: In those dreadful climates where everything is dead nine months out of the year, where the sun warms the air for a few weeks only in order to let the inhabitants know the benefits of which they are deprived and to prolong their misery, in those regions where the earth yields whatever it yields only after much labor and where the source of life seems to reside more in the arms than in the heart, men, constantly involved in providing for their subsistence, hardly thought about gentler bonds, everything was confined to physical impulsion, opportunity dictated choice, ease dictated preference. Idleness, which feeds the passions, yielded to labor, which represses them. Before they could think about living happily, men had to think about living. Mutual need united them far more effectively than sentiment would have done, society was formed solely through industry, the ever-present danger of perishing did not permit of a language restricted to gesture, and their first word was not *love me* [*aimez-moi*] but *help me* [*aidez-moi*].

The two expressions, although quite similar, are pronounced in a very different tone [of voice]. Not feeling, but understanding had to be conveyed; so that it was a matter not of energy but of clarity. In the place of accent, which was not forthcoming from the heart, they used strong, [easily] perceived articulations, and if the form of the language to some extent made any natural impression, that impression contributed still further to its harshness.

Indeed, men of the North are not without passions, but theirs are passions of another kind. In warm climates the passions are voluptuous, related to love and softness. Nature does so much for those who live there, that there is almost nothing left for them to do. As long as an Asian has women and rest, he is content. But in the North, where people consume a great deal and the soil is barren, men, subject to so many needs, are easily irritated; everything that happens around them worries them; since they have a hard time subsisting, the poorer they are, the more they cling to the little they have; to get close to them is to threaten their lives. That is what accounts for their irascible temperament, so quick to lash out furiously at everything that offends them. Their most natural utterings [*voix*] therefore are those of anger and threats, and they are invariably accompanied by strong articulations which make them harsh and noisy.

REFLECTIONS ON THESE DIFFERENCES

Such, in my opinion, are the most general physical causes of the characteristic difference between primitive languages. Southern languages must have been lively, resonant, accentuated, eloquent, and often obscure because of their vigor; northern languages must have been muted, crude, articulated, shrill, monotone and clear, more because of their words than because of good construction. Modern languages, though they have been intermingled and recast hundreds of times, still retain something of these differences: French, English, German are the private languages of men who help one another, who argue with one another in a deliberate manner, or of excited men who get angry; but the ministers of the Gods proclaiming the sacred mysteries, wise men giving laws to their people, leaders swaying the masses must speak Arabic or Persian.[10] Our languages are better written than spoken, and it is more pleasant to read us than it is to listen to us. In contrast, oriental languages lose their life and warmth when they are written down: only half the meaning is conveyed by the words, all its vigor is in the accents. To form an opinion about the genius of the Orientals from their books is like painting a man's portrait from his corpse.

In order to assess men's actions properly, one has to consider them in all their relations, and that is something we are simply not taught to do. When we put ourselves in the place of others, we always put ourselves in their place as circumstances have modified us, not as they must have modified them, and when we think that we are judging them in the light of reason, we are merely comparing their prejudices with ours. Because he can read a little Arabic, a man smiles as he peruses the Koran; if he had heard Mohammed himself proclaim it in that eloquent rhythmic language, in that rich and persuasive voice which seduced the ear before it did the heart, constantly infusing his succinct sayings with the accent of enthusiasm, he would have prostrated himself and cried: *Great Prophet, Messenger of God, Lead us to glory, to martyrdom; we want to conquer or to die for you.* Fanaticism always appears ludicrous to us, because it has no voice to command a hearing among us. Even our fanatics are not true fanatics; they are merely knaves or fools. Instead of inflections for men inspired, our languages provide only cries for men possessed by the Devil.

THE ORIGIN OF MUSIC

Together with the first utterings [*voix*], either the first articulations or the first sounds were formed, depending on the kind of passion that dictated them. Anger wrests [from us] threatening cries which the tongue and the palate articulate; but the voice of tenderness is gentler: it is modulated by the glottis and becomes a sound. Its accents, however, are more or less frequent, its inflections more or less acute depending on the sentiment that accompanies it. Thus cadence and sounds are born together with syllables: passion rouses all of the [vocal] organs to speech and adorns the voice with

---

[10] Turkish is a northern language.

their full brilliance; thus verse, song, speech have a common origin. Around the fountains which I have mentioned, the first speeches were the first songs: the periodic and measured recurrences of rhythm, the melodious inflections of accents, caused poetry and music to be born together with language; or rather, all this was nothing other than language itself in those happy climates and those happy ages when the only pressing needs that required another's collaboration were needs born of the heart.

The first stories, the first declamations, the first laws were in verse; poetry was discovered before prose; it had to be so, since the passions spoke before reason did. The same was true of music: at first there was no music other than melody, nor any other melody than the varied sound of speech; accents made up the song, quantities made up measure, and people spoke as much by sonorities and rhythm as by articulations and utterings. To say and to sing were formerly one, says Strabo; and, he adds, this shows poetry to be the source of eloquence.[11] He should have said that both sprang from the same source and were initially the same thing. In view of the way in which the earliest societies united, was it surprising that the first stories were set in verse and that the first laws were sung? Is it surprising that the first Grammarians subordinated their art to music and were at one and the same time teachers of both?

A language that has only articulations and utterings [*voix*] is therefore in possession of only half its resources: true, it conveys ideas; but in order to convey sentiments and images it still needs rhythm and sounds [or sonorities], that is to say a melody; that is what the Greek language had, and ours lacks.

We are always astounded by the prodigious effects of eloquence, poetry, and music among the Greeks. We can make no sense of them, because we no longer experience anything like them, and all we can bring ourselves to do, in view of the strong evidence regarding them, is to pretend that we believe them as a concession to our scholars.[12] Burette, having transcribed some pieces of Greek music as best he could into our musical notation, was so naïve as to have these pieces performed at the Academy of Belles Lettres, and the Academicians were so forbearing as to listen to them. I rather admire such an experiment in a country whose music all other nations find indecipherable. Given any foreign Musician you please a solo from a French opera to perform, and I defy you to recognize any part of it. Yet these very Frenchmen took it upon them-

---

[11]*Geogr[aphy]*, B[oo]k I.

[12]"Archytas and Aristoxenus, indeed, thought grammar comprehended under music, and that the same persons taught both subjects. . . . But so did Eupolis, in whose work Prodamus teaches both music and letters. And Maricas, that is to say Hyperbolus, acknowledges that the musicians teach him nothing but letters." Quintilian, B[oo]k I, ch[apter] 10.

selves to pass judgment on the melody of one of Pindar's Odes set to Music two thousand years ago![13]

I have read that American Indians, seeing the amazing effects of fire-arms, used to pick musket balls up off the ground, and, after hurling them with a loud outcry, were utterly surprised to find that they had not killed anyone. Our orators, our musicians, our scholars are like those Indians. The wonder is not that we no longer achieve with our music what the Greeks achieved with theirs; the wonder would, rather, be that the same effects could be produced with such very different instruments.

OF MELODY

Man is modified by his senses, unquestionably; but because we fail to distinguish between modifications, we confuse their causes; we attribute both too much and too little power to sensations; we do not realize that often they affect us not only as sensations but as signs or images, and that their moral effects also have moral causes. Just as the sentiments which painting arouses in us are not due to colors, the power which music exercises over our souls is not the product of sounds. Beautiful colors, nicely modulated, give the eye pleasure, but that pleasure is purely sensory. It is the drawing, the imitation that endows these colors with life and soul, it is the passions which they express that succeed in arousing our own, the objects which they represent that succeed in affecting us. Interest and sentiment do not depend on colors; the lines of a touching painting touch us in an etching as well; remove them from the Painting, and the colors will cease to have any effect.

Melody does in music exactly what drawing does in painting; it indicates the lines and shapes, of which the chords and sounds are but the colors; but, it will be said, melody is no more than a succession of sounds; undoubtedly; but by the same token drawing is also nothing more than an arrangement of colors. An orator uses ink to set down his writings: does that mean that ink is a most eloquent liquid?

Suppose a country where they had no idea of drawing, but where many people who spent their lives combining, mixing, grading colors, believed that they excelled in painting; those people would argue about our paint-

[13]Some allowance must probably always be made for Greek exaggeration, but to make such allowances to a point where all differences vanish is really too great a concession to modern prejudice. "It was," says the Abbé Terrasson, "when the music of the Greeks at the time of Amphion or of Orpheus was at the level at which we now find it in the towns farthest removed from the capital, that it interrupted the flow of rivers, attracted oaks, and caused rocks to move. Nowadays, when it has reached a very high level of perfection, it is much beloved, its beauties are even understood, but it leaves everything in place. The same was true of the verses of Homer, a poet born in times which, in comparison with the times that followed, still preserved something of the childhood of the human spirit. Men were enthralled by his verses, whereas nowadays they merely enjoy and appreciate the verses of good poets." There is no denying that the Abbé Terrasson was occasionally philosophic, but he certainly gives no proof of it in this passage.

ing exactly as we argue about the music of the Greeks. If they were told about the emotion which beautiful paintings arouse in us and the charm of being moved by a pathetic scene, their scholars would immediately delve into the matter, comparing their colors with ours, seeing whether our green is more delicate or our red more brilliant; they would inquire what combinations of colors have the power to cause weeping and what others to arouse anger. The Burettes of that country would patch together a few ragtag scraps of our paintings; whereupon people would ask themselves with some astonishment what is so wonderful about that coloration.

But if, in a neighboring nation, someone began tracing a line, a sketch, some as yet unfinished figure, it would all be regarded as so much scribbling, as willful and baroque painting, and for the sake of preserving [good] taste they would restrict themselves to that simple beauty which really expresses nothing but causes beautiful modulations, large slabs of strong color, extended transitions between hues, to vibrate without a single line.

Finally they might perhaps by dint of progress get to the experiment with the prism. Straightway some famous artist would be sure to erect a fancy system on the basis of it. Gentlemen, he would say to them, if we are to philosophize properly we must go back to the physical causes. Here you have the resolution of light, the primary colors, their relationships, their proportions, the true principles of the pleasure you derive from painting. All this mysterious talk about drawing, respresentation, shape is pure imposture on the part of French painters who think that with their imitations they can arouse I know not what movements in the soul, when it is well known that there are only sensations. You hear wonderful reports about their painting, but look at my hues.

French painters, he would continue, may have noticed the rainbow; nature may have endowed them with some taste for nuance and some instinct for coloration. I, however, have shown you the great, the true principles of the art. What am I saying, of the art? Of all the arts, Gentlemen, of all the Sciences. The analysis of colors, the measurement of prismatic refractions provide you with the only precise relations to be found in nature, with the rule for all relations. Now, everything in the universe is only relations. One therefore knows everything once one knows how to paint, one knows everything once one knows how to match colors.

What would we say about a painter so lacking in sense and taste as to reason this way and stupidly to limit the pleasure painting gives us to the physical aspects of his art? What would we say about a musician who, filled with similar prejudices, believed that harmony alone is the source of the great effects of music? We would send the former off to paint the woodwork, and condemn the other to compose French operas.

As painting, then, is not the art of combining colors in ways pleasing to the eye, music is not the art of combining sounds in ways pleasing to the ear. If there were no more than that to them, they would both be natural sciences, not fine arts. Imitation alone raises them to that rank. What makes painting one of the imitative arts? Drawing. What makes music another? Melody.

OF HARMONY

The beauty of sounds is by nature; their effect is entirely physical; it is due to the interaction of the different particles of air set in motion by the sounding body and by all of its constituent parts, [continuing] perhaps to infinity: all of these taken together, produce a pleasant sensation: everyone in the universe will take pleasure in listening to beautiful sounds; but unless this pleasure is enlivened by familiar melodic inflections it will not be [totally] delightful, it will not become utter pleasure [*volupté*]. The songs which to us are the most beautiful will only moderately affect an ear completely unaccustomed to them; it is a language for which one has to have the Dictionary.

Regarding harmony properly so called, the situation is even less auspicious. Since all of its beauties are by convention, it does not in any way appeal to ears untutored in it; to experience and to appreciate it requires long-standing familiarity with it. Rude ears perceive our consonances as mere noise. It is not surprising that when the natural proportions are altered, natural pleasure disappears.

A sound carries with it all of its accompanying overtones, so related [to it] in terms of intensity and intervals as to produce its most perfect harmony. Add to it the third or fifth or some other consonant interval, and what you have done is not to augment it but to double it; you retain the relation of interval while changing that of intensity: by emphasizing one consonant interval and not the others, you upset the proportion. By trying to do better than nature, you do worse. Your ear and your taste are spoiled by a misunderstanding of art. By nature there is no other harmony than unison.

M. Rameau contends that comparatively simple trebles naturally suggest their basses, and that a person with a true but untrained ear will naturally sing this bass. That is a musician's prejudice, contradicted by all experience. A person who has never heard either bass or harmony will not only fail to find them on his own, he will even dislike them if he should hear them, and he will very much prefer simple unison.

Even if a thousand years were spent reckoning the relations of sounds and the laws of harmony, how could that art ever be turned into an art of imitation, what would be the principle of this supposed imitation, of what is harmony the sign, and what have chords in common with our passions?

Ask the same question about melody, and the answer is immediately evident, it is in the reader's mind all along. By imitating the inflections of the voice, melody expresses plaints, cries of suffering or of joy, threats, moans; all the vocal signs of the passions fall within its province. It imitates the accents of [various] languages as well as the idiomatic expressions commonly associated in each one of them with given movements of the soul; it not only imitates, it speaks; and its language, though inarticulate, is lively, ardent, passionate, and a hundred times more vigorous than speech itself. This is where musical imitation acquires its power, and song its hold on sensitive hearts. In some [musical] systems, harmony can contribute to these [effects] by linking the succession of sounds in accordance with a few laws of modulation, by making intonations more accurate and providing the ear with reliable evidence of this accuracy, by reconciling barely perceptible inflections and fixing them to consonant, connected intervals. But by placing constraints on melody at the same time, harmony deprives it of energy and expressiveness, it eliminates the passionate accent in favor of intervals, it restricts to only two modes songs that should have as many modes as there are tones of voice, and it eradicates and destroys a great many sounds or intervals that do not fit into its system; in a word, it separates song and speech to such an extent that these two languages contend, thwart one another, deprive one another of any truth, and cannot be united in the treatment of a passionate subject without appearing absurd. That is why the people always find it ridiculous to have strong, serious passions expressed in song; for they know that in our languages these passions have no musical inflections at all, and that men of the north no more die singing than do Swans.

By itself, harmony is not even adequate to express what would seem to fall entirely within its province. Thunder, murmuring waters, winds, storms are but poorly rendered by simple chords. Do what you may, mere noise says nothing to the mind; objects have to speak in order to make themselves heard; in every imitation, some sort of discourse must always complement the voice of nature. A musician who tries to render noise with noise errs; he knows neither the weaknesses nor the strengths of his art; he judges of it without taste or insight; teach him that he must render noise with song, that if he wished to make frogs croak, he would have to make them sing; for it is not enough for him merely to imitate, he must do so in a way that both moves and pleases, otherwise his dreary imitation is as nought, and by failing to arouse anyone's interest, it fails to make any impression.

THAT OUR LIVELIEST SENSATIONS OFTEN ACT BY WAY OF MORAL IMPRESSIONS

As long as sounds continue to be considered exclusively in terms of the excitation they trigger in our nerves, the true principles of music and of its power over men's hearts will remain elusive. In a melody, sounds act on us not only as sounds but as signs of our affections, of our sentiments; that is how they arouse in us the [e]motions which they express and the image of which we recognize in them. Something of this moral effect can be discerned even in animals. One Dog's barking attracts another. When my cat hears me imitate a miaowing, he is immediately alert, restless, tense. As soon as he notices that it is I, imitating the sounds of a cat, he sits back and relaxes. What accounts for this difference in impressions, since there is none in the excitation of the nerve fibers, and the cat itself was initially deceived?

If the major impact our sensations have upon us is not due to moral causes, then why are we so sensitive to impressions which are meaningless to barbarians? Why does music that most moves us seem but an empty noise to the ear of a Carib? Are his nerves of a different nature from ours, why are they not excited in the same way, or why do the same excitations affect some people so strongly and others hardly at all?

As proof of the physical power of sounds, people refer to the cure of Tarantula bites. The example proves the opposite. It is not the case that absolute sounds or the same tunes are the indicated cure for everyone who has been stung by that insect; rather, each one of them requires tunes with a melody he knows and lyrics he can understand. An Italian requires Italian tunes, a Turk would require Turkish tunes. One is affected only by accents that are familiar; the nerves respond to them only insofar as the mind inclines them to it; one has to understand the language in which one is being addressed if one is to be moved by what one is told. Bernier's Cantatas are said to have cured a French musician of the fever; they would have given one to a musician of any other nation.

The same differences can be observed in relation to all the other senses, down to the crudest of them. Let a man, with his hand resting and his glance focusing on one and the same object, alternately believe that it is and that it is not alive; although what strikes his senses is the same, what a difference in the impression! The roundness, whiteness, firmness, gentle warmth, springy resistance, rhythmic swelling are pleasant but dull to the touch, once he no longer believes that underneath them he can feel the throbbing and beating of a heart full of life.

I know only one sense the reactions of which are without any moral component: taste. That is why a sweet tooth is the dominant vice only of people who feel nothing.

Whoever wishes to philosophize about the power of sensations must therefore begin by distinguishing between exclusively sensory impressions and the intellectual and moral impressions which we receive by way of the senses but of which the senses are merely the occasional causes; let him avoid the error of attributing to sensible objects a power which they either lack or derive from the affections of the soul which they represent to us. Colors and sounds can do much as representations and signs, and little as simple objects of sensation. Sequences of sounds or of chords may perhaps give me a moment's pleasure; but in order to delight and to move me, these sequences must provide something that is neither sound nor chord, and will succeed in moving me in spite of myself. Even songs that are merely pleasant but say nothing, become boring; for it is not so much the ear that conveys pleasure to the heart as the heart that conveys it to the ear. I believe that if these ideas had been explored more adequately, much foolish speculation about ancient music could have been avoided. But in this century, when every effort is made to materialize all the operations of the soul and to deprive human sentiments of all morality, I should be greatly surprised if the new philosophy did not prove as fatal to good taste as it does to virtue.

FALSE ANALOGY BETWEEN COLORS AND SOUNDS

Physical observations have occasioned every kind of absurdity in discussions of the fine arts. The analysis of sound has revealed the same relations as has the analysis of light. Straightway the analogy was seized upon, without regard for experience or reason. The systematizing spirit has jumbled everything and, since it proved impossible to paint for the ears, it was decided to sing to the eyes. I have seen the famous clavichord on which music was supposedly produced with colors; what a gross misunderstanding of how nature operates it was, not to see that the effect of colors is due to their permanence and that of sounds to their succession.

The full wealth of coloration is spread out all at once over the face of the earth. Everything is seen at first glance; but the more one looks, the more one is enchanted. One need only go on admiring and contemplating forever.

The same is not true of sound; nature does not analyze it and separate out its harmonics; on the contrary, it hides them under the appearance of unison; or if, sometimes, it does separate them in the modulated song of man or in the warbling of certain birds, it does so successively and one after the other; it inspires songs, not chords, it dictates melody, not harmony. Colors are the ornament of inanimate beings; all matter is colored; but sounds proclaim movement; the voice proclaims a being endowed with sense; only animate bodies sing. It is not the mechanical flutist that plays the flute, but the engineer who measured the flow of air and made the fingers move.

Thus every sense has its own proper realm. The realm of music is time, that of painting is space. To multiply the number of sounds heard all at once, or to present colors one after the other, is to alter their economy, it is to substitute the eye for the ear, and the ear for the eye.

You say: just as every color is determined by the angle of refraction of the ray that causes it, so is every sound determined by the number of vibrations of the sounding body in a given span of time. Now, since the relations between these angles and these numbers are the same, the analogy is obvious. Granted; but it is an analogy of reason, not of sensation, and [besides], it is not to the point. In the first place, the angle of refraction is both perceptible and measurable, whereas the number of vibrations is neither. Sounding bodies being subject to the influence of the air constantly change their size and the sounds they give forth. Colors last, sounds vanish, and one can never be certain that the sounds that arise next are the same as those that have just died away. Moreover, every color is absolute, independent, whereas every sound is for us only relative, and distinct only by contrast. By itself a sound has no absolute character by which it might be recognized; it is low or high, loud or soft in relation to another sound; in itself it is none of these. Nor is a given sound by nature anything within the harmonic system: it is neither tonic, nor dominant, nor harmonic, nor fundamental; for all of these properties are only relationships, and since the entire system can vary from low to high, every sound changes its rank and position in the system as the system changes in degree. But the properties of colors are not at all functions of relationships. Yellow is yellow, independently of red and of blue; it is everywhere perceptible and recognizable, and as soon as its angle of refraction has been determined we can be sure of obtaining the same yellow every time.

Colors are not in the colored bodies but in the light; an object must be illuminated in order to be visible. Sounds also need a moving agent, and in order for them to exist, the sounding body has to be set in motion. Sight here enjoys a further advantage: for the constant emanation [of light] from the stars is the natural agency by which sight is acted upon, whereas nature by itself engenders few sounds and, short of believing in the harmony of the heavenly spheres, living beings are needed to product it.

Painting is thus seen to be closer to nature, while music is more closely related to human art. Music is also felt to [involve our] interest more than does painting, precisely because it brings man closer to man and always gives us some idea about our own kind. Painting is often dead and inanimate; it can transport you to the middle of a desert; but as soon as vocal signs strike your ear, they herald a being like yourself, they are, so to speak, the organs of the soul, and if they also depict solitude, they tell you that you are not alone in it. Birds whistle, man alone sings; and it is not possible to hear a song or a symphony without immediately telling oneself: another being endowed with sense is present.

One of the great advantages the musician enjoys is that he can paint things that cannot be heard, whereas the Painter cannot represent things that cannot be seen; and the greatest wonder of an art that acts solely through movement is that it can fashion it even into an image of repose. Sleep, the quiet of night, solitude, and silence itself have a place in the spectacles of music. It is known that noise can produce the effect of silence and silence the effect of noise, as when one falls asleep while being read to in an even and monotonous voice and wakes up the moment the reading stops. But the effect of music on us is more profound, in that it excites in us through one of the senses, affects similar to those that can be aroused through another; and since that relation is perceptible only if the impression is strong, painting, which lacks the requisite strength, cannot imitate music as music imitates it. Though the whole of nature be asleep, he who contemplates it does not sleep; and the musician's art consists in substituting for the imperceptible image of the object, that of the [e]motions which that object's presence excites in the beholder's heart. It will not only churn up the sea, fan the flames of a conflagration, cause rivers to run, rain to fall, and streams to swell, but will also depict the desolation of dreadful deserts, dusk the walls of a subterranean dungeon, appease the storm, clear and still the air and, from the orchestra, spread renewed freshness through the woodlands. It will not represent these things directly, but it will excite in the soul the very same sentiments which one experiences upon seeing them.

A MUSICIANS' ERROR THAT IS HARMFUL TO THEIR ART

Note how everything constantly brings us back to the moral effects about which I have spoken, and how far the musicians who account for the impact of sounds solely in terms of the action of air and the excitation of [nerve] fibers are from understanding wherein the power of this art consists. The more closely they assimilate it to purely physical impressions, the farther away they remove it from its origin, and the more they also deprive it of its primitive energy. By abandoning the accents of speech and adhering exclusively to the rules of harmony, music becomes noisier to the ear and less pleasing to the heart. It has already ceased to speak; soon it will no longer sing, and once that happens it will no longer, for all its chords and harmony, have any effect on us.

THAT THE MUSICAL SYSTEM OF THE GREEKS HAS NO RELATION WHATSOEVER TO OURS

How did these changes come about? By a natural change in the character of languages. It is well known that our harmony is a gothic invention.

People who claim to discover the system of the Greeks in ours talk foolishness. The system of the Greeks was absolutely not harmonic in our sense of the term, except for what was required to tune instruments according to perfect consonances. All peoples with stringed instruments have to tune them by consonances, whereas those without them exhibit inflections in their songs which we call false because they do not fit into our system and we have no notations for them. This has been observed in the songs of American savages; and it should also have been observed in the various intervals of Greek music if it had been studied with less partiality for our own music.

The Greeks divided their Scale into tetrachords as we divide our keyboard into octaves; and the same divisions recurred regularly in each of their tetrachords as they do in each of our octaves, a similarity which would not have been preserved in the unity of the harmonic mode, and would not even have been imagined. But since one proceeds by smaller intervals when speaking than when singing, it was natural for them to view the repetition of tetrachords in their oral melody as we do the repetition of octaves in our harmonic melody.

The only consonances they acknowledged are the consonances they call perfect; they excluded thirds and sixths from this class. Why did they do so? Because they did not know, or at least in practice excluded the minor interval of the whole tone, and their consonances were not tempered in any degree; as a consequence all their major thirds were too great and their minor thirds too small by a comma, and so their major and minor sixths were reciprocally altered in the same way. Now, try to imagine what notions of harmony and what harmonic modes are possible once thirds and sixths are excluded from the class of consonances! If, with a true sense for harmony, they had perceived the consonances which they did allow, then these consonances would at least have been implicit in their songs, and the unsounded consonance of the root sequences would have lent its name to the diatonic sequences it implied. Far from having fewer consonances than we, they would have had more; and, for example, since they understood the bass *do sol*, they would have called the second *do re* a consonance.

But, someone might object, why diatonic sequences? Because of an instinct that inclines us to choose the most convenient inflections in an accented and singing language: because the voice took a middle course between the extreme glottal modifications that are required in order constantly to sound the large intervals of consonances on the one hand, and the difficulty of controlling intonation in the very complicated relationships of smaller intervals on the other, it naturally hit on intervals smaller than consonances and simpler than commas; which is not to say that smaller intervals did not also serve a function in the more pathetic forms.

HOW MUSIC DEGENERATED

As language became perfected, melody imperceptibly lost some of its former vigor by imposing new rules on itself, and the calculation of intervals replaced delicacy of inflection. That, for example, is how the enharmonic genus gradually fell into disuse. Once theater had assumed a fixed form, all singing in it was restricted to prescribed modes; and as the rules for imitation were multiplied, the language of imitation grew weaker.

The study of philosophy and the progress of reasoning having perfected grammar, deprived language of the lively and passionate tone that had originally made it so songlike. Composers, who at first had been in the pay of Poets and worked only under their direction and as it were at their dictation, became independent of them at the time of Melanippides and Philoxenus. It is about this license that Music complains so bitterly in a comedy by Pherecrates, a passage of which has been preserved for us by Plutarch. Thus as melody began to be less closely tied to discourse, it imperceptibly assumed a separate existence, and music became increasingly independent of words. That was also the period when the wonders gradually ceased which it had wrought when it was but the accent and the harmony of poetry, and when it endowed poetry with a power over the passions which speech has since exercised only over the reason. Indeed, once Greece abounded in Sophists and Philosophers it no longer had famous poets or musicians. In cultivating the art of convincing [men], the art of moving [them] was lost. Even Plato, jealous of Homer and Euripides, decried the one and was incapable of imitating the other.

Soon servitude added its influence to that of philosophy. Greece in chains lost the fire that warms only free souls, and she never recovered for the praise of her tyrants the tone in which she had sung her Heroes. The influx of Romans further diluted what harmony and accent the language had kept. Latin is a duller and a less musical tongue and, on adopting music, harmed it. The way people sang in the capital came little by little to affect the singing in the provinces; the theaters of Rome had a harmful effect on those of Athens; by the time Nero was carrying off prizes, Greece had ceased to deserve them; and the same melody shared by two languages suited each of them less well.

Finally the catastrophe occurred which destroyed the progress of the human spirit, without eliminating the vices that were its product: Europe, overrun by barbarians and subjugated by ignorant men, at one and the same time lost her sciences, her arts, and the universal instrument of both, a harmonious and perfected language. These crude men whom the North had fathered, gradually accustomed all ears to the coarseness of their [vocal] organ; their harsh voices, devoid of accents, were noisy without being sonorous. The Emperor Julian compared the speech of the Gauls to the croaking of frogs. Since all of their articulations were as grating as their voices were nasal and dull, they could impart brilliance to their singing only by stressing vowel sounds in order to cover up the profusion and the harshness of their consonants.

This noisy singing, combined with the inflexibility of their [vocal] organ, compelled these newcomers as well as the subject peoples who imitated them, to make all sounds more sustained in order to make them intelligible. Labored articulation and stressed sounds contributed equally to rob melody of all sense of measure and rhythm. Since the hardest thing to pronounce was always the transition from one sound to the next, the best they could do was to pause at each sound as long as possible, increase its volume, and let it burst forth as vehemently as possible. Soon song was nothing but a dreary and slow succession of drawled and shouted sounds, devoid alike of sweetness, measure, and grace; and although some scholars have maintained that in Latin singing the distinction between long and short syllables had to be observed, it is in any event certain that verse was sung like prose, and that not feet, nor rhythm, nor any kind of measured song were of any further concern.

Since song was thus deprived of all melody and consisted solely in the volume and duration of sounds, it must eventually have suggested ways in which it might be made still more resonant with the aid of consonances. Several voices, constantly drawing out in unison endlessly long sounds, chanced upon a few chords which made the noise seem pleasant to them by accentuating it: and that is how the use of descant and of counterpoint began.

For I know not how many centuries, musicians kept going in circles about vain questions which they debated because they did not know the principle of an effect which they knew [perfectly well]. Even the most tireless reader could not stand eight to ten long chapters of verbiage in Jean de Muris for the sake of finding out whether it is the fifth or the fourth which should be the lower interval in an octave divided into two consonances; and four hundred years later, equally dreary lists of all the basses that must carry a sixth instead of a fifth are still to be found in Bontempi. In the meantime, however, harmony imperceptibly took the direction prescribed to it by analysis, until finally the invention of the minor mode and of dissonances introduced into it the arbitrariness in which it abounds, and which only prejudice prevents us from perceiving.[14]

---

[14] By reducing the whole of harmony to the very simple principle of the resonance of strings in their aliquot [or constituent] parts, M. Rameau bases the minor mode and the dissonance on his supposed findings that a vibrating sonorous string induces vibrations in longer strings at the lower twelfth and the lower major seventeenth. According to him these strings vibrate and quiver over their entire length, but do not resonate. That strikes me as very odd physics; it is rather as if one were to say that the sun is shining but it is impossible to see anything.

Once melody was forgotten and the attention of musicians had focused entirely on harmony, everything gradually turned toward this new object; form, mode, scale, everything acquired a new complexion: harmonic successions came to determine the sequence of parts. Once this sequence had usurped the name of melody, it indeed became impossible to fail to recognize its mother's features in this new melody; and as our musical system thus gradually became purely harmonic, it is not surprising that spoken accent should have suffered as a result, and that for us music should have lost all of its vigor.[15]

That is how singing gradually became an art entirely separate from speech, from which it originates; how the harmonic aspects of sounds caused the inflections of the voice to be forgotten; and how music, restricted to the exclusively physical effect of combinations of vibrations, finally came to be deprived of the moral effects it used to produce when it was doubly the voice of nature.

THE RELATION OF LANGUAGES TO GOVERNMENTS

This progress[ion] is neither accidental nor arbitrary; it is due to the vicissitudes of things. Languages are naturally formed according to men's needs; they change and become transformed as these same needs change. In ancient times, when persuasion served in lieu of public force, eloquence was necessary. Of what use would it be today, when public force replaces persuasion? It requires neither art nor figures of speech to say *such is my pleasure*. What discourses then remain to be addressed to the people assembled? Sermons. And why should those who deliver them care whether they persuade the people, since the people do not award privileges? Popular languages have become as thoroughly useless to us as has eloquence. Societies have assumed their final forms; nothing can be changed in them anymore except by arms and cash, and since there is nothing left to say to the people but *give money*, it is said with posters on street corners or with soldiers in private homes; for this there is no need to assemble anyone: on the contrary, subjects must be kept scattered; that is the first maxim of modern politics.

[15] Since these longer strings produce only the sound of the highest note because they are divided, vibrate, and resonate in unison with it, they blend their sound with its sounds, and thus seem not to emit any sound of their own. The error consists in believing that they were seen to have vibrated over their entire length, and in not having observed the nodes carefully. We know from experience, and M. Tartini has confirmed it, that two strings which form any given harmonic interval can make their fundamental heard in the bass even without a third string: but a single string has no other fundamental than its own; it produces no resonance or vibration in its multiples, but only in its unison and its aliquot [or constituent] parts. Since sound has no other cause than the vibration of the sounding body, and since the effect always follows the unimpeded action of the cause, it is nonsense to separate vibrations from resonance.

Some languages are conducive to liberty; namely, the sonorous, rhythmic, harmonious languages in which speech can be made out from far away. Ours are made for the buzz in the Sultan's Council Chamber. Our preachers agonize, work themselves into a sweat in the Churches, and still no one has any idea of what they have said. After they have worn themselves out shouting for an hour, they leave the pulpit half-dead. Surely it was not worth the effort.

Among the ancients it was easy to be heard by the people in a public square; one could speak in one for an entire day without strain. Generals delivered formal speeches to their Troops; they could make themselves heard without wearing themselves out. Modern historians who included formal speeches in their histories have made themselves a laughingstock. Imagine someone delivering a formal speech in French to the people of Paris in the Place Vendôme. If he shouts at the top of his voice, people will hear that he is shouting, but they will not make out a single word. Herodotus read his history to the people of Greece assembled out of doors, and he met with universal applause. Nowadays, an academician who reads a paper at a public session can hardly be heard at the back of the hall. The reason there are fewer mountebanks in the marketplaces of France than of Italy is not that in France people listen to them less, but only that they cannot hear them as well. M. d'Alembert believes that a French recitative could be delivered in the Italian manner; it would have to be spoken directly into the ear, or it would simply not be heard. Now, I maintain that any language in which it is not possible to make oneself understood by the people assembled is a servile language; it is impossible for a people to remain free and speak that language.

On the Theatre: A Letter to
M. d'Alembert

To ask if the theatre is good or bad in itself is to pose too vague a question; it is to examine a relation before having defined the terms. The theatre is made for the people, and it is only by its effects on the people that one can determine its absolute qualities. There can be all sorts of entertainment. There is, from people to people, a prodigious diversity of morals [manners], temperaments, and characters. Man is one; I admit it! But man modified by religions, governments, laws, customs, prejudices, and climates becomes so different from himself that one ought not to seek among us for what is good for men in general, but only what is good for them in this time or that country. Thus the plays of Menander, made for the Athenian theatre, were out of place in Rome's. Thus the gladiatorial combats which, during the republic, animated the courage and valor of the Romans, only inspired the population of Rome, under the emperors, with the love of blood and cruelty. The same object offered to the same people at different times taught men at first to despise their own lives and, later, to make sport of the lives of others.

The sorts of entertainment are determined necessarily by the pleasure they give and not by their utility. If utility is there too, so much the better. But the principal object is to please; and, provided that the people enjoy themselves, this object is sufficiently attained. This alone will always prevent our being able to give these sorts of institutions all the advantages they are susceptible of; and it is a gross self-deception to form an idea of perfection for them that could not be put into practice without putting off those whom one wants to instruct. It is from this that is born the diversity of entertainments according to the diverse tastes of nations. An intrepid, grave, and cruel people wants deadly and perilous festivals in which valor and composure shine. A ferocious and intense people wants blood, combat, and terrible passions. A voluptuous people wants music and dances. A gallant people wants love and civility. A frivolous people wants joking and ridicule. *Trahit sua quemque voluptas*. To please them, there must be entertainments which promote their penchants, whereas what is needed are entertainments which would moderate them.

The stage is, in general, a painting of the human passions, the original of which is in every heart. But if the painter neglected to flatter these passions, the spectators would soon be repelled and would not want to see themselves in a light which made them despise themselves. So that, if he gives an odious coloring to some passions, it is only to those that are not general and are naturally hated. Hence the author, in this respect, only follows public sentiment. And then, these repulsive passions are always used to set off others, if not more legitimate, at least more to the liking of the spectators. It is only reason that is good for nothing on the stage. A man without passions or who always mastered them could not attract anyone. And it has already been observed that a Stoic in tragedy would be an insufferable figure. In comedy he would, at most, cause laughter.

Let no one then attribute to the theatre the power to change sentiments or morals [manners], which it can only follow and embellish. An author who would brave the general taste would soon write for himself alone. When Molière transformed the comic stage, he attacked modes and ridiculous traits. But, for all of that, he did not shock the public's taste.[1] He followed or expanded on it, just as Cornéille, on his part, did. It was the old theatre which was beginning to shock this taste, because, in an age grown more refined, the theatre preserved its initial coarseness. So, also, the general taste having changed since the time of these two authors, if their masterpieces were now to be presented for the first time, they would inevitably fail. The connoisseurs can very well admire them forever; if the public still admires them, it is more for shame at recanting than from a real sentiment for their beauties. It is said that a good play never fails. Indeed, I believe it; this is because a good play never shocks the morals [manners][2] of its time. Who doubts that the best play of Sophocles would fall flat in our theatre? We would be unable to put ourselves in the places of men who are totally dissimilar to us.

Any author who wants to depict alien morals [manners] for us nevertheless takes great pains to make his play correspond to our morals [manners].

---

[1]Although he anticipated public taste by only a bit, Molière himself had difficulty in succeeding; the most perfect of his works failed at its birth because he presented it too soon and the public was not yet ripe for the *Misanthrope*.

All of this is founded on an evident maxim, i.e., that a people often follows practices which it despises or which it is ready to despise as soon as someone dares to set the example for it. When, in my day, the puppet rage was ridiculed, what was said in the theatre was only the reflection of what was thought by even those who spent their days at that silly amusement. But the constant tastes of a people, its customs, its old prejudices, ought to be respected on the stage. Never has a poet come off well who violated this law.

[2] I say the tastes or morals [manners] indifferently. For although the one is not the other, they always have a common origin and undergo the same revolutions. This does not imply that good taste and good morals [manners] always reign at the same time; this is an assertion which requires clarification and discussion. But that a certain state of taste always answers to a certain state of morals [manners] is indisputable.

Without this precaution, one never succeeds, and even the success of those who have taken it often has grounds very different from those supposed by a superficial observer. If the *Arlequin sauvage* is so well received by audiences, is it thought that this is a result of their taste for the character's sense and simplicity, or that a single one of them would want to resemble him? It is, all to the contrary, that this play appeals to their turn of mind, which is to love and seek out new and singular ideas. Now there is nothing newer for them than what has to do with nature. It is precisely their aversion for the ordinary which sometimes leads them back to the simple things.

It follows from these first observations that the general effect of the theatre is to strengthen the national character, to augment the natural inclinations, and to give a new energy to all the passions. In this sense it would seem that, its effect being limited to intensifying and not changing the established morals [manners], the drama would be good for the good and bad for the vicious. Even in the first case it would remain to be seen if the passions did not degenerate into vices from being too much excited. I know that the poetic theatre claims to do exactly the opposite and to purge the passions in exciting them. But I have difficulty understanding this rule. Is it possible that in order to become temperate and prudent we must begin by being intemperate and mad?

"Oh no! It is not that," says the partisans of the theatre. "Tragedy certainly intends that all the passions which it portrays move us; but it does not always want our emotion to be the same as that of the character tormented by a passion. More often, on the contrary, its purpose is to excite sentiments in us opposed to those it lends its characters." They say, moreover, that if authors abuse their power of moving hearts to excite an inappropriate interest, this fault ought to be attributed to the ignorance and depravity of the artists and not to the art. They say, finally, that the faithful depiction of the passions and of the sufferings which accompany them suffices in itself to make us avoid them with all the care of which we are capable.

To become aware of the bad faith of all these responses, one need only consult his own heart at the end of a tragedy. Do the emotion, the disturbance, and the softening which are felt within onself and which continue after the play give indication of an immediate disposition to master and regulate our passions? Are the lively and touching impressions to which we become accustomed and which return so often, quite the means to moderate our sentiments in the case of need? Why should the image of the sufferings born of the passions efface that of the transports of pleasure and joy which are also seen to be born of them and which the authors are careful to adorn even more in orer to render their plays more enjoyable? Do we not know that all the passions are sisters and that one alone suffices for arousing a thousand, and that to combat one by the other is only the way to make the heart more sensitive to them all? The only instrument which serves to purge them is reason, and I have already said that reason has no effect in the theatre. It is true that we do not share the feelings of all the characters; for, since their interests are opposed, the author must indeed make us prefer one of them; otherwise we would have no contact at all with the play. But far from choosing, for that reason, the passions which he wants to make us like, he is forced to choose those which we like already. What I have said of the sorts of entertainment ought to be understood even more of the interest which is made dominant in them. At London a drama is interesting when it causes the French to be hated; at Tunis, the noble passion would be piracy; at Messina, a delicious revenge; at Goa, the honor of burning Jews. If an author[3] shocks these maxims, he will write a very fine play to which no one will go. And then this author must be taxed with ignorance, with having failed in the first law of his art, in the one which serves as the basis for all the others, which is, to succeed. Thus the theatre purges the passions that one does not have and foments those that one does. Is that a well-administered remedy?

Hence, there is a combination of general and particular causes which keeps the theatre from being given that perfection of which it is thought to be susceptible and from producing the advantageous effects that seem to be expected from it. Even if this perfection is supposed to be as great as it can be, and the people as well disposed as could be wished, nevertheless these effects would be reduced to nothing for want of means to make them felt. I know of only three instruments with which the morals [manners] of a people can be acted upon: the force of the laws, the empire of opinion, and the appeal of pleasure. Now the laws have no access to the theatre where the least constraint would make it a pain and not an amusement.[4] Opinion does not depend on the theatre, since, rather than giving the law to the public, the theatre receives the law from it. And, as to the pleasure that can be had in the theatre, its whole effect is to bring us back more often.

Let us see if there can be other means. The theatre, I am told, directed

---

[3] In order to see this, let a man, righteous and virtuous, but simple and crude, with neither love nor gallantry and who speaks no fine phrases, be put on the French stage; let a prudent man without prejudices be put on it, one who, having been affronted by a bully, refuses to go and have his throat cut by the offender; and let the whole theatrical art be exhausted in rendering these characters as appealing to the French people as is the Cid: I will be wrong, if it succeeds.

[4] The laws can determine the subjects of the plays, and their form, and the way to play them; but the laws cannot force the public to enjoy them. The emperor Nero sang at the theatre and had all those who fell asleep put to death; still he could not keep everybody awake. And the pleasure of a short nap came close to costing Vespasian his life. Noble Actors of the Paris Opera, if you had enjoyed the imperial power, I should not now complain about having lived too long.

as it can and ought to be, makes virtue lovable and vice odious. What? Before there were dramas, were not virtuous men loved, were not the vicious hated, and are these sentiments feebler in the places that lack a theatre? The theatre makes virtue lovable . . . It accomplishes a great miracle in doing what nature and reason do before it! The vicious are hated on the *stage*. . . . Are they loved in society when they are known to be such? Is it quite certain that this hate is the work of the author rather than of the crimes that he makes the vicious commit? Is it quite certain that the simple account of these crimes would produce less horror in us than all the colors with which he has painted them? If his whole art consists in producing malefactors for us in order to render them hateful, I am unable to see what is so admirable in this art, and we get, in this regard, only too many lessons without need of this one. Dare I add a suspicion which comes to me? I suspect that any man, to whom the crimes of Phaedra or Medea were told beforehand, would hate them more at the beginning of the play than at the end. And if this suspicion is well founded, then what are we to think of this much-vaunted effect of the theatre?

I should like to be clearly shown, without wasting words, how it could produce sentiments in us that we did not have and could cause us to judge moral beings otherwise than we judge them by ourselves? How puerile and senseless are these vain pretensions when examined closely! If the beauty of virtue were the product of art, virtue would have long since been disfigured! As for me, even if I am again to be regarded as wicked for daring to assert that man is born good, I think it and believe that I have proved it. The source of the concern which attaches us to what is decent and which inspires us with aversion for evil is in us and not in the plays. There is no art for producing this concern, but only for taking advantage of it. The love of the beautiful[5] is a sentiment as natural to the human heart as the love of self; it is not born out of an arrangement of scenes; the author does not bring it; he finds it there; and out of this pure sentiment, to which he appeals, are born the sweet tears that he causes to flow.

Imagine a play as perfect as you like. Where is the man who, going for the first time, does not go already convinced of what is to be proved in it and already predisposed toward those whom he is meant to like? But this is not the question; what is important is to act consistently with one's principles and to imitate the people whom one esteems. The heart of man is always right concerning that which has no personal relation to himself. In the quarrels at which we are purely spectators, we immediately take the

---

[5] We have to do with the morally beautiful here. Whatever the philosophers may say of it, this love is innate to man and serves as principle to his conscience. (I can cite as an example of this the little play *Nanine*, which has caused the audience to grumble and is only protected by the great reputation of its author. All this is only because honor, virtue, and the pure sentiments of nature are preferred in it to the impertinent prejudice of social station.)

side of justice, and there is no act of viciousness which does not give us a lively sentiment of indignation so long as we receive no profit from it. But when our interest is involved, our sentiments are soon corrupted. And it is only then that we prefer the evil which is useful to us to the good that nature makes us love. Is it not a necessary effect of the constitution of things that the vicious man profits doubly, from his injustice and the probity of others? What more advantageous treaty could he conclude than one obliging the whole world, excepting himself, to be just, so that everyone will faithfully render unto him what is due him, while he renders to no one what he owes? He loves virtue, unquestionably; but he loves it in others because he hopes to profit from it. He wants none of it for himself because it would be costly to him. What then does he go to see at the theatre? Precisely what he wants to find everywhere: lessons of virtue for the public, from which he excepts himself, and people sacrificing everything to their duty while nothing is exacted from him.

I hear it said that tragedy leads to pity through fear. So it does; but what is this pity? A fleeting and vain emotion which lasts no longer than the illusion which produced it; a vestige of natural sentiment soon stifled by the passions; a sterile pity which feeds on a few tears and which has never produced the slightest act of humanity. Thus, the sanguinary Sulla cried at the account of evils he had not himself committed. Thus, the tyrant of Phera hid himself at the theatre for fear of being seen groaning with Andromache and Priam, while he heard without emotion the cries of so many unfortunate victims slain daily by his orders. Tacitus reports that Valerius Asiaticus, calumniously accused by the order of Messalina, who wanted him to perish, defended himself before the emperor in a way that touched this prince very deeply and drew tears from Messalina herself. She went into the next room in order to regain her composure after having, in the midst of her tears, whispered a warning to Vitellius not to let the accused escape. I never see one of these weeping ladies in the boxes at the theatre, so proud of their tears, without thinking of the tears of Messalina for the poor Valerius Asiaticus.

If, according to the observation of Diogenes Laertius, the heart is more readily touched by feigned ills than real ones, if theatrical imitations draw forth more tears than would the presence of the objects imitated, it is less because the emotions are feebler and do not reach the level of pain, as the Abbé du Bos believes,[6] than because they are pure and without mixture of anxiety for ourselves. In giving our tears to these fictions, we have satisfied all the rights of humanity without having to give anything more of

---

[6] He says that the poet afflicts us only so much as we wish, that he makes us like his heroes only so far as it pleases us. This is contrary to all experience. Many people refrain from going to tragedy because they are moved to the point of discomfort; others, ashamed of crying at the theatre, do so nevertheless in spite of themselves; and these effects are not rare enough to be only exceptions to the maxim of this author.

ourselves; whereas unfortunate people in person would require attention from us, relief, consolation, and work, which would involve us in their pains and would require at least the sacrifice of our indolence, from all of which we are quite content to be exempt. It could be said that our heart closes itself for fear of being touched at our expense.

In the final accounting, when a man has gone to admire fine actions in stories and to cry for imaginary miseries, what more can be asked of him? Is he not satisfied with himself? Does he not applaud his fine soul? Has he not acquitted himself of all that he owes to virtue by the homage which he has just rendered it? What more could one want of him? That he practice it himself? He has no role to play; he is no actor.

The more I think about it, the more I find that everything that is played in the theatre is not brought nearer to us but made more distant. When I see the *Comte d'Essex,* the reign of Elizabeth is ten centuries removed in my eyes, and, if an event that took place yesterday at Paris were played, I should be made to suppose it in the time of Molière. The theatre has rules, principles, and a morality apart, just as it has a language and a style of dress that is its own. We say to ourselves that none of this is suitable for us, and that we should think ourselves as ridiculous to adopt the virtues of its heroes as it would be to speak in verse or to put on Roman clothing. This is pretty nearly the use of all these great sentiments and of all these brilliant maxims that are vaunted with so much emphasis—to relegate them forever to the stage, and to present virtue to us as a theatrical game, good for amusing the public but which it would be folly seriously to attempt introducing into society. Thus the most advantageous impression of the best tragedies is to reduce all the duties of man to some passing and sterile emotions that have no consequences, to make us applaud our courage in praising that of others, our humanity in pitying the ills that we could have cured, our charity in saying to the poor, God will help you!

To be sure, a simpler style can be adopted on the stage, and the tone of the theatre can be reconciled in the drama with that of the world. But in this way, morals [manners] are not corrected; they are depicted, and an ugly face does not appear ugly to him who wears it. If we wish to correct them by caricaturing them, we leave the realm of probability and nature, and the picture no longer produces an effect. Caricature does not render objects hateful; it only renders them ridiculous. And out of this arises a very great difficulty; afraid of being ridiculous, men are no longer afraid of being vicious. The former cannot be remedied without promoting the latter. Why, you will ask, must I suppose this to be a necessary opposition? Why, Sir? Because the good do not make evil men objects of derision, but crush them with their contempt, and nothing is less funny or laughable than virtue's indignation. Ridicule, on the other hand, is the favorite arm of vice. With it, the respect that the heart owes to virtue is attacked at its root, and the love that is felt for it is finally extinguished.

Thus everything compels us to abandon this vain idea that some wish to give us of the perfection of a form of theatre directed toward public utility. It is an error, said the grave Muralt, to hope that the true relations of things will be faithfully presented in the theatre. For, in general, the poet can only alter these relations in order to accommodate them to the taste of the public. In the comic, he diminishes them and sets them beneath man; in the tragic, he extends them to render them heroic and sets them above humanity. Thus they are never to his measure, and we always see beings other than our own kind in the theatre. I add that this difference is so true and so well recognized that Aristotle makes a rule of it in his poetics: *Comoedia enim deteriores, Tragoedia meliores quam nunc sont imitari conantur.* Here is a well-conceived imitation, which proposes for its object that which does not exist at all and leaves, between defect and excess, that which is as a useless thing! But of what importance is the truth of the imitation, provided the illusion is there? The only object is to excite the curiosity of the public. These productions of wit and craft, like most others, have for their end only applause. When the author receives it and the actors share in it, the play has reached its goal, and no other advantage is sought. Now, if the benefit is non-existent, the harm remains; and since the latter is indisputable, the issue seems to me to be settled. But let us turn to some examples which will make the solution clearer.

§

I believe I can assert as a truth easy to prove, on the basis of those mentioned above, that the French theatre, with all of its faults, is nevertheless pretty nearly as perfect as it can be, whether from the point of view of pleasure or that of utility, and that these two advantages are in a relation that cannot be disturbed without taking from one more than would be given the other, which would make the theatre even less perfect. This is not to say that a man of genius could not invent a kind of play preferable to those which are established. But this new kind, needing the talents of the author to sustain itself, will necessarily die with him. And his successors, lacking the same resources, will always be forced to return to the common means of interesting and of pleasing. What are these means in our theatre? Celebrated actions, great names, great virtues in tragedy; comic situations and the amusing in comedy; and always love in both.[7] I ask in what way morals [manners] can profit from all this?

I will be told that in these plays crime is always punished and virtue always rewarded. I answer that, even if this were so, most tragic actions

---

[7] The Greeks did not need to found the principal interest of their tragedy on love and actually did not do so. Our tragedy does not have the same resources and could not do without this interest. The reason for this difference will be seen in what follows.

are only pure fables, events known to be inventions of the poet, and so do not make a strong impression on the audience; as a result of showing them that we want to instruct them, we no longer instruct them. I answer, moreover, that these punishments and rewards are always effected by such extraordinary means that nothing similar is expected in the natural course of human things. Finally, I answer by denying the fact. It is not, nor can it be, generally true. For, since this end is not the one toward which authors direct their plays, they are likely to attain it rarely; and often it would be an obstacle to success. Vice or virtue?—what is the difference, provided that the public is overawed by an impression of greatness? So the French stage, undeniably the most perfect, or at least, the most correct which has ever existed, is no less the triumph of the great villains than of the most illustrious heroes: witness Catalina, Mahomet, Atreus and many others.

I am well aware that one must not look to the catastrophe to judge the moral effect of a tragedy and that, in this respect, the end is fulfilled when the virtuous unfortunate is the object of more concern than the happy guilty party! This does not prevent the pretended rule from being violated in such a case. As there is no one who would not prefer to be Britannicus than Nero, I agree that we ought to consider the play which puts them on the stage to be a good one in this respect, even though Britannicus perishes in it. But, according to the same principle, what judgment must we bring to a tragedy in which, although the criminals are punished, they are presented to us in so favorable a light that our sympathies are entirely with them? Where Cato, the greatest of humans, plays the role of a pedant; where Cicero, the savior of the republic—Cicero, who of all those who have borne the name of fathers of their country was the first to have it and the only one to merit it—is shown as a vile orator, a coward; while the infamous Catalina, covered with crimes that we would not dare to mention, ready to slay all his magistrates and to reduce his country to ashes, has the role of a great man and gains by his talents, his firmness, and his courage all the esteem of the audience? For all that he may have had a strong character, if you please, was he any the less for that a hateful villain? And was it necessary to lend to the crimes of a brigand the coloring of a hero's exploits? To what else does the moral of such a play lead if not the encouragement of Catalinas and to the bestowing on clever knaves of the benefits of the public esteem owed to the virtuous? But such is the taste that must be flattered on the stage; such are the morals [manners] of an educated age. Knowledge, wit, and courage alone have our admiration. And thou, modest Virtue, thou remain'st ever unhonored! Blind men that we are, amidst so much enlightenment! Victims of our own mad applause, will we never learn how much contempt and hate are deserved by any man who abuses the genius and the talent that nature gave him, to the hurt of humankind?

Atrée and *Mahomet* do not even use the feeble device of a final catastrophe. The monster who serves as hero in each of these two plays comfortably finishes his crimes and enjoys their benefits; one of the two states the matter, in fitting terms, in the last verse of the tragedy:

Finally I harvest the fruits of my crimes.

I am prepared to believe that the audience, sent home with this fine maxim, will not conclude that crime pays in pleasure and enjoyment. But I ask, what will the play in which this maxim is set up as an example have profited them?

As for *Mahomet*, the fault of attaching the public admiration to the guilty party, who is really worthy of exactly the opposite, would be even greater if the author had not taken care to bring attention and veneration to a second character in such a way as to remove, or at least to balance, the terror and amazement which Mahomet inspires. Above all, the scene they have together is conducted with so much art that Mahomet, without being out of character, without losing any of the superiority belonging to him, is nevertheless eclipsed by the simple common sense and intrepid virtue of Zopire.[8] To dare to put two such interlocutors face to face, an author was needed who was well aware of his powers. I have never heard spoken all the praise of which this scene, in particular, seems to me to be worthy; but I do not know another in the French theatre where the hand of a master is more visibly imprinted, and where the sacred character of virtue more visibly triumphs over the elevation of genius.

Another consideration which tends to justify this play is that its purpose is not only to expose crimes but, in particular, the crimes of fanaticism, for the sake of teaching the people to understand it and to defend themselves against it. Unhappily, such efforts are quite useless and are not always without danger. Fanaticism is not an error, but a blind and stupid fury that reason can never confine. The only secret for preventing it from coming to birth is to restrain those who excite it. You can very well demonstrate to madmen that their chiefs are fooling them; they are no less fervent in following them. Once fanaticism exists, I see only one way left to stop its progress; that is to use its own arms against it. It has nothing to do with

[8]I remember having found more warmth and elevation in Omar in his relations with Zopire than in Mahomet himself; and I took this for a fault. In thinking it over, I changed my mind. Omar, carried away by his fanaticism, ought to speak of his master only with that transport of zeal and admiration which raises him above humanity. But Mahomet is not a fanatic; he is an imposter who, knowing that there is no question of playing the inspired prophet with Zopire, seeks to win him with an affected tone of confidence and through ambitious motives. This reasonable posture renders him necessarily less brilliant than Omar; he is so by the very fact that he is greater and is better able to judge men. He himself says this or makes it understood throughout the scene. It was hence my fault if I did not recognize this; but that is what happens to us little authors. In wishing to censure the writings of our masters, our thoughtlessness causes us to pick out a thousand faults which are beauties for men of judgment.

reasoning or convincing. One must leave philosophy behind, close the books, take the sword, and punish the imposters. What is more, I fear, with regard to Mahomet, that his greatness of soul diminishes the atrocity of his crimes by a great deal in the eyes of the spectators, and that such a play, given before people capable of choosing, would create more Mahomets than Zopires. At least, it is quite certain that such examples are not at all encouraging for virtue.

The black Atreus has none of these excuses; the horror which he inspires is a pure loss. He teaches us nothing other than to shudder at his crime; and, although he is great only in his rage, there is no other figure in the whole play who is capable, by his character, of sharing the public's attention with him. For, as to the mawkish Plisthenes, I do not know how he can be endured in such a tragedy. Seneca put no love in his; and since the modern author was able to bring himself to follow Seneca in all the rest, he would have done well to have imitated him in this too. Indeed, one must have a very flexible heart to tolerate amorous conversations along with Atreus' scenes.

Before finishing with this play, I cannot refrain from mentioning a merit in it which will, perhaps, seem to be a fault to many people. The role of Thyestes is, perhaps of all that have ever been put on our stage, the one that most approaches the taste of the ancients. He is not a courageous hero; he is not a model of virtue; it could not be said, either, that he is a criminal.[9] He is a weak man and nevertheless involves our sympathy on this basis alone: he is a man and unfortunate. It seems, also, on this basis alone, that the feeling which he inspires is extremely tender and moving. For this man is very close to each of us; heroism, on the other hand, overwhelms us even more than it moves us, because, after all, what has it to do with us? Would it not be desirable if our sublime authors deigned to descend a little from their customary great heights and touched us sometimes with simple suffering humanity, for fear that having pity only for unhappy heroes we shall pity no one? The ancients had heroes and put men on their stages; we, on the contrary, put only heroes on the stage and hardly have any men. The ancients spoke of humanity in less-studied phrases, but they knew how to exercise it better.

---

[9] The proof of this is that he attracts us. As to the fault for which he is punished, it is old, it is quite enough atoned for, and finally, it is a small thing for a villain in the theatre; a villain in the theatre is not understood to be such if he does not cause us to shudder in horror.

The Social Contract

INTRODUCTORY NOTE

I wish to enquire whether, taking men as they are and laws as they can be made, it is possible to establish some just and certain rule of administration in civil affairs. In this investigation I shall always strive to reconcile what right permits with what interest prescribes, so that justice and utility may not be severed.

BOOK ONE

Man was born free, and everywhere he is in chains. Many a one believes himself the master of others, and yet he is a greater slave than they. How has this change come about? I do not know. What can render it legitimate? I believe that I can settle this question.

If I considered only force and the results that proceed from it, I should say that so long as a people is compelled to obey and does obey, it does well; but that, so soon as it can shake off the yoke and does shake it off, it does better; for, if men recover their freedom by virtue of the same right by which it was taken away, either they are justified in resuming it, or there was no justification for depriving them of it. But the social order is a sacred right which serves as a foundation for all others. This right, however, does not come from nature. It is therefore based on conventions. The question is to know what these conventions are. Before coming to that, I must establish what I have just laid down.

The earliest of all societies and the only natural one, is the family; yet children remain attached to their father only so long as they have need of him for their own preservation. As soon as this need ceases, the natural bond is dissolved. The children being freed from the obedience which they owed to their father, and the father from the cares which he owed to his children, become equally independent. If they remain united, it is no longer naturally but voluntarily; and the family itself is kept together only by convention.

118

This common liberty is a consequence of man's nature. His first law is to attend to his own preservation, his first cares are those which he owes to himself; and as soon as he comes to years of discretion, being sole judge of the means adapted for his own preservation, he becomes his own master.

The family is, then, if you will, the primitive model of political societies; the chief is the analogue of the father, while the people represent the children; and all, being born free and equal, alienate their liberty only for their own advantage. The whole difference is that, in the family, the father's love for his children repays him for the care that he bestows upon them; while, in the State, the pleasure of ruling makes up for the chief's lack of love for his people.

Grotius denies that all human authority is established for the benefit of the governed, and he cites slavery as an instance. His invariable mode of reasoning is to establish right by fact.[1] A juster method might be employed, but none more favorable to tyrants.

It is doubtful, then, according to Grotius, whether the human race belongs to a hundred men, or whether these hundred men belong to the human race; and he appears throughout his book to incline to the former opinion, which is also that of Hobbes. In this way we have mankind divided like herds of cattle, each of which has a master, who looks after it in order to devor it.

Just as a herdsman is superior in nature to his herd, so chiefs, who are the herdsmen of men, are superior in nature to their people. Thus, according to Philo's account, the Emperor Caligula reasoned, inferring truly enough from this analogy that kings are gods, or that men are brutes.

The reasoning of Caligula is tantamount to that of Hobbes and Grotius. Aristotle, before them all, had likewise said that men are not naturally equal, but that some are born for slavery and others for dominion.

Aristotle was right, but he mistook the effect for the cause. Every man born in slavery is born for slavery; nothing is more certain. Slaves lose everything in their bonds, even the desire to escape from them; they love their servitude as the companions of Ulysses loved their brutishness.[2] If, then, there are slaves by nature, it is because there have been slaves contrary to nature. The first slaves were made such by force; their cowardice kept them in bondage.

I have said nothing about King Adam nor about Emperor Noah, the father of three great monarchs who shared the universe, like the children of Saturn with whom they are supposed to be identical. I hope that my moderation will give satisfaction; for, as I am a direct descendant of one of

---

[1] "Learned researches in public law are often nothing but the history of ancient abuses; and to devote much labor to studying them is misplaced pertinacity" (*Treatise on the Interests of France in relation to her Neighbours*, by the Marquis d'Argenson). That is exactly what Grotius did.

[2] See a small treatise by Plutarch entitled *That Brutes employ Reason*.

these princes, and perhaps of the eldest branch, how do I know whether, by examination of titles, I might not find myself the lawful king of the human race? Be that as it may, it cannot be denied that Adam was sovereign of the world, as Robinson was of his island, so long as he was its sole inhabitant; and it was an agreeable feature of that empire that the monarch, secure on his throne, had nothing to fear from rebellions, or wars, or conspirators.

The strongest man is never strong enough to be always master, unless he transforms his power into right, and obedience into duty. Hence the right of the strongest—a right apparently assumed in irony, and really established in principle. But will this phrase never be explained to us? Force is a physical power; I do not see what morality can result from its effects. To yield to force is an act of necessity, not of will; it is at most an act of prudence. In what sense can it be a duty?

Let us assume for a moment this pretended right. I say that nothing results from it but inexplicable nonsense; for if force constitutes right, the effect changes with the cause, and any force which overcomes the first succeeds to its rights. As soon as men can disobey with impunity, they may do so legitimately; and since the strongest is always in the right, the only thing is to act in such a way that one may be the strongest. But what sort of a right is it that perishes when force ceases? If it is necessary to obey by compulsion, there is no need to obey from duty; and if men are no longer forced to obey, obligation is at an end. We see, then, that this word *right* adds nothing to force; it here means nothing at all.

Obey the powers that be. If that means, Yield to force, the precept is good but superfluous; I reply that it will never be violated. All power comes from God, I admit; but every disease comes from him too; does it follow that we are prohibited from calling in a physician? If a brigand should surprise me in the recesses of a wood, am I bound not only to give up my purse when forced, but am I also morally bound to do so when I might conceal it? For, in effect, the pistol which he holds is a superior force.

Let us agree, then, that might does not make right, and that we are bound to obey none but lawful authorities. Thus my original question ever recurs.

Since no man has any natural authority over his fellow-men, and since force is not the source of right, conventions remain as the basis of all lawful authority among men.

If an individual, says Grotius, can alienate his liberty and become the slave of a master, why should not a whole people be able to alienate theirs, and become subject to a king? In this there are many equivocal terms requiring explanation; but let us confine ourselves to the word *alienate*. To alienate is to give or sell. Now, a man who becomes another's slave does not give himself; he sells himself at the very least for his subsistence. But why does a nation sell itself? So far from a king supplying his subjects with their subsistence, he draws his from them; and, according to Rabelais, a king does not live on a little. Do subjects, then, give up their persons on condition that their property also shall be taken? I do not see what is left for them to keep.

It will be said that the despot secures to his subjects civil peace. Be it so; but what do they gain by that, if the wars which his ambition brings upon them, together with his insatiable greed and the vexations of his administration, harass them more than their own dissensions would? What do they gain by it if this tranquillity is itself one of their miseries? Men live tranquilly also in dungeons; is that enough to make them contented there? The Greeks confined in the cave of the Cyclops lived peacefully until their turn came to be devoured.

To say that a man gives himself for nothing is to say what is absurd and inconceivable; such an act is illegitimate and invalid, for the simple reason that he who performs it is not in his right mind. To say the same thing of a whole nation is to suppose a nation of fools; and madness does not confer rights.

Even if each person could alienate himself, he could not alienate his children; they are born free men; their liberty belongs to them, and no one has a right to dispose of it except themselves. Before they have come to years of discretion, the father can, in their name, stipulate conditions for their preservation and welfare, but not surrender them irrevocably and unconditionally; for such a gift is contrary to the ends of nature, and exceeds the rights of paternity. In order, then, that an arbitrary government might be legitimate, it would be necessary that the people in each generation should have the option of accepting or rejecting it; but in that case such a government would no longer be arbitrary.

To renounce one's liberty is to renounce one's quality as a man, the rights and also the duties of humanity. For him who renounces everything there is no possible compensation. Such a renunciation is incompatible with man's nature, for to take away all freedom from his will is to take away all morality from his actions. In short, a convention which stipulates absolute authority on the one side and unlimited obedience on the other is vain and contradictory. Is it not clear that we are under no obligations whatsoever towards a man from whom we have a right to demand everything? And does not this single condition, without equivalent, without exchange, involve the nullity of the act? For what right would my slave have against me, since all that he has belongs to me? His rights being mine, this right of me against myself is a meaningless phrase.

Grotius and others derive from war another origin for the pretended right of slavery. The victor having, according to them, the right of slaying the vanquished, the latter may purchase his life at the cost of his freedom; an agreement so much the more legitimate that it turns to the advantage of both.

But it is manifest that this pretended right of slaying the vanquished in no way results from the state of war. Men are not naturally enemies, if only for the reason that, living in their primitive independence, they have no mutual relations sufficiently durable to constitute a state of peace or a state of war. It is the relation of things and not of men which constitutes war; and since the state of war cannot arise from simple personal relations, but only from real relations, private war—war between man and man— cannot exist either in the state of nature, where there is no settled owner- ship, or in the social state, where everything is under the authority of the laws.

Private combats, duels, and encounters are acts which do not constitute a state of war; and with regard to the private wars authorized by the Establishments of Louis IX, King of France, and suspended by the Peace of God, they were abuses of the feudal government, an absurd system if ever there was one, contrary both to the principles of natural right and to all sound government.

War, then, is not a relation between man and man, but a relation between State and State, in which individuals are enemies only by acci- dent, not as men, nor even as citizens,[3] but as soldiers; not as members of the fatherland, but as its defenders. In short, each State can have as enemies only other States and not individual men, inasmuch as it is impos- sible to fix any true relation between things of different kinds.

This principle is also conformable to the established maxims of all ages and to the invariable practice of all civilized nations. Declarations of war are not so much warnings to the powers as to their subjects. The foreigner, whether king, or nation, or private person, that robs, slays, or detains subjects without declaring war against the government, is not an enemy, but a brigand. Even in open war, a just prince, while he rightly takes possession of all that belongs to the State in an enemy's country, respects the person and property of individuals; he respects the rights on which his own are based. The aim of war being the destruction of the hostile State, we have a right to slay its defenders so long as they have arms in their

---

[3] The Romans, who understood and respected the rights of war better than any nation in the world, carried their scruples so far in this respect that no citizen was allowed to serve as a volunteer without enlisting expressly against the enemy, and by name against a certain enemy. A legion in which Cato the younger made his first campaign under Popilius having been re-formed, Cato the elder wrote to Popilius that, if he consented to his son's continuing to serve under him, it was necessary that he should take a new military oath, because, the first being annulled, he could no longer bear arms against the enemy (Cicero, *De Officiis* I., 11). And Cato also wrote to his son to abstain from appearing in battle until he had taken this new oath. I know that it will be possible to urge against me the siege of Clusium and other particular cases; but I cite laws and customs (Livy, V. 35–37). No nation has transgressed its laws less frequently than the Romans, and no nation has had laws so admirable.

hands; but as soon as they lay them down and surrender, ceasing to be enemies or instruments of the enemy, they become again simply men, and no one has any further right over their lives. Sometimes it is possible to destroy the State without killing a single one of its members; but war confers no right except what is necessary to its end. These are not the principles of Grotius; they are not based on the authority of poets, but are derived from the nature of things, and are founded on reason.

With regard to the right of conquest, it has no other foundation than the law of the strongest. If war does not confer on the victor the right of slaying the vanquished, this right, which he does not possess, cannot be the foundation of a right to enslave them. If we have a right to slay an enemy only when it is impossible to enslave him, the right to enslave him is not derived from the right to kill him; it is, therefore, an iniquitous bargain to make him purchase his life, over which the victor has no right, at the cost of his liberty. In establishing the right of life and death upon the right of slavery, and the right of slavery upon the right of life and death, is it not manifest that one falls into a vicious circle?

Even if we grant this terrible right of killing everybody, I say that a slave made in war, or a conquered nation, is under no obligation at all to a master, except to obey him so far as compelled. In taking an equivalent for his life the victor has conferred no favor on the slave; instead of killing him unprofitably, he has destroyed him for his own advantage. Far, then, from having acquired over him any authority in addition to that of force, the state of war subsists between them as before, their relation even is the effect of it; and the exercise of the rights of war supposes that there is no treaty of peace. They have made a convention. Be it so; but this convention, far from terminating the state of war, supposes its continuance.

Thus, in whatever way we regard things, the right of slavery is invalid, not only because it is illegitimate, but because it is absurd and meaningless. These terms, *slavery* and *right,* are contradictory and mutually exclusive. Whether addressed by a man to a man, or by a man to a nation, such a speech as this will always be equally foolish: "I make an agreement with you wholly at your expense and wholly for my benefit, and I shall observe it as long as I please, while you also shall observe it as long as I please."

THAT IT IS ALWAYS NECESSARY TO GO BACK TO A FIRST CONTRACT

If I should concede all that I have so far refuted, those who favor despotism would be no farther advanced. There will always be a great difference between subduing a multitude and ruling a society. When isolated men, however numerous they may be, are subjected one after another to a single person, this seems to me only a case of master and slaves, not of a nation and its chief; they form, if you will, an aggregation, but not an association, for they have neither public property nor a body politic. Such a man, had he enslaved half the world, is never anything but an individual; his interest, separated from that of the rest, is never anything but a private interest. If he dies, his empire after him is left disconnected and disunited, as an oak dissolves and becomes a heap of ashes after the fire has consumed it.

A nation, says Grotius, can give itself to a king. According to Grotius, then, a nation is a nation before it gives itself to a king. This gift itself is a civil act, and presupposes a public resolution. Consequently, before examining the act by which a nation elects a king, it would be proper to examine the act by which a nation becomes a nation, for this act, being necessarily anterior to the other, is the real foundation of the society.

In fact, if there were no anterior contract, where, unless the election were unanimous, would be the obligation upon the minority to submit to the decision of the majority? And whence do the hundred who desire a master derive the right to vote on behalf of ten who do not desire one? The law of the plurality of votes is itself established by convention, and presupposes unanimity once at least.

I assume that men have reached a point at which the obstacles that endanger their preservation in the state of nature overcome, by their resistance, the forces which each individual can exert with a view to maintaining himself in that state. Then this primitive condition can no longer subsist, and the human race would perish unless it changed its mode of existence.

Now, as men cannot create any new forces, but only combine and direct those that exist, they have no other means of self-preservation than to form by aggregation a sum of forces which may overcome the resistance, to put them in action by a single motive power, and to make them work in concert.

This sum of forces can be produced only by the combination of many; but the strength and freedom of each man being the chief instruments of his preservation, how can he pledge them without injuring himself, and without neglecting the cares which he owes to himself? This difficulty, applied to my subject, may be expressed in these terms:

"To find a form of association which may defend and protect with the whole force of the community the person and property of every associate, and by means of which each, coalescing with all, may nevertheless obey only himself, and remain as free as before." Such is the fundamental problem of which the social contract furnishes the solution.

The clauses of this contract are so determined by the nature of the act that the slightest modification would render them vain and ineffectual; so that, although they have never perhaps been formally enunciated, they are everywhere the same, everywhere tacitly admitted and recognized, until, the social pact being violated, each man regains his original rights and recovers his natural liberty, whilst losing the conventional liberty for which he renounced it.

These clauses, rightly understood, are reducible to one only, viz. the total alienation to the whole community of each associate with all his rights; for, in the first place, since each gives himself up entirely, the conditions are equal for all; and, the conditions being equal for all, no one has any interest in making them burdensome to others.

Further, the alienation being made without reserve, the union is as perfect as it can be, and an individual associate can no longer claim anything; for, if any rights were left to individuals, since there would be no common superior who could judge between them and the public, each, being on some point his own judge, would soon claim to be so on all; the state of nature would still subsist, and the association would necessarily become tyrannical or useless.

In short, each giving himself to all, gives himself to nobody; and as there is not one associate over whom we do not acquire the same rights which we concede to him over ourselves, we gain the equivalent of all that we lose, and more power to preserve what we have.

If, then, we set aside what is not of the essence of the social contract, we shall find that it is reducible to the following terms: "Each of us puts in common his person and his whole power under the supreme direction of the general will; and in return we receive every member as an indivisible part of the whole."

Forthwith, instead of the individual personalities of all the contracting parties, this act of association produces a moral and collective body, which is composed of as many members as the assembly has voices, and which receives from this same act its unity, its common self (*moi*), its life, and its will. This public person, which is thus formed by the union of all the individual members, formerly took the name of *city*, and now takes that of *republic* or *body politic*, which is called by its members *State* when it is passive, *sovereign* when it is active, *power* when it is compared to similar bodies. With regard to the associates, they take collectively the name of *people*, and are called individually, *citizens*, as participating in the sovereign power, and *subjects*, as subjected to the laws of the State. But these terms are often confused and are mistaken one for another; it is sufficient to know how to distinguish them when they are used with complete precision.

We see from this formula that the act of association contains a reciprocal engagement between the public and individuals, and that every individual, contracting so to speak with himself, is engaged in a double relation, viz. as a member of the sovereign towards individuals, and as a member of the State towards the sovereign. But we cannot apply here the maxim of civil law that no one is bound by engagements made with himself; for there is a great difference between being bound to oneself and to a whole of which one forms part.

We must further observe that the public resolution which can bind all subjects to the sovereign in consequence of the two different relations under which each of them is regarded cannot, for a contrary reason, bind the sovereign to itself, and that accordingly it is contary to the nature of the body politic for the sovereign to impose on itself a law which it cannot transgress. As it can only be considered under one and the same relation, it is in the position of an individual contracting with himself; whence we see that there is not, nor can be, any kind of fundamental law binding upon the body of the people, not even the social contract. This does not imply that such a body cannot perfectly well enter into engagements with others in what does not derogate from this contract; for, with regard to foreigners, it becomes a simple being, an individual.

But the body politic or sovereign, deriving its existence only from the sanctity of the contract, can never bind itself, even to others, in anything that derogates from the original act, such as alienation of some portion of itself, or submission to another sovereign. To violate the act by which it exists would be to annihilate itself; and what is nothing produces nothing.

So soon as the multitude is thus united in one body, it is impossible to injure one of the members without attacking the body, still less to injure the body without the members feeling the effects. Thus duty and interest alike oblige the two contracting parties to give mutual assistance; and the men themselves should seek to combine in this twofold relationship all the advantages which are attendant on it.

Now, the sovereign, being formed only of the individuals that compose it, neither has nor can have any interest contrary to theirs; consequently the sovereign power needs no guarantee towards its subjects, because it is impossible that the body should wish to injure all its members; and we shall see hereafter that it can injure no one as an individual. The sovereign, for the simple reason that it is so, is always everything that it ought to be.

But this is not the case as regards the relation of subjects to the sovereign, which, notwithstanding the common interest, would have no security for the performance of their engagements, unless it found means to ensure their fidelity.

Indeed, every individual may, as a man, have a particular will contrary to, or divergent from, the general will which he has as a citizen; his private interest may prompt him quite differently from the common interest; his absolute and naturally independent existence may make him regard what he owes to the common cause as a gratuitous contribution, the loss of which will be less harmful to others than the payment of it will be burdensome to him; and, regarding the moral person that constitutes the State as an imaginary being because it is not a man, he would be willing to enjoy the rights of a citizen without being willing to fulfill the duties of a subject. The progress of such injustice would bring about the ruin of the body politic.

In order, then, that the social pact may not be a vain formulary, it tacitly includes this engagement, which can alone give force to the others,—that whoever refuses to obey the general will shall be constrained to do so by the whole body; which means nothing else than that he shall be forced to be free; for such is the condition which, uniting every citizen to his native land, guarantees him from all personal dependence, a condition that ensures the control and working of the political machine, and alone renders legitimate civil engagements, which, without it, would be absurd and tyrannical, and subject to the most enormous abuses.

The passage from the state of nature to the civil state produces in man a very remarkable change, by substituting in his conduct justice for instinct, and by giving his actions the moral quality that they previously lacked. It is only when the voice of duty succeeds physical impulse, and law succeeds appetite, that man, who till then had regarded only himself, sees that he is obliged to act on other principles, and to consult his reason before listening to his inclinations. Although, in this state, he is deprived of many advantages that he derives from nature, he acquires equally great ones in return; his faculties are exercised and developed; his ideas are expanded; his feelings are ennobled; his whole soul is exalted to such a degree that, if the abuses of this new condition did not often degrade him below that from which he has emerged, he ought to bless without ceasing the happy moment that released him from it for ever, and transformed him from a stupid and ignorant animal into an intelligent being and a man.

Let us reduce this whole balance to terms easy to compare. What man loses by the social contract is his natural liberty and an unlimited right to anything which tempts him and which he is able to attain; what he gains is civil liberty and property in all that he posseses. In order that we may not be mistaken about these compensations, we must clearly distinguish natural liberty, which is limited only by the powers of the individual, from civil liberty, which is limited by the general will; and possession, which is nothing but the result of force or the right of first occupancy, from property, which can be based only on a positive title.

Besides the preceding, we might add to the acquisitions of the civil state moral freedom, which alone renders man truly master of himself; for the impulse of mere appetite is slavery, while obedience to a self-prescribed law is liberty. But I have already said too much on this head, and the philosophical meaning of the term *liberty* does not belong to my present subject.

Every member of the community at the moment of its formation gives himself up to it, just as he actually is, himself and all his powers, of which the property that he possesses forms part. By this act, possession does not change its nature when it changes hands, and become property in those of the sovereign; but, as the powers of the State (*cité*) are incomparably greater than those of an individual, public possession is also, in fact, more secure and more irrevocable, without being more legitimate, at least in respect of foreigners; for the State, with regard to its members, is owner of all their property by the social contract, which, in the State, serves as the basis of all rights; but with regard to other powers, it is owner only by the right of first occupancy which it derives from individuals.

The right of first occupancy, although more real than that of the strongest, becomes a true right only after the establishment of that of property. Every man has by nature a right to all that is necessary to him; but the positive act which makes him a proprietor of certain property excludes him from all the residue. His portion having been allotted, he ought to confine himself to it, and he has no further right to the undivided property. That is why the right of first occupancy, so weak in the state of nature, is respected by every member of a State. In this right men regard not so much what belongs to others as what does not belong to themselves.

In order to legalize the right of first occupancy over any domain whatsoever, the following conditions are, in general, necessary; first, the land must not yet be inhabited by any one; secondly, a man must occupy only the area required for his subsistence; thirdly, he must take possession of it, not by an empty ceremony, but by labor and cultivation, the only mark of ownership which, in default of legal title, ought to be respected by others.

Indeed, if we accord the right of first occupancy to necessity and labor, do we not extend it as far as it can go? Is it impossible to assign limits to this right? Will the mere setting foot on common ground be sufficient to give an immediate claim to the ownership of it? Will the power of driving away other men from it for a moment suffice to deprive them for ever of the right of returning to it? How can a man or a people take possession of an immense territory and rob the whole human race of it except by a punishable usurpation, since other men are deprived of the place of residence and the sustenance which nature gives to them in common? When Nuñez Balbao on the sea-shore took possession of the Pacific Ocean and of the whole of South America in the name of the crown of Castille, was this sufficient to dispossess all the inhabitants, and exclude from it all the princes in the world? On this supposition, such ceremonies might have been multiplied vainly enough; and the Catholic king in his cabinet might, by a single stroke, have taken possession of the whole world, only cutting off afterwards from his empire what was previously occupied by other princes.

We perceive how the lands of individuals, united and contiguous, become public territory, and how the right of sovereignty, extending itself from the subjects to the land which they occupy, becomes at once real and personal; which places the possessors in greater dependence, and makes their own powers a guarantee for their fidelity—an advantage which ancient monarchs do not appear to have clearly perceived, for, calling themselves only kings of the Persians or Scythians or Macedonians, they seem to have regarded themselves as chiefs of men rather than as owners of countries. Monarchs of to-day call themselves more cleverly kings of France, Spain, England, etc.; in thus holding the land they are quite sure of holding its inhabitants.

The peculiarity of this alienation is that the community, in receiving the property of individuals, so far from robbing them of it, only assures them lawful possession, and changes usurpation into true right, enjoyment into ownership. Also, the possessors being considered as depositaries of the public property, and their rights being respected by all the members of the State, as well as maintained by all its power against foreigners, they have, as it were, by a transfer advantageous to the public and still more to themselves, acquired all that they have given up—a paradox which is easily explained by distinguishing between the rights which the sovereign and the proprietor have over the same property, as we shall see hereafter.

It may also happen that men begin to unite before they possess anything, and that afterwards occupying territory sufficient for all, they enjoy it in common or share it among themselves, either equally or in proportions fixed by the sovereign. In whatever way this acquisition is made, the right which every individual has over his property is always subordinate to the right which the community has over all; otherwise there would be no stability in the social union, and no real force in the exercise of sovereignty.

I shall close this chapter and this book with a remark which ought to serve as a basis for the whole social system; it is that instead of destroying natural equality, the fundamental pact, on the contrary, substitutes a moral and lawful equality for the physical inequality which nature imposed upon men, so that, although unequal in strength or intellect, they all become equal by convention and legal right.[4]

BOOK TWO

The first and most important consequence of the principles above established is that the general will alone can direct the forces of the State

[4]Under bad governments this equality is only apparent and illusory; it serves only to keep the poor in their misery and the rich in their usurpations. In fact, laws are always useful to those who possess and injurious to those that have nothing; whence it follows that the social state is advantageous to men only so far as they all have something, and none of them has too much.

according to the object of its institution, which is the common good; for if the opposition of private interests has rendered necessary the establishment of societies, the agreement of these same interests has rendered it possible. That which is common to these different interests forms the social bond; and unless there were some point in which all interests agree, no society could exist. Now, it is solely with regard to this common interest that the society should be governed.

I say, then, that sovereignty, being nothing but the exercise of the general will, can never be alienated, and that the sovereign power, which is only a collective being, can be represented by itself alone; power indeed can be transmitted, but not will.

In fact, it is not possible that a particular will should agree on some point with the general will, it is at least impossible that this agreement should be lasting and constant; for the particular will naturally tends to preferences, and the general will to equality. It is still more impossible to have a security for this agreement; even though it should always exist, it would not be a result of art, but of chance. The sovereign may indeed say: "I will now what a certain man wills, or at least what he says that he wills;" but he cannot say: "What that man wills to-morrow, I shall also will," since it is absurd that the will should bind itself as regards the future, and since it is not incumbent on any will to consent to anything contrary to the welfare of the being that wills. If, then, the nation simply promises to obey, it dissolves itself by that act and loses its character as a people; the moment there is a master, there is no longer a sovereign, and forthwith the body politic is destroyed.

This does not imply that the orders of the chiefs cannot pass for decisions of the general will, so long as the sovereign, free to oppose them, refrains from doing so. In such a case the consent of the people should be inferred from the universal silence. This will be explained at greater length.

§

For the same reason that sovereignty is inalienable it is indivisible; for the will is either general,[5] or it is not; it is either that of the body of the people, or that of only a portion. In the first case, this declared will is an act of sovereignty and constitutes law; in the second case, it is only a particular will, or an act of magistracy—it is at most a decree.

But our publicists, being unable to divide sovereignty in its principle, divide it in its object. They divide it into force and will, into legislative power and executive power; into rights of taxation, of justice, and of war;

[5]That a will may be general, it is not always necessary that it should be unanimous, but it is necessary that all votes should be counted; any formal exclusion destroys the generality.

into internal administration and power of treating with foreigners—sometimes confounding all these departments, and sometimes separating them. They make the sovereign a fantastic being, formed of connected parts; it is as if they composed a man of several bodies, one with eyes, another with arms, another with feet, and nothing else. The Japanese conjurers, it is said, cut up a child before the eyes of the spectators; then, throwing all its limbs into the air, they make the child come down again alive and whole. Such almost are the jugglers' tricks of our publicists; after dismembering the social body, by a deception worthy of the fair, they recombine its parts, nobody knows how.

This error arises from their not having formed exact notions about the sovereign authority, and from their taking as parts of this authority what are only emanations from it. Thus, for example, the acts of declaring war and making peace have been regarded as acts of sovereignty, which is not the case, since neither of them is a law, but only an application of the law, a particular act which determines the case of the law, as will be clearly seen when the idea attached to the word *law* is fixed.

By following out the other divisions in the same way, it would be found that, whenever the sovereignty appears divided, we are mistaken in our supposition; and that the rights which are taken as parts of that sovereignty are all subordinate to it, and always suppose supreme wills of which these rights are merely executive.

It would be impossible to describe the great obscurity in which this want of precision has involved the conclusions of writers on the subject of political right when they have endeavored to decide upon the respective rights of kings and peoples on the principles that they had established. Every one can see, in chapters III and IV of the first book of Grotius, how that learned man and his translator Barbeyrac become entangled and embarrassed in their sophisms, for fear of saying too much or not saying enough according to their views, and so offending the interests that they had to conciliate. Grotius, having taken refuge in France through discontent with his own country, and wishing to pay court to Louis XIII., to whom his book is dedicated, spares no pains to despoil the people of all their rights, and, in the most artful manner, bestow them on kings. This also would clearly have been the inclination of Barbeyrac, who dedicated his translation to the king of England, George I. But unfortunately the expulsion of James II., which he calls an abdication, forced him to be reserved and to equivocate and evade, in order not to make William appear a usurper. If these two writers had adopted true principles, all difficulties would have been removed, and they would have been always consistent; but they would have spoken the truth with regret, and would have paid court only to the people. Truth, however, does not lead to fortune, and the people confer neither embassies, nor professorships, nor pensions.

§

It follows from what precedes that the general will is always rightful and always tends to the public advantage; but it does not follow that the resolutions of the people are always the right ones. Men always desire their own good, but do not always discern it; the people are never corrupted, though often deceived, and it is only then that they seem to will what is evil.

There is often a great deal of difference between the will of all and the general will; the latter regards only the common interest, while the former has regard to private interests, and is merely a sum of particular wills, but take away from these same wills the pluses and minuses which cancel one another,[6] and the general will remains as the sum of the differences.

If the people came to a resolution when adequately informed and without any communication among the citizens, the general will would always result from the great number of slight differences, and the resolution would always be good. But when factions, partial associations, are formed to the detriment of the whole society, the will of each of these associations becomes general with reference to its members, and particular with reference to the State; it may then be said that there are no longer as many voters as there are men, but only as many voters as there are associations. The differences become less numerous and yield a less general result. Lastly, when one of these associations becomes so great that it predominates over all the rest, you no longer have as the result a sum of small differences, but a single difference; there is then no longer a general will, and the opinion which prevails is only a particular opinion.

It is important, then, in order to have a clear declaration of the general will, that there should be no partial association in the State, and that every citizen should express only his own opinion.[7] Such was the unique and sublime institution of the great Lycurgus. But if there are partial associations, it is necessary to multiply their number and prevent inequality, as Solon, Numa, and Servius did. These are the only proper precautions for ensuring that the general will may always be enlightened, and that the people may not be deceived.

---

[6]"Every interest," says the Marquis d'Argenson, "has different principles. The accord of two particular interests is formed by opposition to that of a third." He might have added that the accord of all interests is formed by opposition to that of each. Unless there were different interests, the common interest would scarcely be felt and would never meet with any obstacle; everything would go of itself, and politics would cease to be an art.

[7]"It is true," says Machiavelli, "that some divisions injure the State, while some are beneficial to it; those are injurious to it which are accompanied by cabals and factions; those assist it which are maintained without cabals, without factions. Since, therefore, no founder of a State can provide against enmities in it, he ought at least to provide that there shall be no cabals" (*History of Florence*, Book VII).

§

In order to discover the rules of association that are most suitable to nations, a superior intelligence would be necessary who could see all the passions of men without experiencing any of them; who would have no affinity with our nature and yet know it thoroughly; whose happiness would not depend on us, and who would nevertheless be quite willing to interest himself in ours; and, lastly, one who, storing up for himself with the progress of time a far-off glory in the future, could labour in one age and enjoy in another.[8] Gods would be necessary to give laws to men.

The same argument that Caligula adduced as to fact, Plato put forward with regard to right, in order to give an idea of the civil or royal man whom he is in quest of in his work the *Statesman*. But if it is true that a great prince is a rare man, what will a great lawgiver be? The first has only to follow the model which the other has to frame. The latter is the mechanician who invents the machine, the former is only the workman who puts it in readiness and works it. "In the birth of societies," says Montesquieu, "it is the chiefs of the republics who frame the institutions, and afterwards it is the institutions which mold the chiefs of the republics."

He who dares undertake to give institutions to a nation ought to feel himself capable, as it were, of changing human nature; of transforming every individual, who in himself is a complete and independent whole, into part of a greater whole, from which he receives in some manner his life and his being; of altering man's constitution in order to strengthen it; of substituting a social and moral existence for the independent and physical existence which we have all received from nature. In a word, it is necessary to deprive man of his native powers in order to endow him with some which are alien to him, and of which he cannot make use without the aid of other people. The more thoroughly those natural powers are deadened and destroyed, the greater and more durable are the acquired powers, the more solid and perfect also are the institutions; so that if every citizen is nothing, and can be nothing, except in combination with all the rest, and if the force acquired by the whole be equal or superior to the sum of the natural forces of all the individuals, we may say that legislation is at the highest point of perfection which it can attain.

The lawgiver is in all respects an extraordinary man in the State. If he ought to be so by his genius, he is not less so by his office. It is not magistracy nor sovereignty. This office, which constitutes the republic, does not enter into its constitution; it is a special and superior office, having nothing in common with human government; for, if he who rules

---

[8]A nation becomes famous only when its legislation is beginning to decline. We are ignorant during how many centuries the institutions of Lycurgus conferred happiness on the Spartans before they were known to the rest of Greece.

men ought not to control legislation, he who controls legislation ought not to rule men; otherwise his laws, being ministers of his passions, would often serve only to perpetuate his acts of injustice; he would never be able to prevent private interests from corrupting the sacredness of his work.

When Lycurgus gave laws to his country, he began by abdicating his royalty. It was the practice of the majority of the Greek towns to entrust to foreigners the framing of their laws. The modern republics of Italy often imitated this usage; that of Geneva did the same and found it advantageous.[9] Rome, at her most glorious epoch, saw all the crimes of tyranny spring up in her bosom, and saw herself on the verge of destruction, through uniting in the same hands legislative authority and sovereign power.

Yet the Decemvirs themselves never arrogated the right to pass any law on their sole authority. Nothing that we propose to you, they said to the people, can pass into law without your consent. Romans, be yourselves the authors of the laws which are to secure your happiness.

He who frames laws, then, has, or ought to have, no legislative right, and the people themselves cannot, even if they wished, divest themselves of this incommunicable right, because, according to the fundamental compact, it is only the general will that binds individuals, and we can never be sure that a particular will is conformable to the general will until it has been submitted to the free votes of the people. I have said this already, but it is not useless to repeat it.

Thus we find simultaneously in the work of legislation two things that seem incompatible—an enterprise surpassing human powers and, to execute it, an authority that is a mere nothing.

Another difficulty deserves attention. Wise men who want to speak to the vulgar in their own language instead of in a popular way will not be understood. Now, there are a thousand kinds of ideas which it is impossible to translate into the language of the people. Views very general and objects very remote are alike beyond its reach; and each individual, approving of no other plan of government than that which promotes his own interests, does not readily perceive the benefits that he is to derive from the continual deprivations which good laws impose. In order that a newly formed nation might approve sound maxims of politics and observe the fundamental rules of state-policy, it would be necessary that the effect should become the cause; that the social spirit, which should be the work of the institution, should preside over the institution itself, and that men should be, prior to the laws, what they ought to become by means of them. Since, then, the lawgiver cannot employ either force or reasoning,

---

[9]Those who consider Calvin only as a theologian are but little acquainted with the extent of his genius. The preparation of our wise edicts, in which he had a large share, does him as much credit as his *Institutes*. Whatever revolution time may bring about in our religion, so long as love of country and of liberty is not extinct among us, the memory of that great man will not cease to be revered.

he must needs have recourse to an authority of a different order, which can compel without violence and persuade without convincing.

It is this which in all ages has constrained the founders of nations to resort to the intervention of heaven, and to give the gods the credit for their own wisdom, in order that the nations, subjected to the laws of the State as to those of nature, and recognizing the same power in the formation of man and in that of the State, might obey willingly, and bear submissively the yoke of the public welfare.

The lawgiver puts into the mouths of the immortals that sublime reason which soars beyond the reach of common men, in order that he may win over by divine authority those whom human prudence could not move.[10] But it does not belong to every man to make the gods his oracles, nor to be believed when he proclaims himself their interpreter. The great soul of the lawgiver is the real miracle which must give proof of his mission. Any man can engrave tables of stone, or bribe an oracle, or pretend secret intercourse with some divinity, or train a bird to speak in his ear, or find some other clumsy means to impose on the people. He who is acquainted with such means only will perchance be able to assemble a crowd of foolish persons; but he will never found an empire, and his extravagant work will speedily perish with him. Empty deceptions form but a transient bond; it is only wisdom that makes it lasting. The Jewish law, which still endures, and that of the child of Ishmael, which for ten centuries has ruled half the world, still bear witness to-day to the great men who dictated them; and whilst proud philosophy or blind party spirit sees in them nothing but fortunate impostors, the true statesman admires in their systems the great and powerful genius which directs durable institutions.

It is not necessary from all this to infer with Warburton that politics and religion have among us a common aim, but only that, in the origin of nations, one serves as an instrument of the other.

§

As an architect, before erecting a large edifice, examines and tests the soil in order to see whether it can support the weight, so a wise lawgiver does not begin by drawing up laws that are good in themselves, but considers first whether the people for whom he designs them are fit to endure them. It is on this account that Plato refused to legislate for the Arcadians and Cyrenians, knowing that these two peoples were rich and could not tolerate equality; and it is on this account that good laws and

---

[10] "It is true," says Machiavelli, "there never was in a nation any promulgator of extraordinary laws who had not recourse to God, because otherwise they would not have been accepted; for there are many advantages recognized by a wise man which are not so self-evident that they can convince others" (*Discourses on Titus Livius*, Book I, chapter 11).

worthless men were to be found in Crete, for Minos had only disciplined a people steeped in vice.

A thousand nations that have flourished on the earth could never have borne good laws; and even those that might have done so could have succeeded for only a very short period of their whole duration. The majority of nations, as well as of men, are tractable only in their youth; they become incorrigible as they grow old. When once customs are established and prejudices have taken root, it is a perilous and futile enterprise to try and reform them; for the people cannot even endure that their evils should be touched with a view to their removal, like those stupid and cowardly patients that shudder at the sight of a physician.

But just as some diseases unhinge men's minds and deprive them of all remembrance of the past, so we sometimes find, during the existence of States, epochs of violence, in which revolutions produce an influence upon nations such as certain crises produce upon individuals, in which horror of the past supplies the place of forgetfulness, and in which the State, inflamed by civil wars, springs forth so to speak from its ashes, and regains the vigor of youth in issuing from the arms of death. Such was Sparta at the time of Lycurgus, such was Rome after the Tarquins, and such among us moderns were Holland and Switzerland after the expulsion of their tyrants.

But these events are rare; they are exceptions, the explanation of which is always found in the particular constitution of the excepted State. They could not even happen twice with the same nation; for it may render itself free so long as it is merely barbarous, but can no longer do so when the resources of the State are exhausted. Then commotions may destroy it without revolutions being able to restore it, and as soon as its chains are broken, it falls in pieces and ceases to exist; henceforward it requires a master and not a deliverer. Free nations, remember this maxim: "Liberty may be acquired but never recovered."

Youth is not infancy. There is for nations as for men a period of youth, or, if you will, of maturity, which they must await before they are subjected to laws; but it is not always easy to discern when a people is mature, and if the time is anticipated, the labor is abortive. One nation is governable from its origin, another is not so at the end of ten centuries. The Russians will never be really civilized, because they have been civilized too early. Peter had an imitative genius; he had not the true genius that creates and produces anything from nothing. Some of his measures were beneficial, but the majority were ill-timed. He saw that his people were barbarous, but he did not see that they were unripe for civilization; he wished to civilize them, when it was necessary only to discipline them. He wished to produce at once Germans or Englishmen, when he should have begun by making Russians; he prevented his subjects from ever becoming what they might have been, by persuading them that they were what they were not. It is in this way that a French tutor trains his pupil to shine for a moment in childhood, and then to be for ever a nonentity. The Russian Empire will desire to subjugate Europe, and will itself be subjugated. The Tartars, its subjects or neighbors, will become its masters and ours. This revolution appears to me inevitable. All the kings of Europe are working in concert to accelerate it.

BOOK THREE

Liberty, not being a fruit of all climates, is not within the reach of all peoples. The more we consider this principle established by Montesquieu, the more do we perceive its truth; the more it is contested, the greater opportunity is given to establish it by new proofs.

In all the governments of the world, the public person consumes, but produces nothing. Whence, then, comes the substance it consumes? From the labor of its members. It is the superfluity of individuals that supplies the necessaries of the public. Hence it follows that the civil State can subsist only so long as men's labor produces more than they need.

Now this excess is not the same in all countries of the world. In several it is considerable, in others moderate, in others nothing, in others a minus quantity. This proportion depends on the fertility due to climate, on the kind of labor which the soil requires, on the nature of its products, on the physical strength of its inhabitants, on the greater or less consumption that is necessary to them, and on several other like proportions of which it is composed.

On the other hand, all governments are not of the same nature; there are some more or less wasteful; and the differences are based on this other principle, that the further the public contributions are removed from their source, the more burdensome they are. We must not measure this burden by the amount of the imposts, but by the distance they have to traverse in order to return to the hands from which they have come. When this circulation is prompt and well-established, it matters not whether little or much is paid; the people are always rich, and the finances are always prosperous. On the other hand, however little the people may contribute, if this little does not revert to them, they are soon exhausted by constantly giving; the State is never rich and the people are always in beggary.

It follows from this that the more the distance between the people and the government is increased, the more burdensome do the tributes become; therefore, in a democracy the people are least encumbered, in an aristocracy they are more so, and in a monarchy they bear the greatest weight. Monarchy, then, is suited only to wealthy nations; aristocracy, to States moderate both in wealth and size; democracy, to small and poor States.

Indeed, the more we reflect on it, the more do we find in this the difference between free and monarchical States. In the first, everything is

used for the common advantage; in the others, public and private resources are reciprocal, and the former are increased by the diminution of
the latter; lastly, instead of governing subjects in order to make them
happy, despotism renders them miserable in order to govern them.

There are, then, in every climate natural causes by which we can assign
the form of government which is adapted to the nature of the climate, and
even say what kind of inhabitants the country should have.

Unfruitful and barren places, where the produce does not repay the
labor, ought to remain uncultivated and deserted, or should only be peopled by savages; places where men's toil yields only bare necessaries
ought to be inhabited by barbarous nations; in them any polity would be
an impossibility. Places where the excess of the produce over the labor is
moderate are suitable for free nations; those in which abundant and fertile
soil yields much produce for little labor are willing to be governed
monarchically, in order that the superfluity of the subjects may be consumed by the luxuries of the Prince; for it is better that this excess should
be absorbed by the government than squandered by private persons.
There are exceptions, I know; but these exceptions themselves confirm
the rule, in that, sooner or later, they produce revolutions which restore
things to their natural order.

We should always distinguish general laws from the particular causes
which may modify their effects. If the whole south should be covered with
republics, and the whole north with despotic States, it would not be less
true that, through the influence of climate, despotism is suitable to warm
countries, barbarism to cold countries, and a good polity to intermediate
regions. I see, however, that while the principle is admitted, its application may be disputed; it will be said that some cold countries are very
fertile, and some southern ones very unfruitful. But this is a difficulty only
for those who do not examine the matter in all its relations. It is necessary,
as I have already said, to reckon those connected with labor, resources,
consumption, etc.

Let us suppose that the produce of two districts equal in area is in the
ratio of five to ten. If the inhabitants of the former consume four and those
of the latter nine parts, the surplus produce of the first will be one-fifth,
and that of the second one-tenth. The ratio between these two surpluses
being then inversely as that of the produce of each, the district which
yields only five will give a surplus double that of the district which produces ten.

But it is not a question of double produce, and I do not think that
anyone dare, in general, place the fertility of cold countries even on an
equality with that of warm countries. Let us, however, assume this equality; let us, if you will, put England in the scales with Sicily, and Poland
with Egypt; more to the south we shall have Africa and India; more to the
north we shall have nothing. For this equality in produce what a differ-

ence in the cultivation! In Sicily it is only necessary to scratch the soil; in England what care is needed to till it! But where more exertion is required to yield the same produce, the surplus must necessarily be very small.

Consider, besides this, that the same number of men consume much less in warm countries. The climate demands that people should be temperate in order to be healthy; Europeans who want to live as at home all die of dysentery and dyspepsia. "We are," says Chardin, "carnivorous beasts, wolves in comparison with Asiatics. Some attribute the temperance of the Persians to the fact that their country is scantily cultivated; I believe, on the contrary, that their country is not very abundant in provisions because the inhabitants need very little. If their frugality," he continues, "resulted from the poverty of the country, it would be only the poor who would eat little, whereas it is the people generally; and more or less would be consumed in each province, according to the fertility of the country, whereas the same abstemiousness is found throughout the kingdom. They pride themselves greatly on their mode of living, saying that it is only necessary to look at their complexions, to see how much superior they are to those of Christians. Indeed, the complexions of the Persians are smooth; they have beautiful skins, delicate and clear; while the complexions of their subjects, the Armenians, who live in European fashion, are rough and blotched, and their bodies are coarse and heavy."

The nearer we approach to the Equator, the less do the people live upon. They eat scarcely any meat; rice, maize, *cuzcuz*, millet, cassava, are their ordinary foods. There are in India millions of men whose diet does not cost a half-penny a day. We see even in Europe palpable differences in appetite between northern and southern nations. A Spaniard will live for eight days on a German's dinner. In countries where men are most voracious luxury is directed to matters of consumption; in England it is displayed in a table loaded with meats; in Italy you are regaled with sugar and flowers.

Again, luxury in dress presents similar differences. In climates where the changes of the seasons are sudden and violent, garments are better and simpler; in those where people dress only for ornament, splendor is more sought after than utility, for clothes themselves are a luxury. At Naples you will see men every day walking to Posilippo with gold-embroidered coats, and no stockings. It is the same with regard to buildings; everything is sacrificed to magnificence when there is nothing to fear from injury by the atmosphere. In Paris and in London people must be warmly and comfortably housed; in Madrid they have superb drawing-rooms, but no windows that shut, while they sleep in mere closets.

The foods are much more substantial and nutritious in warm countries; this is a third difference which cannot fail to influence the second. Why do people eat so many vegetables in Italy? Because they are good, nourishing, and of excellent flavor. In France, where they are grown only on water, they are not nourishing and count almost for nothing on the table; they do not, however, occupy less ground, and they cost at least as much labor to cultivate. It is found by experience that the wheats of Barbary, inferior in other respects to those of France, yield much more flour, and that those of France, in their turn, yield much more than wheats of the north. Whence we may infer that a similar gradation is observable generally, in the same direction, from the Equator to the Pole. Now is it not a manifest disadvantage to have in an equal quantity of produce a smaller quantity of nutriment?

To all these different considerations I may add one which springs from, and strengthens, them; It is that warm countries have less need of inhabitants than cold countries, but would be able to maintain a greater number; hence a double surplus is produced, always to the advantage of despotism. The greater the surface occupied by the same number of inhabitants, the more difficult to rebellions become, because measures cannot be concerted promptly and secretly, and because it is always easy for the government to discover the plans and cut off communications. But the more closely packed a numerous population is, the less power has a government to usurp the sovereignty; the chiefs deliberate as securely in their cabinets as the prince in his council, and the multitude assemble in the squares as quickly as the troops in their quarters. The advantage, then, of a tyrannical government lies in this, that it acts at great distances. By help of the points of support which it procures, its power increases with the distance, like that of levers.[11] That of the people, on the other hand, acts only when concentrated; it evaporates and disappears as it extends, like the effect of powder scattered on the ground, which takes fire only grain by grain. The least populous countries are thus the best adapted for tyranny; wild beasts reign only in deserts.

§

When, then, it is asked absolutely which is the best government, an insoluble and likewise indeterminate question is propounded; or, if you will, it has as many correct solutions as there are possible combinations in the absolute and relative positions of the nations.

But if it were asked by what sign it can be known whether a given people is well or ill governed, that would be a different matter, and the question of fact might be determined.

[11]This does not contradict what I said before (Book II, chapter ix.) on the inconveniences of large States; for there it was a question of the authority of the government over its members, and here it is a question of its power against its subjects. Its scattered members serve as points of support to it for operating at a distance upon the people, but it has no point of support for acting on its members themselves. Thus, the length of the lever is the cause of its weakness in the one case, and of its strength in the other.

It is, however, not settled, because every one wishes to decide it in his own way. Subjects extol the public tranquillity, citizens the liberty of individuals; the former prefer security of possessions, the latter, that of persons; the former are of opinion that the best government is the most severe, the latter maintain that it is the mildest; the one party wish that crimes should be punished and the other that they should be prevented; the one party think it well to be feared by their neighbors, the other party prefer to be unacquainted with them; the one party are satisfied when money circulates, the other party demand that the people should have bread. Even though there should be agreement on these and other similar points, would further progress be made? Since moral quantities lack a precise mode of measurement, even if people were in accord about the sign, how could they be so about the valuation of it?

For my part, I am always astonished that people fail to recognize a sign so simple, or that they should have the insincerity not to agree about it. What is the object of political association? It is the preservation and prosperity of its members. And what is the surest sign that they are preserved and prosperous? It is their number and population. Do not, then, go and seek elsewhere for this sign so much discussed. All other things being equal, the government under which, without external aids, without naturalizations, and without colonies, the citizens increase and multiply most, is infallibly the best. That under which a people diminishes and decays is the worst. Statisticians, it is now your business; reckon, measure, compare.[12]

---

[12]On the same principle must be judged the centuries which deserve preference in respect of the prosperity of the human race. Those in which literature and art were seen to flourish have been too much admired, without the secret object of their cultivation being penetrated, without their fatal consequences being considered: *Idque apud imperitos humanitas vocabatur, quum pars servitutis esset.* Shall we never detect in the maxims of books the gross self-interest which makes the authors speak? No, whatever they may say, when, notwithstanding its brilliancy, a country is being depopulated, it is untrue that all goes well, and it is not enough that a poet should have an income of 100,000 livres for his epoch to be the best of all. The apparent repose and tranquillity of the chief men must be regarded less than the welfare of nations as a whole, and especially that of the most populous States. Hail lays waste a few cantons, but it rarely causes scarcity. Riots and civil wars greatly startle the chief men; but they do not produce the real misfortunes of nations, which may even be abated, while it is being disputed who shall tyrannize over them. It is from their permanent condition that their real prosperity or calamities spring; when all is left crushed under the yoke, it is then that everything perishes; it is then that the chief men, destroying them at their leisure, *ubi solitudinem faciunt, pacem appellant.* When the broils of the great agitated the kingdom of France, and the coadjutor of Paris carried a poniard in his pocket to the *Parlement,* that did not prevent the French nation from living happily and harmoniously in free and honorable ease. Greece of old flourished in the midst of the most cruel wars; blood flowed there in streams, but the whole country was peopled with men. It seemed, said Machiavelli, that amid murders, proscriptions, and civil wars, our republic became more powerful; the virtues of its citizens, their morals, their independence, were more effectual in strengthening it than all its dissensions had been in weakening it. A little agitation gives energy to men's minds, and what makes the race truly prosperous is not so much peace as liberty.

§

As the particular will acts incessantly against the general will, so the government makes a continual effort against the sovereignty. The more this effort is increased, the more is the constitution altered; and as there is here no other corporate will which, by resisting that of the Prince, may produce equilibrium with it, it must happen sooner or later that the Prince at length oppresses the sovereign and violates the social treaty. Therein is the inherent and inevitable vice which, from the birth of the body politic, tends without intermission to destroy it, just as old age and death at length destroy the human body.

There are two general ways by which a government degenerates, viz. when it contracts, or when the State is dissolved.

The government contracts when it passes from the majority to the minority, that is, from democracy to aristocracy, and from aristocracy to royalty. That is its natural tendency.[13] If it retrograded from the minority to the majority, it might be said to relax; but this inverse progress is impossible.

In reality, the government never changes its form except when its

---

[13]The slow formation and the progress of Venice in her lagoons present a notable example of this succession; it is indeed astonishing that, after more than twelve hundred years, the Venetians seem to be still only in the second stage, which began with the *Serrar di Consiglio* in 1198. As for the ancient Doges, with whom they are reproached, whatever the *Squittinio della libertà veneta* may say, it is proved that they were not their sovereigns.

People will not fail to bring forward as an objection to my views the Roman Republic, which followed, it will be said, a course quite contrary, passing from monarchy to aristocracy, and from aristocracy to democracy. I am very far from regarding it in this way.

The first institution of Romulus was a mixed government, which speedily degenerated into despotism. From peculiar causes the State perished before its time, as we see a new-born babe die before attaining manhood. The expulsion of the Tarquins was the real epoch of the birth of the Republic. But it did not at first assume a regular form, because, through not abolishing the patrician order, only a half of the work was done. For, in this way, the hereditary aristocracy, which is the worst of legitimate administrations, remaining in conflict with the democracy, the form of the government, always uncertain and fluctuating, was fixed, as Machiavelli has shown, only on the institution of the tribunes; not till then was there a real government and a true democracy. Indeed, the people then were not only sovereign, but also magistrates and judges; the Senate was only a subordinate tribunal for moderating and concentrating the government; and the consuls themselves, although patricians, although chief magistrates, although generals with absolute authority in war, were in Rome only the presidents of the people.

From that time, moreover the government seemed to follow its natural inclination, and tend strongly to aristocracy. The patriciate abolishing itself as it were, the aristocracy was no longer in the body of patricians as it is at Venice and Genoa, but in the body of the Senate, composed of patricians and plebeians, and also in the body of tribunes when they began to usurp an active power; for words make no difference in things, and when a nation has chiefs to govern for them, whatever name those chiefs bear, they always form an aristocracy.

From the abuses of aristocracy sprang the civil wars and the triumvirate. Sulla, Julius Cæsar, Augustus, became in fact real monarchs; and at length, under the despotism of Tiberius, the State was broken up. Roman history, then, does not belie my principle, but confirms it.

exhausted energy leaves it too weak to preserve itself; and if it becomes still more relaxed as it extends, its force will be annihilated, and it will no longer subsist. We must therefore concentrate the energy as it dwindles; otherwise the State which it sustains will fall into ruin.

The dissolution of the State may occur in two ways.

Firstly, when the Prince no longer administers the State in accordance with the laws; and, secondly, when he usurps the sovereign power. Then a remarkable change takes place—the State, and not the government, contracts; I mean that the State dissolves, and that another is formed within it, which is composed only of the members of the government, and which is to the rest of the people nothing more than their master and their tyrant. So that as soon as the government usurps the sovereignty, the social compact is broken, and all the ordinary citizens, rightfully regaining their natural liberty, are forced, but not morally bound, to obey.

The same thing occurs also when the members of the government usurp separately the power which they ought to exercise only collectively; which is no less a violation of the laws, and occasions still greater disorder. Then there are, so to speak, as many Princes as magistrates; and the State, not less divided than the government, perishes or changes its form.

When the State is broken up, the abuse of the government, whatever it may be, takes the common name of *anarchy*. To distinguish, democracy degenerates into *ochloracy*, aristocracy into *oligarchy;* I should add that royalty degenerates into *tyranny;* but this last word is equivocal and requires explanation.

In the vulgar sense a tyrant is a king who governs with violence and without regard to justice and the laws. In the strict sense, a tyrant is a private person who arrogates to himself the royal authority without having a right to it. It is in this sense that the Greeks understand the word tyrant; they bestowed it indifferently on good and bad princes whose authority was not legitimate.[14] Thus *tyrant* and *usurper* are two words perfectly synonymous.

To give different names to different things, I call the usurper of royal authority a *tyrant*, and the usurper of sovereign power a *despot*. The tyrant is he who, contrary to the laws, takes upon himself to govern according to the laws; the despot is he who sets himself above the laws themselves. Thus the tyrant cannot be a despot, but the despot is always a tyrant.

---

[14] *Omnes enim et habentur et dicuntur tyranni, qui potestate utuntur perpetua in ea civitate quae libertate usa est* (Corn. Nep., *in Miltiad.*, cap. viii). It is true that Aristotle (*Mor. Nicom.*, Book VIII, cap. x.) distinguishes the tyrant from the king, by the circumstance that the former governs for his own benefit, and the latter only for the benefit of his subjects; but besides the fact that, in general, all the Greek authors have taken the word *tyrant* in a different sense, as appears especially from Xenophon's *Hiero*, it would follow from Aristotle's definition that, since the beginning of the world, not a single king has yet existed.

§

Such is the natural and inevitable tendency of the best constituted governments. If Sparta and Rome have perished, what State can hope to endure for ever? If we wish to form a durable constitution, let us, then, not dream of making it eternal. In order to succeed we must not attempt the impossible, nor flatter ourselves that we are giving to the work of men a stability which human things do not admit of.

The body politic, as well as the human body, begins to die from its birth, and bears in itself the causes of its own destruction. But both may have a constitution more or less robust, and fitted to preserve them a longer or shorter time. The constitution of man is the work of nature; that of the State is the work of art. It does not rest with men to prolong their lives; it does rest with them to prolong that of the State as far as possible, by giving it the best constitution practicable. The best constituted will come to an end, but not so soon as another, unless some unforeseen accident brings about its premature destruction.

The principle of political life is in the sovereign authority. The legislative power is the heart of the State; the executive power is its brain, giving movement to all the parts. The brain may be paralyzed and yet the individual may live. A man remains an imbecile and lives; but so soon as the heart ceases its functions, the animal dies.

It is not by laws that the State subsists, but by the legislative power. The law of yesterday is not binding to-day; but tacit consent is presumed from silence, and the sovereign is supposed to confirm continually the laws which it does not abrogate when able to do so. Whatever it has once declared that it wills, it wills always, unless the declaration is revoked.

Why, then, do people show so much respect for ancient laws? It is on account of their antiquity. We must believe that it is only the excellence of the ancient laws which has enabled them to be so long preserved; unless the sovereign had recognized them as constantly salutary, it would have revoked them a thousand times. That is why, far from being weakened, the Laws are ever acquiring fresh vigor in every well-constituted State; the prejudice in favor of antiquity renders them more venerable every day; while, wherever laws are weakened as they grow old, this fact proves that there is no longer any legislative power, and that the State no longer lives.

BOOK FOUR

So long as a number of men in combination are considered as a single body, they have but one will, which relates to the common preservation and to the general well-being. In such a case all the forces of the State are vigorous and simple, and its principles are clear and luminous; it has no confused and conflicting interests; the common good is everywhere plainly manifest and only good sense is required to perceive it. Peace, union, and equality are foes to political subtleties. Upright and simple-minded men are hard to deceive because of their simplicity; allurements and refined pretexts do not impose upon them; they are not even cunning enough to be dupes. When, in the happiest nation in the world, we see troops of peasants regulating the affairs of the State under an oak and always acting wisely, can we refrain from despising the refinements of other nations, who make themselves illustrious and wretched with so much art and mystery?

A State thus governed needs very few laws; and in so far as it becomes necessary to promulgate new ones, this necessity is universally recognized. The first man to propose them only gives expression to what all have previously felt, and neither factions nor eloquence will be needed to pass into law what every one has already resolved to do, so soon as he is sure that the rest will act as he does.

What deceives reasoners is that, seeing only States that are ill-constituted from the beginning, they are impressed with the impossibility of maintaining such a policy in those States; they laugh to think of all the follies to which a cunning knave, an insinuating speaker, can persuade the people of Paris or London. They know not that Cromwell would have been put in irons by the people of Berne, and the Duke of Beaufort imprisoned by the Genevese.

But when the social bond begins to be relaxed and the State weakened, when private interests begin to make themselves felt and small associations to exercise influence on the State, the common interest is injuriously affected and finds adversaries; unanimity no longer reigns in the voting; the general will is no longer the will of all; opposition and disputes arise, and the best counsel does not pass uncontested.

/Lastly, when the State, on the verge of ruin, no longer subsists except in a vain and illusory form, when the social bond is broken in all hearts, when the basest interest shelters itself impudently under the sacred name of the public welfare, the general will becomes dumb; all, under the guidance of secret motives, no more express their opinions as citizens than if the State had never existed; and, under the name of laws, they deceitfully pass unjust decrees which have only private interest as their end.

Does it follow from this that the general will is destroyed or corrupted? No; it is always constant, unalterable, and pure; but it is subordinated to others which get the better of it. Each, detaching his own interest from the common interest, sees clearly that he cannot completely separate it; but his share in the injury done to the State appears to him as nothing in comparison with the exclusive advantage which he aims at appropriating to himself. This particular advantage being excepted, he desires the general welfare for his own interests quite as strongly as any other. Even in selling his vote for money, he does not extinguish in himself the general will, but eludes it. The fault that he commits is to change the state of the question, and to answer something different from what he was asked; so that, instead of saying by a vote: "It is beneficial to the State," he says: "It is beneficial to a certain man or a certain party that such or such a motion should pass." Thus the law of public order in assemblies is not so much to maintain in them the general will as to ensure that it shall always be consulted and always respond.

I might in this place make many reflections on the simple right of voting in every act of sovereignty—a right which nothing can take away from the citizens—and on that of speaking, proposing, dividing, and discussing, which the government is always very careful to leave to its members only; but this important matter would require a separate treatise, and I cannot say everything in this one.

§

We see from the previous chapter that the manner in which public affairs are managed may give a sufficiently trustworthy indication of the character and health of the body politic. The more that harmony reigns in the assemblies, that is, the more the voting approaches unanimity, the more also is the general will predominant; but long discussions, dissensions, and uproar proclaim the ascendancy of private interests and the decline of the State.

This is not so clearly apparent when two or more orders enter into its constitution, as, in Rome, the patricians and plebeians, whose quarrels often disturbed the *comitia*, even in the palmiest days of the Republic; but this exception is more apparent than real, for, at that time, by a vice inherent in the body politic, there were, so to speak, two States in one; what is not true of the two together is true of each separately. And, indeed, even in the most stormy times, the *plebiscita* of the people, when the Senate did not interfere with them, always passed peaceably and by a large majority of votes; the citizens having but one interest, the people had but one will.

At the other extremity of the circle unanimity returns; that is, when the citizens, fallen into slavery, have no longer either liberty or will. Then fear and flattery change votes into acclamations; men no longer deliberate, but adore or curse. Such was the disgraceful mode of speaking in the Senate under the Emperors. Sometimes it was done with ridiculous precautions. Tacitus observes that under Otho the senators, in overwhelming Vitellius with execrations, affected to make at the same time a frightful noise, in order that, if he happened to become master, he might not know what each of them had said.

From these different considerations are deduced the principles by which we should regulate the method of counting votes and of comparing opinions, according as the general will is more or less easy to ascertain and the State more or less degenerate.

There is but one law which by its nature requires unanimous consent, that is, the social compact; for civil association is the most voluntary act in the world; every man being born free and master of himself, no one can, under any pretext whatever, enslave him without his assent. To decide that the son of a slave is born a slave is to decide that he is not born a man.

If, then, at the time of the social compact, there are opponents of it, their opposition does not invalidate the contract, but only prevents them from being included in it; they are foreigners among citizens. When the State is established, consent lies in residence; to dwell in the territory is to submit to the sovereignty.[15]

Excepting this original contract, the vote of the majority always binds all the rest, this being a result of the contract itself. But it will be asked how a man can be free and yet forced to conform to wills which are not his own. How are opponents free and yet subject to laws they have not consented to?

I reply that the question is wrongly put. The citizen consents to all the laws, even to those which are passed in spite of him, and even to those which punish him when he dares to violate any of them. The unvarying will of all the members of the State is the general will; it is through that that they are citizens and free.[16] When a law is proposed in the assembly of the people, what is asked of them is not exactly whether they approve the proposition or reject it, but whether it is conformable or not to the general will, which is their own; each one in giving his vote expresses his opinion thereupon; and from the counting of the votes is obtained the declaration of the general will. When, therefore, the opinion opposed to my own prevails, that simply shows that I was mistaken, and that what I considered to be the general will was not so. Had my private opinion prevailed, I should have done something other than I wished; and in that case I should not have been free.

This supposes, it is true, that all the marks of the general will are still in

[15]This must always be understood to relate to a free State; for otherwise family, property, want of an asylum, necessity, or violence, may detain an inhabitant in a country against his will; and then his residence alone no longer supposes his consent to the contract or to the violation of it.

[16]At Genoa we read in front of the prisons and on the fetters of the galley-slaves the word, *Libertas*. This employment of the device is becoming and just. In reality, it is only the malefactors in all States who prevent the citizens from being free. In a country where all such people are in the galleys the most perfect liberty will be enjoyed.

the majority; when they cease to be so, whatever side we take, there is no longer any liberty.

In showing before how particular wills were substituted for general wills in public resolutions, I have sufficiently indicated the means practicable for preventing this abuse; I will speak of it again hereafter. With regard to the proportional number of votes for declaring this will, I have also laid down the principles according to which it may be determined. The difference of a single vote destroys unanimity; but between unanimity and equality there are many unequal divisions, at each of which this number can be fixed according to the condition and requirements of the body politic.

Two general principles may serve to regulate these proportions: the one, that the more important and weighty the resolutions, the nearer should the opinion which prevails approach unanimity; the other, that the greater the despatch requisite in the matter under discussion, the more should we restrict the prescribed difference in the division of opinions; in resolutions which must be come to immediately the majority of a single voted should suffice. The first of these principles appears more suitable to laws, the second to affairs. Be that as it may, it is by their combination that are established the best proportions which can be assigned for the decision of a majority.

§

With regard to the elections of the Prince and the magistrates, which are, as I have said, complex acts, there are two modes of procedure, viz. choice and lot. Both have been employed in different republics, and a very complicated mixture of the two is seen even now in the election of the Doge of Venice.

"Election by lot," says Montesquieu, "is of the nature of democracy." I agree, but how is it so? "The lot," he continues, "is a mode of election which mortifies no one; it leaves every citizen a reasonable hope of serving his country." But these are not the reasons.

If we are mindful that the election of the chiefs is a function of government and not of sovereignty, we shall see why the method of election by lot is more in the nature of democracy, in which the administration is by so much the better as its acts are less multiplied.

In every true democracy, the magistracy is not a boon but an onerous charge, which cannot fairly be imposed on one individual rather than on another. The law alone can impose this burden on the person upon whom the lot falls. For then, the conditions being equal for all, and the choice not being dependent on any human will, there is no particular application to alter the universality of the law.

In an aristocracy the Prince chooses the Prince, the government is maintained by itself, and voting is rightly established.

The instance of the election of the Doge of Venice, far from destroying this distinction, confirms it; this composite form is suitable in a mixed government. For it is an error to take the government of Venice as a true aristocracy. If the people have no share in the government, the nobles themselves are numerous. A multitude of poor *Barnabotes* never come near any magistracy, and have for their nobility only the empty title of Excellency and the right to attend the Great Council. This Great Council being as numerous as our General Council at Geneva, its illustrious members have no more privileges than our simple citizens (*citoyens*). It is certain that, setting aside the extreme disparity of the two Republics, the burgesses (*la bourgeoisie*) of Geneva exactly correspond to the Venetian order of patricians; our natives (*natifs*) and residents (*habitants*) represent the citizens and people of Venice; our peasants (*paysans*) represent the subjects of the mainland; in short, in whatever way we consider this Republic apart from its size, its government is no more aristocratic than ours. The whole difference is that, having no chief for life, we have not the same need for election by lot.

Elections by lot would have few drawbacks in a true democracy, in which, all being equal as well in character and ability as in sentiments and fortune, the choice would become almost indifferent. But I have already said that there is no true democracy.

When choice and lot are combined, the first should be employed to fill the posts that require peculiar talents, such as military appointments; the other is suitable for those in which good sense, justice, and integrity are sufficient, such as judicial offices, because, in a well-constituted State, these qualities are common to all the citizens.

Neither lot nor voting has any place in a monarchical government. The monarch being by right sole Prince and sole magistrate, the choice of his lieutenants belongs to him alone. When the Abbé de Saint-Pierre proposed to multiply the councils of the King of France and to elect the members of them by ballot, he did not see that he was proposing to change the form of government.

It would remain for me to speak of the method of recording and collecting votes in the assembly of the people; but perhaps the history of the Roman policy in that respect will explain more clearly all the principles which I might be able to establish. It is not unworthy of a judicious reader to see in some detail how public and private affairs were dealt with in a council of 200,000 men.

§

When an exact relation cannot be established among the constituent parts of the State, or when indestructible causes are incessantly changing their relations, a special magistracy is instituted, which is not incorporated with the others, but which replaces each term in its true relation, forming a connexion or middle term either between the Prince and the people, or between the Prince and the sovereign, or if necessary between both at once.

This body, which I shall call the *tribuneship*, is the guardian of the laws and of the legislative power. It sometimes serves to protect the sovereign against the government, as the tribunes of the people did in Rome; sometimes to support the government against the people, as the Council of Ten now does in Venice; and sometimes to maintain an equilibrium among all parts, as the ephors did in Sparta.

The tribuneship is not a constituent part of the State, and should have no share in the legislative or in the executive power; but it is in this very circumstance that its own power is greatest; for, while unable to do anything, it can prevent everything. It is more sacred and more venerated, as defender of the laws, than the Prince that executes them and the sovereign that enacts them. This was very clearly seen in Rome, when those proud patricians, who always despised the people as a whole, were forced to bow before a simple officer of the people, who had neither auspices nor jurisdiction.

The tribuneship, wisely moderated, is the strongest support of a good constitution; but if its power be ever so little in excess, it overthrows everything. Weakness is not natural to it; and provided it has some power, it is never less than it should be.

It degenerates into tyranny when it usurps the executive power, of which it is only the moderator, and when it wishes to make the laws which it should only defend. The enormous power of the ephors, which was without danger so long as Sparta preserved her morality, accelerated the corruption when it had begun. The blood of Agis, slain by these tyrants, was avenged by his successor; but the crime and the punishment of the ephors alike hastened the fall of the republic, and, after Cleomenes, Sparta was no longer of any account. Rome, again, perished in the same way; and the excessive power of the tribunes, usurped by degress, served at last, with the aid of laws framed on behalf of liberty, as a shield for the emperors who destroyed her. As for the Council of Ten in Venice, it is a tribunal of blood, horrible both to the patricians and to the people; and, far from resolutely defending the laws, it has only served since their degradation for striking secret blows which men dare not remark.

The tribuneship, like the government, is weakened by the multiplication of its members. When the tribunes of the Roman people, at first two in number and afterwards five, wished to double this number, the Senate allowed them to do so, being quite sure of controlling some by means of others, which did not fail to happen.

The best means of preventing the usurpations of such a formidable body, a means of which no government has hitherto availed itself, would be, not to make this body permanent, but to fix intervals during which it should remain suspended. These intervals, which should not be long enough to allow abuses time to become established, can be fixed by law in such a manner that it may be easy to shorten them in case of need by means of extraordinary commissions.

This method appears to me free from objection, because, as I have said, the tribuneship, forming no part of the constitution, can be removed without detriment; and it seems to me efficacious, because a magistrate newly established does not start with the power that his predecessor had, but with that which the law gives him.

§

The inflexibility of the laws, which prevents them from being adapted to emergencies, may in certain cases render them pernicious, and thereby cause the ruin of the State in a time of crisis. The order and tardiness of the forms require a space of time which circumstances sometimes do not allow. A thousand cases may arise for which the legislator has not provided and to perceive that everything cannot be foreseen is a very needful kind of foresight.

We must therefore not desire to establish political institutions so firmly as to take away the power of suspending their effects. Even Sparta allowed her laws to sleep.

But only the greatest dangers can outweigh that of changing the public order, and the sacred power of the laws should never be interfered with except when the safety of the country is at stake. In these rare and obvious cases, the public security is provided for by a special act, which entrusts the care of it to the most worthy man. This commission can be conferred in two ways, according to the nature of the danger.

If an increase in the activity of the government suffices to remedy this evil, we may concentrate it in one or two of its members; in that case it is not the authority of the laws which is changed but only the form of their administration. But if the danger is such that the formal process of law is an obstacle to our security, a supreme head is nominated, who may silence all the laws and suspend for a moment the sovereign authority. In such a case the general will is not doubtful, and it is clear that the primary intention of the people is that the State should not perish. In this way the suspension of the legislative power does not involve its abolition; the magistrate who silences it can make it speak; he dominates it without having power to represent it; he can do everything but make laws.

The first method was employed by the Roman Senate when it charged the consuls, by a consecrated formula, to provide for the safety of the

Republic. The second was adopted when one of the two consuls nominated a dictator,[17] a usage of which Alba had furnished the precedent to Rome.

At the beginning of the Republic they very often had recourse to the dictatorship, because the State had not yet a sufficiently firm foundation to be able to maintain itself by the vigor of its constitution alone.

Public morality rendering superfluous at that time many precautions that would have been necessary at another time, there was no fear either that a dictator would abuse his authority or that he would attempt to retain it beyond the term. On the contrary, it seemed that so great a power must be a burden to him who was invested with it, such haste did he make to divest himself of it, as if to take the place of the laws were an office too arduous and too dangerous.

Therefore it is the danger, not of abuse, but of its degradation, that makes me blame the indiscreet use of this supreme magistracy in early times; for whilst it was freely used at elections, at dedications, and in purely formal matters, there was reason to fear that it would become less formidable in case of need, and that the people would grow accustomed to regard as an empty title that which was only employed in empty ceremonies.

Towards the close of the Republic, the Romans, having become more circumspect, used the dictatorship sparingly with as little reason as they had formerly been prodigal of it. It was easy to see that their fear was ill-founded; that the weakness of the capital then constituted its security against the magistrates whom it had within it; that a dictator could, in certain cases, defend the public liberty without ever being able to assail it; and that the chains of Rome would not be forged in Rome itself, but in her armies. The slight resistance which Marius made against Sylla, and Pompey against Cæsar, showed clearly what might be looked for from the authority within against the force without.

This error caused them to commit great mistakes; such, for example, was that of not appointing a dictator in the Catiline affair; for as it was only a question of the interior of the city, or at most of some province of Italy, a dictator, with the unlimited authority that the laws gave him, would have easily broken up the conspiracy, which was suppressed only by a combination of happy accidents such as human prudence could not have foreseen.

Instead of that, the Senate was content to entrust all its power to the consuls; whence it happened that Cicero, in order to act effectively, was constrained to exceed his authority in a material point, and that, although the first transports of joy caused his conduct to be approved, he was afterwards justly called to account for the blood of citizens shed contrary to

---

[17]This nomination was made by night and in secret as if they were ashamed to set a man above the laws.

the laws, a reproach which could not have been brought against a dictator. But the consul's eloquence won over everybody; and he himself, although a Roman, preferred his own glory to his country's good, and sought not so much the most certain and legitimate means of saving the State as the way to secure the whole credit of this affair.[18] Therefore he was justly honored as the liberator of Rome and justly punished as a violator of the laws. However brilliant his recall may have been, it was certainly a pardon.

Moreover, in whatever way this important commission may be conferred, it is important to fix its duration at a very short term which can never be prolonged. In the crises which cause it to be established, the State is soon destroyed or saved; and, the urgent need having passed away, the dictatorship becomes tyrannical or useless. In Rome the dictators held office for six months only, and the majority abdicated before the end of this term. Had the term been longer, they would perhaps have been tempted to prolong it still further, as the Decemvirs did their term of one year. The dictator only had time to provide for the necessity which had led to his election; he had no time to think of other projects.

§

Just as the declaration of the general will is made by the law, the declaration of public opinion is made by the censorship. Public opinion is a kind of law of which the censor is minister, and which he only applies to particular cases in the manner of the Prince.

The censorial tribunal, then, far from being the arbiter of the opinion of the people, only declares it, and so soon as it departs from this position, its decisions are fruitless and ineffectual.

It is useless to distinguish the character of a nation from the objects of its esteem, for all these things depend on the same principle and are necessarily intermixed. In all the nations of the world it is not nature but opinion which decides the choice of their pleasures. Reform men's opinions and their manners will be purified of themselves. People always like what is becoming or what they judge to be so; but it is in this judgment that they make mistakes; the question, then, is to guide their judgment. He who judges the manners judges of honor; and he who judges of honor takes his law from opinion.

The opinions of a nation spring from its constitution. Although the law does not regulate morality, it is legislation that gives it birth, and when legislation becomes impaired, morality degenerates; but then the judgment of the censors will not do what the power of the laws has failed to do.

---

[18]He could not be satisfied about this in proposing a dictator; he dared not nominate himself, and could not feel sure that his colleague would nominate him.

It follows from this that the censorship may be useful to preserve morality, never to restore it. Institute censors while the laws are vigorous; so soon as they have lost their power all is over. Nothing that is lawful has any force when the laws cease to have any.

The censorship supports morality by preventing opinions from being corrupted, by preserving their integrity through wise applications, sometimes even by fixing them when they are still uncertain. The use of seconds in duels, carried to a mad extreme in the kingdom of France, was abolished by these simple words in an edict of the king: "As for those who have the cowardice to appoint seconds." This judgment, anticipating that of the public, immediately decided it. But when the same edicts wanted to declare that it was also cowardice to fight a duel, which is very true, but contrary to common opinion, the public ridiculed this decision, on which its judgment was already formed.

I have said elsewhere[19] that as public opinion is not subject to constraint, there should be no vestige of this in the tribunal established to represent it. We cannot admire too much the art with which this force, wholly lost among the moderns, was set in operation among the Romans and still better among the Lacedæmonians.

A man of bad character having brought forward a good measure in the Council of Sparta, the ephors, without regarding him, caused the same measure to be proposed by a virtuous citizen. What an honor for the one, what a stigma for the other, without praise or blame being given to either! Certain drunkards from Samos[20] defiled the tribunal of the ephors; on the morrow a public edict granted permission to the Samians to be filthy. A real punishment would have been less severe than such impunity. When Sparta pronounced what was or was not honourable, Greece made no appeal from her decisions.

§

Men had at first no kings except the gods and no government but a theocracy. They reasoned like Caligula, and at that time they reasoned rightly. A long period is needed to change men's sentiments and ideas in order that they may resolve to take a fellow-man as a master and flatter themselves that all will be well.

From the single circumstance that a god was placed at the head of every political society, it followed that there were as many gods as nations. Two nations foreign to each other, and almost always hostile, could not long

---

[19]I merely indicate in this chapter what I have treated at greater length in the *Letter to M. d'Alembert.*

[20]They were from another island, which the delicacy of our language forbids us to name on this occasion.

acknowledge the same master; two armies engaged in battle with each other could not obey the same leader. Thus from national divisions resulted polytheism and, from this, theological and civil intolerance, which are by nature the same, as will be shown hereafter.

The fancy of the Greeks that they recognized their own gods among barbarous nations arose from their regarding themselves as the natural sovereigns of those nations. But in our days that is a very ridiculous kind of erudition which turns on the identity of the gods of different nations, as if Moloch, Saturn, and Chronos could be the same god! As if the Baal of the Phœnicians, the Zeus of the Greeks, and the Jupiter of the Latins could be the same! As if there could be anything in common among imaginary beings bearing different names!

But if it is asked why under paganism, when every State had its worship and its gods, there were no wars of religion, I answer that it was for the same reason that each State, having its peculiar form of worship as well as its own government, did not distinguish its gods from its laws. Political warfare was also religious; the departments of the gods were, so to speak, fixed by the limits of the nations. The god of one nation had no right over other nations. The gods of the pagans were not jealous gods; they shared among them the empire of the world; even Moses and the Hebrew nation sometimes countenanced this idea by speaking of the god of Israel. It is true that they regarded as nought the gods of the Canaanites, proscribed nations, devoted to destruction, whose country they were to occupy; but see how they spoke of the divinities of the neighboring nations whom they were forbidden to attack: "The possession of what belongs to Chalmos your god," said Jephthah to the Ammonites, "is it not lawfully your due? By the same title we possess the lands which our conquering god has acquired."[21] In this, it seems to me, there was a well-recognized parity between the rights of Chamos and those of the god of Israel.

But when the Jews, subjected to the kings of Babylon, and afterwards to the kings of Syria, obstinately refused to acknowledge any other god than their own, this refusal being regarded as a rebellion against the conqueror, drew upon them the persecutions which we read of in their history, and of which no other instance appears before Christianity.[22]

Every religion, then, being exclusively attached to the laws of the State which prescribed it, there was no other way of converting a nation than to subdue it, and no other missionaries than conquerors; and the obligation

---

[21]"*Nonne ea quae possidet Chamos deus tuus tibi jure debentur?*" (Judges xi. 24). Such is the text of the Vulgate. Père de Carrières has translated it thus: "Do you not believe that you have a right to possess what belongs to Chamos your god?" I am ignorant of the force of the Hebrew text, but I see that in the Vulgate Jephthah positively acknowledges the right of the god Chamos, and that the French translator weakens this acknowledgement by an "according to you" which is not in the Latin.

[22]There is the strongest evidence that the war of the Phocæans, called a sacred war, was not a war of religion. Its object was to punish sacrilege, and not to subdue unbelievers.

to change their form of worship being the law imposed on the vanquished, it was necessary to begin by conquering before speaking of conversions. Far from men fighting for the gods, it was, as in Homer, the gods who fought for men; each sued for victory from his own god and paid for it with new altars. The Romans, before attacking a place, summoned its gods to abandon it; and when they left the Tarentines their exasperated gods, it was because they then regarded these gods as subjected to their own and forced to pay them homage. They left the vanquished their gods as they left them their laws. A crown for the Capitoline Jupiter was often the only tribute that they imposed.

At last, the Romans having extended their worship and their laws with their empire, and having themselves often adopted those of the vanquished, the nations of this vast empire, since the right of citizenship was granted to all, found insensibly that they had multitudes of gods and religions, almost the same everywhere; and this is why paganism was at length known in the world as only a single religion.

It was in these circumstances that Jesus came to establish on earth a spiritual kingdom, which, separating the religious from the political system, destroyed the unity of the State, and caused the intestine divisions which have never ceased to agitate Christian nations. Now this new idea of a kingdom in the other world having never been able to enter the minds of the pagans, they always regarded Christians as actual rebels who, under cover of a hypocritical submission, only sought an opportunity to make themselves independent and supreme, and to usurp by cunning the authority which, in their weakness, they pretended to respect. This was the cause of persecutions.

What the pagans had feared came to pass. Then everything changed its aspect; the humble Christians altered their tone, and soon this pretended kingdom of the other world became, under a visible chief, the most violent despotism in this world.

As, however, there have always been a Prince and civil laws, a perpetual conflict of jurisdiction has resulted from this double power, which has rendered any good polity impossible in Christian States; and no one has ever succeeded in understanding whether he was bound to obey the ruler or the priest.

Many nations, however, even in Europe or on its outskirts, wished to preserve or to re-establish the ancient system, but without success; the spirit of Christianity prevailed over everything. The sacred worship always retained or regained its independence of the sovereign, and without any necessary connexion with the body of the State. Muhammad had very sound views; he thoroughly unified his political system; and so long as his form of government subsisted under his successors, the khalifs, the government was quite undivided and in that respect good. But the Arabs having become flourishing, learned, polished, effeminate, and indolent, were subjugated by the barbarians, and then the division between the two powers began again. Although it may be less apparent among the Muhammadans than among the Christians, the division nevertheless exists, especially in the sect of Ali; and there are States, such as Persia, in which it is still seen.

Among us, the kings of England have established themselves as heads of the church; and the Tsars have done the same; but by means of this title they have made themselves its ministers rather than its rulers; they have acquired not so much the right of changing it as the power of maintaining it; they are not its legislators but only its princes. Wherever the clergy form a corporation,[23] they are masters and legislators in their own country. There are, then, two powers, two sovereigns, in England and in Russia, just as elsewhere.

Of all Christian authors, the philosopher Hobbes is the only one who has clearly seen the evil and its remedy, and who has dared to propose a reunion of the heads of the eagle and the complete restoration of political unity, without which no State or government will ever be well constituted. But he ought to have seen that the domineering spirit of Christianity was incompatible with his system, and that the interest of the priest would always be stronger than that of the State. It is not so much what is horrible and false in his political theory as what is just and true that has rendered it odious.[24]

---

[23]It must, indeed, be remarked that it is not so much the formal assemblies, like those in France, that bind the clergy into one body, as the communion of churches. Communion and excommunication are the social pact of the clergy, a pact by means of which they will always be the masters of nations and kings. All priests who are of the same communion are fellow citizens, though they are as far asunder as the poles. This invention is a master-piece of policy. There was nothing similar among pagan priests; therefore they never formed a body of clergy.

[24]See, among others, in a letter from Grotius to his brother of the 11th April, 1643, what that learned man approves and what he blames in the book *De Cive*. It is true that, inclined to indulgence, he appears to pardon the author for the good for the sake of the evil, but everyone is not so merciful.

Émile: General Principles of Education

I. EMILE IN INFANCY

Everything is good as it comes from the hands of the Author of Nature; but everything degenerates in the hands of man. He forces one country to nourish the productions of another; one tree to bear the fruits of another. He mingles and confounds the climates, the elements, the seasons; he mutilates his dog, his horse, and his slave; he overturns everything, disfigures everything; he loves deformity, monsters; he will have nothing as Nature made it, not even man; like a saddle-horse, man must be trained for man's service—he must be made over according to his fancy, like a tree in his garden.

Plants are formed by cultivation and men by education. Had man been born tall and strong, his stature and strength would have been useless to him until he had been taught to use them; they would have been injurious to him by preventing others from thinking of assisting him; and, left to himself, he would have died of want before he had known his needs. People pity the lot of the child; they do not see that the human race would have perished if man had not begun by being a child.

We are born weak; we have need of strength: we are born destitute of everything; we have need of assistance: we are born stupid; we have need of judgment. All that we have not at our birth, but which we need when we are grown, is given us by education.

We derive this education from nature, from men, or from things. The internal development of our faculties and organs is the education of nature; the use which we learn to make of this development is the education of men; while the acquisition of personal experience from the objects that affect us is the education of things.

Each one of us is thus formed by three kinds of teachers. The pupil in whom their different lessons are at variance is badly educated, and will never be in harmony with himself; while he in whom they all agree, in whom they all tend to the same end—he alone moves toward his destiny and consistently lives; he alone is well educated.

Now, of these three different educations, that of nature is entirely independent of ourselves, while that of things depends on ourselves only

158

in certain respects. The education we receive of men is the only one of which we are truly the masters; but even this is true only in theory, for who can hope to have the entire direction of the conversation and acts of those who surround a child?

As soon, then, as education becomes an art, it is well-nigh impossible for it to succeed, for no one has in his control all the conditions necessary for its success. All that can be done by dint of effort is to approach the final purpose as nearly as possible; but to attain it we must be aided by fortune.

What is this purpose? It is the very one proposed by nature, as has just been shown. Since the co-operation of the three educations is necessary for their perfection, it is to the one over which we have no control that we must direct the other two. But perhaps this word nature has too vague a meaning; we must here make an attempt to determine it.

Nature, we are told, is but habit. What does this mean? Are there not habits that we contract only through compulsion, and that never stifle nature? Such, for example, is the habit of plants whose vertical direction is impeded. The plant, set at liberty, preserves the inclination it was forced to take; but the sap has not on this account changed its primitive direction, and if the plant continues to grow, its prolongation again becomes vertical. The same is true of the inclinations of men. So long as we remain in the same condition we can preserve those which result from habit and which are the least natural to us; but the moment the situation changes, habit ceases and the natural is restored. Education is certainly nothing but a habit. Now, there are people who forget and lose their education, and others who hold to it. Whence comes this difference? If we were to limit the term nature to habits that are in conformity with Nature, we might spare ourselves this nonsense.

We are born sensible, and from our birth we are affected in different ways by the objects which surround us. As soon as we have the consciousness, so to speak, of our sensations, we are disposed to seek or to shun the objects which produce them: first, according as they are agreeable or disagreeable to us; then, according to the congruity or the incongruity which we find between ourselves and these objects; and, finally, according to the judgments which we derive from them relative to the idea of happiness or perfection which is given us by the reason. These dispositions are extended and strengthened in proportion as we become more susceptible and enlightened; but, constrained by our habits, they change more or less with our opinions. Before this alteration, these dispositions are what I call our nature.

It is, then, to these primitive dispositions that everything should be referred; and this might be done if our three educations were merely different; but what are we to do when they are opposed to one another; when, instead of educating a man for himself, we wish to educate him for others? Then agreement is impossible. Compelled to oppose nature or our social institutions, we must choose between making a man and a citizen, for we can not make both at once.

The natural man is complete in himself; he is the numerical unit, the absolute whole, who is related only to himself or to his fellow-man. Civilized man is but a fractional unit that is dependent on its denominator, and whose value consists in its relation to the whole, which is the social organization. Good social institutions are those which are the best able to make man unnatural, and to take from him his absolute existence in order to give him one which is relative, and to transport the *me* into the common unity, in such a way that each individual no longer feels himself one, but a part of the unit, and is no longer susceptible of feeling save when forming a part of the whole.

In order to be something, to be one's self and always one, we must act as we speak; we must always be decided on the course we ought to take, must take it boldly, and must follow it to the end. I am waiting to be shown this prodigy in order to know whether he is man or citizen, or how he manages to be both at the same time.

From these objects, necessarily opposed one to the other, there come two forms of institutions of contrary nature—the one public and common, the other private and domestic.

Would you form an idea of public education? Read the Republic of Plato. It is not a work on politics, as those think who judge of books by their titles, but it is the finest work on education ever written.

When one would refer us to the land of chimeras, he names the educational system of Plato; though if Lycurgus had formed his only on paper, I should have thought it the more chimerical. Plato has done no more than purify the heart of man; but Lycurgus has made it unnatural.

A system of public instruction no longer exists and can no longer exist, because where there is no longer a country there can no longer be citizens. These two words, *country* and *citizen*, ought to be expunged from modern languages. I have a good reason for saying this, but I do not care to state it, as it has no bearing on my subject.

I do not regard as a system of public instruction these ridiculous establishments called colleges. Nor do I take into account the education of the world, because this education, tending toward two opposite ends, fails to reach either of them; it is fit only to make men double-faced, seeming always to attribute everything to others, but never attributing anything save to themselves. Now these pretenses being common to everybody, deceive no one. They are so many misspent efforts.

Finally, there remains domestic education, or that of nature; but what would a man be worth for others who had been educated solely for himself? If perchance the double object proposed could be realized in a single individual by removing the contradictions in human life, we should remove a great obstacle to man's happiness. To form a conception of such a one, we should need to see him in his perfect state, to have observed his inclinations, to have seen his progress, and to have followed the course of his development. In a word, it would be necessary to know the natural man. I believe that my reader will have made some progress in these researches after having read this essay.

To form this rare creature, what have we to do? Much, doubtless, but chiefly to prevent anything from being done. When all we have to do is to sail before the wind, simple tacking suffices; but if the sea runs high and we wish to hold our place, we must cast anchor. Take care, young pilot, that your cable does not slip, that your anchor does not drag, and that your boat does not drift on shore before you are aware of it!

In the social sphere, where all have their destined places, each should be educated for his own. If an individual who has been trained for his place withdraws from it, he is no longer good for anything. Education is useful only so long as fortune accords with the vocation of parents. In every other case it is harmful to the pupil, were it only for the prejudices which it has given him. In Egypt, where the son was obliged to follow the vocation of his father, education at least had an assured object; but with us, where the classes alone are permanent, and where men are ever passing from one to another, no one knows whether, in educating his son for his own social order, he may not be working in opposition to the son's interest.

In the natural order of things, all men being equal, their common vocation is manhood, and whoever is well trained for that can not fulfill badly any vocation connected with it. Whether my pupil be destined for the army, the church, or the bar, concerns me but little. Regardless of the vocation of his parents, nature summons him to the duties of human life. To live is the trade I wish to teach him.* On leaving my hands, he will not, I grant, be a magistrate, a soldier, or a priest. First of all he will be a man; and all that a man ought to be, he can be when the occasion requires it, just as well as any one else can; and fortune will make him change his place in vain, for he will always be in his own.†

Our real study is that of human destiny. He who knows how best to support the good and the evil of this life is, in my opinion, the best educated; whence it follows that the real education consists less in precepts than in practice. Our instruction begins when we begin to live; our education begins with our birth; and our first teacher is our nurse.

We must, then, generalize our views, and consider in our pupil man in general—man exposed to all the accidents of human life. If men were born attached to their native soil, if the same weather lasted the whole

---

*Qui se totam ad vitam ins ruxit, non desiderat particulatim admoneri, doctus in totum, non quomodo cum uxore aut cum filiis viveret, sed quomodo bene viveret.—SENECA, Ep. 94.

†Occupavi te, fortuna, atque cepi; omnesque aditus tuos interclusi, ut ad me aspirare non posses.— CICERO, Tuscul. v, cap. ix.

year, if the fortune of each were so fixed that it could never change, the current practice would be good in certain respects; the child educated for his special vocation, and never withdrawing from it, would not be exposed to the inconveniences of another. But, considering the mutability of human affairs, and the restless, revolutionary spirit of this century, which overthrows the whole existing order of things once in each generation, can we conceive a more senseless method than that of educating a child as though he were never to leave his chamber, and were always to be surrounded by his attendants? If the unfortunate creature take a single step on the ground, or attempts to descend the stairs, he is lost. This is not teaching him to endure suffering, but is training him to feel it.

We think only of protecting our child, but this is not enough. We ought to teach him to protect himself when he has become a man; to bear the blows of destiny; to brave opulence and misery; to live, if need be, amid the snows of Iceland or on the burning rocks of Malta. It is in vain that you take precaution against his dying, for after all he must die; and even though his death may not result from your solicitudes, they are nevertheless unwise. It is of less consequence to prevent him from dying than to teach him how to live. To live is not to breathe, but to act; it is to make use of our organs, of our senses, of our faculties, of every element of our nature which makes us sensible of our existence. The man who has lived most is not he who has numbered the most years, but he who has had the keenest sense of life. Men have been buried at the age of a hundred who died at the moment of birth. They would have gained by going to their graves in their youth, if up to that time they had really lived.

All our wisdom consists in servile prejudices, all our customs are but servitude, worry, and constraint. Civilized man is born, lives, and dies in a state of slavery. At his birth he is stitched in swaddling-clothes; at his death he is nailed in his coffin; and as long as he preserves the human form he is fettered by our institutions.

A child becomes more precious as he advances in age. To the value of his person there comes to be added that of the care which he has cost; and to the loss of his life there is to be added his apprehension of death. It is then especially of the future that we must think, while guarding his preservation; it is against the ills of youth that we must arm him before he has come upon them; for if the value of life increases up to the age that renders it useful, what folly is it to spare infancy some ills while heaping them up for the age of reason!

Suffering is the lot of man at every period of life. The very care of his preservation is connected with pain. Happy he if in his infancy he knows only physical ills—ills much less cruel and much less painful than others, and which much more rarely than they cause us to renounce life! One does not kill himself from the suffering of the gout; and hardly anything but sufferings of the soul produce despair. We pity the lot of infancy, and it is our own that we should really pity. Our greatest ills come to us from ourselves.

A child cries as soon as it is born, and his first years are spent in tears. At one time we trot and caress him to pacify him, and at another we threaten and beat him to keep him quiet. We either do what pleases him, or we exact of him what pleases us; we either subject ourselves to his whims, or subject him to ours. There is no middle ground; he must either give orders or receive them. And so his first ideas are those of domination and servitude. Before knowing how to speak, he commands; and before knowing how to act, he obeys; and sometimes he is punished before he is able to know his faults, or, rather, to commit any. It is thus that, at an early hour, we pour into his young heart the passions that we straightway impute to nature; and that, after having taken the trouble to make him bad, we complain of finding him such.

Would you, then, have him preserve his original form? Guard it from the moment of the child's birth. As soon as born take possession of him, and do not give him up until he is a man. Save in this way, you will never succeed. As the real nurse is the mother, the real preceptor is the father. Let them agree in the discharge of their functions as well as in the system they follow, and let the child pass from the hands of one into the hands of the other. He will be better educated by a judicious though ignorant father, than by the most skillful teacher in the world; for zeal will much better supply the place of talent than talent the place of zeal.

The first tears of children are prayers, and unless we are on our guard they soon become orders. Children begin by being assisted, but end by being served. Thus out of their very weakness, whence proceeds at first the feeling of their dependence, there presently springs the idea of empire and domination; but this idea being excited not so much by their needs as by our services, there begin to appear, at this point, the moral effects whose immediate cause is not in nature; and already we begin to see why, in this early period of life, it is important to discern the secret intention which dictates the gesture or the cry.

When the child makes the effort and reaches out his hand without saying anything, he expects to reach the object because he does not make a proper estimate of its distance—he has made a mistake; but when he complains and cries while reaching out his hand, he then no longer makes a mistake as to the distance, but is either commanding the object to come to him, or is commanding you to bring him the object. In the first case, carry him to the object slowly, stopping at short intervals; in the second, give no sign whatever of hearing him; the louder he cries the less you should listen to him. It is important to accustom him at an early period neither to command men, for he is not their master, nor things, for they do not hear him. Thus, when a child desires something which he sees or which you wish to give him, it is much better to carry him to the object than to bring this object to him. He draws from this procedure a conclusion suitable to his age, and one which can be suggested to him in no other way.

The Abbé de Saint Pierre called men big children; conversely, we might call children little men. These propositions have their truth as maxims; but as principles they have need of explanation. When Hobbes called a rogue a robust child, he said a thing absolutely contradictory. All wickedness comes from weakness. A child is bad only because he is weak; make him strong, and he will be good. He who can do everything does nothing bad. Of all the attributes of the omnipotent Divinity, goodness is the one which we can spare from his conception with the greatest difficulty. All peoples who have recognized two principles have always regarded the evil as inferior to the good; otherwise they would have made an absurd supposition.

Reason alone teaches us to know good and evil. The conscience, which makes us love the one and hate the other, although independent of the reason, can not be developed without it. Before the age of reason we do good and evil without knowing it; and there is no morality in our actions, although there sometimes may be in the feeling we have from the actions of others as they relate to us. A child wishes to disarrange whatever he sees; he breaks and injures whatever he can reach; he seizes a bird as he would seize a stone, and strangles it without knowing what he does.

Why is this? At first sight philosophy goes on to account for it by natural vices. Pride, the spirit of domination, self-love, the wickedness of man, and, it might be added, the sense of his weakness, make the child eager to do feats of strength, and to prove to himself his own power. But see this infirm and broken old man, brought back by the cycle of human life to the feebleness of infancy. He not only remains immobile and peaceable, but would have everything about him remain so; the least change troubles and disquiets him, and he would see the reign of universal calm. If the original cause were not altered, how could the same impotence, connected with the same passions, produce such different effects in the two ages? And where can we look for this difference in causes, save in the physical condition of the two individuals? The active principle, common to both, is in a state of development in one and in a state of extinction in the other; one is in a state of formation, and the other in a state of decay; one is tending to life and the other to death. The decaying activity is concentrated in the heart of the old man; in that of the child this activity is superabundant and extends itself outward; he is conscious of life enough, so to speak, to animate his whole environment. Whether he makes or unmakes matters not; it suffices that he changes the state of things, and every change is an action. Though he seems to have a greater inclination to destroy, this is not through badness. The activity which forms is always slow; and as that which destroys is more rapid, it is better adapted to his vivacity.

At the same time that the Author of Nature gives to children this active principle, he takes care that it should do but little harm, by giving them but little strength to indulge themselves in it; but as soon as they come to consider the people who surround them as instruments which they can employ, they make use of them to follow their inclinations, and to supplement their own feebleness. This is how they become troublesome, tyrannical, imperious, depraved, unconquerable; a progress which does not come from a natural spirit of domination, but which gives them this spirit; for it does not require a long experience to feel how agreeable it is to act through the hands of others, and to need only to set the tongue a-going in order to set the universe in motion.

This principle once known, we see clearly the point at which we abandon the order of nature. We see what must be done in order to maintain ourselves in it.

II. EMILE FROM FIVE TO TWELVE

O men, be humane; it is your foremost duty. Be humane to all classes and to all ages, to everything not foreign to mankind. What wisdom is there for you outside of humanity? Love childhood; encourage its sports, its pleasures, its amiable instincts. Who of you has not sometimes looked back with regret on that age when a smile was ever on the lips, when the soul was ever at peace? Why would you take from those little innocents the enjoyment of a time so short which is slipping from them, and of a good so precious which they can not abuse? Why would you fill with bitterness and sorrow those early years so rapidly passing, which will no more return to them than to you? Fathers, do you know the moment when death awaits your children? Do not prepare for yourselves regrets by taking from them the few moments which Nature has given them. As soon as they can feel the pleasures of existence, allow them to enjoy it; and at whatever hour God may summon them, see to it that they do not die before they have tasted life.

In order not to be running after chimeras, let us not forget what is befitting our condition. Humanity has its place in the order of things, and infancy has its place in the order of human life. We must consider the man in the man, and the child in the child. To assign to each his place, and to fix him there, to adjust human passions according to the constitution of man—this is all that we can do for his well-being. The rest depends on extraneous causes which are not in our power.

We do not know what absolute happiness or unhappiness is. In this life all things are intermingled; we experience no unmixed feeling; we do not remain for two moments in the same state of emotion. The affections of our souls, like the modifications of our bodies, are in a continual flux.

Good and evil are common to us all, but in different degrees. He is the happiest who suffers the least pain; and he the most wretched who feels the fewest pleasures. There are always more sufferings than enjoyments, and this is the difference which is common to all. Human felicity here below is, then, but a negative state, and we must estimate it by the smallest quantity of evils which we suffer.

Every sensation of pain is inseparable from the desire to be delivered from it, and every idea of pleasure is inseparable from the desire to enjoy it. Every desire supposes privation; and all the privations which we feel are painful. It is, then, in the disproportion between our desires and our faculties that our unhappiness consists. A sensible being whose powers should equal his desires would be an absolutely happy being.

Keep the child dependent on things alone, and you will have followed the order of Nature in his education. Offer to his indiscreet caprices only physical obstacles or punishments which result from his actions themselves, and which he recalls on occasion. Without forbidding him to do wrong, it suffices to prevent him from doing it. Only experience or want of power should serve as law for him. Grant nothing to his desires because he demands it, but because he has need of it. Do not let him know what obedience is when he acts, nor what control is when others act for him. Equally in his actions and in yours, let him feel his liberty. If he is lacking in power, supply the exact amount of it which he needs in order to be free and not imperious; and while receiving your aid with a sort of humiliation, let him long for the moment when he will be able to do without it, and when he will have the honor to serve himself.

In order to strengthen the body and to make it grow, Nature resorts to means which ought never to be thwarted. A child must not be constrained to keep still when he wishes to move, nor to move when he wishes to remain quiet. When the will of children has not been spoiled by our fault, they wish nothing that is to no purpose. They must jump, and run, and scream, whenever they have a mind to do so. All their movements are needs of their constitution which is trying to fortify itself; but we should distrust the desires which they themselves have not the power to satisfy. We must then be careful to distinguish the true or natural need from the fancied need which begins to appear, or from that which comes merely from that superabundance of life of which I have spoken.

When a child can ask for what he wants in words, and when, in order to obtain it more quickly, or to overcome a refusal, he supplements his demands with tears, it ought to be firmly refused him. If a real need has made him speak, you ought to know it and to supply the demand at once; but to yield something to his tears is to encourage him to cry the more, to teach him to doubt your good-will, and to believe that importunity goes further with you than kindness. If he does not believe that you are good, he will soon become bad; and if he thinks you weak, he will soon become obstinate. It is important always to grant at the first intimation what we do not mean to refuse. Be not prodigal in refusals, but never recall them.

Be especially on your guard against giving the child empty formulas of politeness which he may use at need as magic words to subject to his caprices all that surrounds him, and to obtain on the instant whatever it pleases him to demand. In the ceremonious education of the wealthy, children are always made politely imperious by prescribing for them the terms which they must employ in order that no one may dare to resist them; they are suppliant neither in tone nor manner, but are even more arrogant when they entreat than when they command, as being more sure of being obeyed. We see at once that, in their mouth, *If you please* signifies *It pleases me*, and that *I beg you* signifies *I command you*. Admirable politeness, which for them amounts merely to a change in the meaning of words, and to an inability ever to speak otherwise than in a tone of command! As for me, I would rather have Émile rude than arrogant; I would much rather have him say, in making a request, *Do this*, than in commanding, *I beg you*. It is not the term which he uses that I care about, but rather the meaning which he connects with it.

There is an excess of severity and an excess of indulgence, and both are equally to be avoided. If you allow children to suffer, you expose their health and their life, and make them actually miserable; if you are overcareful in sparing them every sort of discomfort, you are laying up in store for them great wretchedness by making them delicate and sensitive; you remove them from that condition of men to which they will one day return in spite of you. In order not to expose them to some ills of Nature, you are the author of others which she has not provided for them. You will tell me that I fall into the error of those unwise fathers whom I reproach with sacrificing the happiness of children out of consideration for a remote time which may never come. By no means; for the liberty which I grant my pupil amply rewards him for the slight discomforts to which I allow him to be exposed. I see little vagabonds playing in the snow, purple with cold, benumbed and hardly able to move their fingers. They are at liberty to go and warm themselves, but they do not do it; and if they were forced to go they would feel the rigors of constraint a hundred times more than they feel those of the cold. Of what, then, do you complain? Shall I make your child wretched by exposing him only to the discomforts which he is perfectly willing to suffer? I am doing him good at the present moment by leaving him free; and I am doing him a future good by arming him against ills which he ought to endure. If he could choose between my pupil and yours, do you think he would hesitate for an instant?

Can you conceive that any real happiness is possible for any being outside of his constitution? And is it not to remove man from his constitutional state to desire to exempt him equally from all the ills of his species? This is certainly my belief. In order that man may appreciate great blessings, he must know small evils; such is his nature. If the physical life is too exuberant, the moral life degenerates. The man who has not experienced suffering knows neither human tenderness nor the sweetness of commiseration. He would be touched by nothing, would be unsocial, and a monster among his fellows.

Do you know the surest way of making your child miserable? It is by accustoming him to obtain whatever he desires; for, as his desires are constantly growing through the facility of satisfying them, sooner or later your very inability will force you, in spite of yourself, to resort to a refusal; and this unaccustomed refusal will give him more distress than the very privation of what he desires. First he would have your cane, presently your watch, next the bird which he sees flying in the air, and finally the stars which he sees glittering in the heavens—in a word, he would have everything he sees; and, short of being God himself, how is he to be satisfied?

If these notions of domination and tyranny make men wretched in infancy, what will be their condition when they have become grown, and their relations with other men have begun to extend and multiply? Accustomed to see everything bend before them, what will be their surprise on entering the world to see that everything resists them, and to find themselves crushed under the weight of that universe which they imagined they could move at will! Their insolent airs and puerile vanity bring upon them only mortification, disdain, and raillery; they drink affronts like water; and cruel experiences soon teach them that they know neither their condition nor their strength. Not being able to do everything, they think they can do nothing. So many unaccustomed obstacles dishearten them, so many rebuffs humiliate them, that they become cowardly, timid, and cringing, and fall as much below themselves as they were once raised above themselves.

Considered in itself, is there anything in the world more helpless, more wretched, more at the mercy of everything that surrounds it, than an infant? Is there anything that has such need of pity, attention, and protection, as a child? Does it not seem that he presents a face so benignant and a look so touching solely to the end that every one who approaches him may become interested in his helplessness and run to his assistance? Then what is more shocking, more contrary to propriety, than to see a haughty and stubborn child give orders to all who are about him, and so indiscreet as to lord it over those who have only to abandon him in order to cause him to perish?

On the other hand, who does not see that the helplessness of early life puts so many restraints on children that it is barbarous to add to this enthrallment that of our own caprices, by depriving them of a liberty so contracted, which they can so little abuse, and of which they can be deprived with so little advantage to them and to us? If there is no object so ridiculous as a haughty child, there is none so pitiable as a timorous child. Since civil servitude begins with the age of reason, why anticipate it by private servitude? Let us allow life to have a moment's exemption from that yoke that has not been imposed on us by Nature, and leave to infancy the exercise of that natural liberty which diverts the child, at least for a time, from the vices that are contracted in slavery. Then let those harsh tutors and those fathers who are enslaved to their children come forward with their objections, and, before vaunting their methods, let them once learn the method of Nature.

Your child should obtain nothing because he demands it, but only because he has need of it;* nor should he do anything from obedience, but from necessity. And so the terms obey and command are proscribed from his vocabulary, and still more the terms duty and obligation; but the terms force, necessity, impotency, and constraint, should have a large place in it. Before the age of reason there can be no idea of moral being, or of social relations. Hence, so far as possible, we must shun the use of the words which express them, for fear that the child may at first attach to these words false ideas which we have not the skill or the power to destroy. The first false idea which enters his head is the germ of error and of vice; and it is to this first step that we must pay particular attention. Proceed in such a way that as long as he is affected only by sensuous things all his ideas shall stop at sensation; so proceed that on every hand he may perceive about him only the world of matter; for, unless you do this, you may be sure that he will not listen to you at all, or that he will form of the moral world of which you speak to him fantastic notions which you will never efface from his life.

To reason with children was the grand maxim of Locke, and it is the one chiefly in fashion to-day. Its success, however, does not appear to me to argue very much in its favor; and for my part I know nothing more silly than those children with whom one has reasoned so much. Of all the faculties of man, reason, which, so to speak, is but the aggregate of all the others, is that which is developed with the most difficulty and the latest, and it is this one which we propose to employ to develop the first! The master-work of a good education is to make a reasonable man, and we propose to train up a child through the reason! This is to begin at the end, and to confound the instrument with the work. If children were capable of reasoning, they would have no need of being educated; but by speaking to them from their earliest years in a language they do not understand, we

---

*We should recollect that as pain is often a necessity, pleasure is sometimes a need. There is, then, but one simple desire of children, which should never be gratified—that of being obeyed. Whence it follows that in whatever they demand we must give especial attention to the motive which leads them to demand it. Whenever it is possible, grant whatever can give them a real pleasure; but always refuse them what they demand merely through caprice, or in order to exert an act of authority.

accustom them to be satisfied with words, to pass judgment on everything said to them, to esteem themselves just as wise as their teachers, and to become disputatious and stubborn; and whatever we expect to obtain from them by reasonable motives we never obtain save by motives of selfishness, fear, or vanity, which we are always obliged to add to the first.

Treat your pupil according to his age. At the start put him in his place, and hold him there so firmly that he will no longer be tempted to leave it. Then, before knowing what wisdom is, he will practice the most important of its lessons. Never command him to do anything whatever, not the least thing in the world. Never allow him to imagine that you assume to have any authority over him. Let him know merely that he is weak and that you are strong; that by virtue of his condition and your own he is necessarily at your mercy. Let him know this, let him learn it, let him feel it; and at an early hour let him feel on his proud head the harsh yoke which Nature imposes on man, the heavy yoke of necessity under which every finite creature must bend. Let him see this necessity in things, but never in the caprice* of men. Let the rein which holds him be force, and not authority. Do not forbid him to do what he ought to abstain from doing; but prevent him from doing it without explanation and without argument. Whatever you allow him to do, allow him to do it at the first suggestion, without solicitation, especially without entreaty and without conditions. Give your assent with cheerfulness, and never refuse save with reluctance; but let all your refusals be irrevocable. Let no importunity shake your resolution; but, once pronounced, let it be a brazen wall against which he will not have exhausted his strength a half-dozen times before he gives up trying to overthrow it.

It is in this way that you will make the child patient, calm, resigned, peaceable, even when his wishes have not been gratified; for it is in the nature of man to endure patiently the necessity of things, but not the ill-will of others.

It is very strange that, so long as men have concerned themselves with the education of children, they have devised no other instrument for managing them then emulation, jealousy, envy, vanity, covetousness, and debasing fear, all of them passions of the most dangerous sort, the most prompt to ferment and the most fit to corrupt the soul, even before the body is formed. With each item of precocious instruction which we would cause to enter their heads, we plant a vice in the depths of their hearts. Senseless instructors think they are doing marvels while making their pupils bad in order to teach them what goodness is; and then they gravely tell us, *such is man!* Yes, such is the man whom you have made.

You have tried all instruments save one, the only one which can

---

*We may be sure that the child will regard as a caprice every will which is contrary to his own, and of which he does not see the reason. Now, a child sees no reason in anything which opposes his own whims.

succeed—well-regulated liberty. We should not undertake the education of a child unless we know how to conduct him where we will, simply by the laws of the possible and the impossible. The sphere of each being equally unknown, we extend it or contract it about him as we will. We enchain him or urge him forward or hold him back with nothing but the restraint of necessity, without a murmur on his part; and we make him supple and docile through the mere force of things, without giving occasion for any vice to germinate in him; for the passions are never aroused so long as they are of no effect.

Do not give your pupil any sort of verbal lesson, for he is to be taught only by experience. Inflict on him no species of punishment, for he does not know what it is to be in fault. Never make him ask your pardon, for he does not know how to offend you. Divested of all morality in his actions, he can do nothing which is morally wrong, and which merits either chastisement or reprimand.

I see that the reader, already dismayed, is judging of this child by his own. But he is mistaken. The perpetual restraint under which you hold your pupils irritates their spirits; and the more they are held in constraint under your eyes, the more turbulent they become the moment they regain their liberty. They must needs compensate themselves, when they can, for the harsh constraint in which you hold them. Two pupils from the city will do more mischief in the country than the youth of a whole village. Shut up a little gentleman and a little peasant in the same room, and the first will have overturned and broken everything before the second has stirred from his place. Why is this, unless the first is in haste to abuse a moment of license; while the other, always sure of his liberty, is never in haste to make use of it? And yet, village children, often humored or thwarted, are still very far from the condition in which I would have them kept.

Shall I venture to state, at this point, the most important, the most useful rule, of all education? It is not to gain time, but to lose it. Ye ordinary readers, pardon my paradoxes, for they must be uttered, by any one who reflects; and, whatever you may say to it, I would much rather be a man of paradoxes than a man of prejudices. The most dangerous period in human life is the interval between birth and the age of twelve. It is the time when errors and vices germinate, and when, as yet, there is no instrument to destroy them; and when the instrument comes, the roots have gone down so deep that the time has passed for pulling them out. If children leaped at a single bound from the state of nurslings to the age of reason, the current education might be the best for them; but in accordance with natural progress they require an education of a totally different sort. They must do nothing with their soul until it has all its faculties; for it is impossible for the soul to perceive the torch which you present to it while it is blind, and to follow in the boundless field of ideas a route which the reason traces so faintly even for the sharpest eyes.

The first education, then, ought to be purely negative. It consists not at all in teaching virtue or truth, but in shielding the heart from vice, and the mind from error. If you could do nothing and allow nothing to be done; if you could bring your pupil sound and robust to the age of twelve years without his being able to distinguish his right hand from his left—from your very first lessons the eyes of his understanding would be open to reason. Without prejudice and without habit, he would have nothing in him which could counteract the effect of your endeavors. Ere long he would become in your hands the wisest of men; and, while beginning with doing nothing, you will have produced a prodigy of education.

III. EMILE FROM TWELVE TO FIFTEEN

At the age of twelve or thirteen the strength of the child is developed much more rapidly than his needs. The most violent, the most terrible, has not yet made itself felt in him. But slightly sensitive to the bad effects of air and weather, he braves them without danger; the growing warmth of his body takes the place of clothing; his appetite serves him instead of condiments; whatever can nourish him satisfies one of his age; if he is sleepy, he stretches himself on the ground and sleeps. He sees himself surrounded on all sides by everything that is necessary for him; no imaginary need torments him; he is unaffected by opinion; his desires reach no further than his arms. He is not only able to find a sufficiency in himself, but he has strength in excess of his needs; and this is the only time in his life when he will be in this condition.

I foresee an objection. I shall not be told that the child has more needs than I ascribe to him, but it will be denied that he has the power that I attribute to him. People will not reflect that I am speaking of my own pupil, and not of those walking dolls for whom it is a journey to go from one room to another, who are so boxed up as to labor for breath, and carry about burdens of pasteboard. I shall be told that manly strength manifests itself only at the period of manhood; and that the vital forces, elaborated in special organs and distributed through the whole body, can alone give to the muscles that consistency, activity, tone, and spring which are needed to produce real strength. This is the philosophy of books, but I appeal to experience. Out in your fields I see large boys tilling the earth, dressing vines, holding the plow, handling a cask of wine, and driving a wagon, just as their father would. They would be taken for men if the sound of their voices did not betray them. Even in our cities, young artisans, such as blacksmiths, sledge-tool makers, and farriers, are almost as robust as their masters, and would be hardly less skillful if they had been properly trained. If there is any difference—and I grant that there is—it is much less, I repeat, than that between the vehement desires of a man and the moderate desires of a child. Moreover, it is not simply a question of physical strength, but especially of that strength and capacity of mind which supplies and directs it.

This interval when the power of the individual is greater than his desires, although it is not the period of his greatest absolute strength is, as I have said, the period of his greatest relative strength. It is the most precious period of life, a period which comes but once; it is very short, and all the shorter, as we shall subsequently see, because it is the more important that it be well employed.

What, then, shall our pupil do with that surplus of faculties and powers which he has on hand at present, but which he will stand in need of at a subsequent period of life? He will endeavor to employ it in tasks which may profit him when the occasion comes; he will project into the future, so to speak, that which is superfluous for the time being. The robust child will make provisions for the feeble man; but he will place these stores neither in coffers which can be stolen from him, nor in barns which are not his own. In order that he may really appropriate his acquisitions to himself, it is in his arms, in his head, and in himself, that he will lodge them. This, then, is the period of labor, of instruction, and of study; and observe, it is not I who have arbitrarily made this choice, but it is Nature herself who indicates it.

Human intelligence has its limits; and not only is man unable to know everything, but he can not even know completely the little that other men know. Since the contradictory of every false proposition is a truth, the number of truths is as inexhaustible as the number of errors. There is, then, a choice in the things which ought to be taught, as well as in the time which is fit for learning them. Of the knowledges which are within our reach, some are false, some are useless, and others serve to nourish the pride of him who has them. The small number of those which really contribute to our well-being are alone worthy the pursuit of a wise man, and consequently of a child whom we wish to render such. It is not at all necessary to know everything, but merely that which is useful.

From this small number we must still subtract the truths which require, for being comprehended, an understanding already formed; such as those which suppose a knowledge of the relations of man to man, which a child cannot acquire; or those which, while true in themselves, dispose an inexperienced mind to think falsely on other subjects.

We are thus reduced to a circle which is very small with respect to the existence of things; but yet what an immense sphere this circle forms with respect to the mind of a child! What rash hands shall dare to touch the veil which darkens the human understanding? What abysses I see dug by our vain sciences about this young unfortunate! O thou who art to conduct him in his perilous paths, and to draw from before his eyes the sacred curtain of Nature, tremble! In the first place, make very sure of his head and your own, and have a fear lest either or both become giddy. Beware of the specious attractions of falsehood and of the intoxicating fumes of pride. Remember, ever remember, that ignorance has never been productive of evil, but that error alone is dangerous, and that we do not miss our way through what we do not know, but through what we falsely think we know.

His progress in geometry may serve you as a certain test and measure for the development of his intelligence; but as soon as he can discern what is useful and what is not, it is important to use much tact and skill to interest him in speculative studies. If you wish, for example, to have him find a mean proportional between two lines, begin in such a way as to make it necessary for him to find a square equal to a given rectangle. If two mean proportionals are required, we must first interest him in the problem of the duplication of the cube, etc. Observe how we are gradually approaching the moral notions which distinguish good from evil. Up to this time we have known no law save that of necessity; we now have regard to that which is useful; and we shall soon come to what is proper and good.

The same instinct animates the different faculties of man. To the activity of the body, which seeks to develop itself, succeeds the activity of the mind, which seeks to be instructed. At first, children are merely restless, then they are curious; and this curiosity, well directed, is the motive power of the age which we have now reached. Let us always distinguish the inclinations which come from Nature from those which come from opinion. There is an ardor for knowledge which is founded merely on the desire to be esteemed wise; but there is another which springs from a curiosity natural to man for all that can interest him from near or from far. The innate desire for well-being, and the impossibility of fully satisfying this desire, cause him to seek without intermission means for contributing to it. Such is the first principle of curiosity—a principle natural to the human heart, but the development of which takes place only in proportion to the growth of our passions and our intelligence. Imagine a philosopher banished to a desert isle with his instruments and his books, sure of spending there in solitude the rest of his days; he will hardly occupy himself longer with the solar system, with the laws of attraction, or with the differential calculus. Perhaps he will not open a single book during the remainder of his life; but he will never refrain from visiting his isle, even to the remotest corner, however great it may be. Let us then likewise reject from our primary studies those branches of knowledge for which man has not a natural taste, and let us limit ourselves to those which instinct leads us to pursue.

The earth is the isle of the human race; and the object which strikes our eyes the most forcibly is the sun. The moment we begin to go beyond ourselves, our first observations will naturally fall on these two objects. Thus the philosophy of almost all savage peoples is occupied wholly with the imaginary divisions of the earth and the divinity of the sun.

"What a leap!" some one will possibly say. A moment ago we were occupied simply with what touches us, with what immediately surrounds us; but all at once we are scouring the globe, and leaping to the extremities of the universe. This sudden transition is the effect of our progress in power, and of our mental inclinations. In our state of feebleness and insufficiency, the care of self-preservation wraps us up within ourselves; while in our state of potency and strength, the desire to give extension to our being carries us out of ourselves and makes us reach out as far as it is possible for us to go; but, as the intellectual world is still unknown to us, our thought goes no farther than our eyes, and our understanding widens only with the space which it measures.

Let us transform our sensations into ideas, but let us not jump abruptly from sensible objects to intellectual objects; for it is through the first that we are to reach the second. In the first movements of the mind, let the senses always be its guides; let there be no book but the world, and no other instruction than facts. The child who reads does not think—he merely reads; he is not receiving instruction, but is learning words.

Make your pupil attentive to natural phenomena, and you will soon make him curious; but, in order to nourish his curiosity, never be in haste to satisfy it. Ask questions that are within his comprehension, and leave him to resolve them. Let him know nothing because you have told it to him, but because he has comprehended it himself; he is not to learn science, but to discover it. If you ever substitute in his mind authority for reason, he will no longer reason; he will be but the sport of others' opinions.

You wish to teach this child geography, and you go in search of globes, spheres, and maps. What machines! Why all these representations? Why not begin by showing him the object itself, so that he may know, at least, what you are talking about!

On a fine evening you go out to walk in a favorable place where the horizon, happily unclouded, allows a full view of the setting sun, and you observe the objects which make it possible to recognize the place of his setting. On the morrow, in order to take an airing, you return to the same place before the sun has risen. You see his coming announced from afar by flashes of fire which he shoots forth before him. The conflagration increases; the earth seems all in flames. From their brightness we expect the sun long before he comes into view; at each moment we think we see him approaching, but at last he comes. A brilliant point darts forth like lightning and at once fills all space; the veil of shadows is effaced and falls. Man recognizes his place of sojourn and finds it embellished. During the night the verdure has acquired new vigor; the rising day which illumines it, and the early rays which gild it, show it covered with a brilliant tracery of dew which reflects light and colors to the eye. The birds unite in chorus, and salute in concert the father of life. At this moment not one is silent; their chirping, still feeble, is slower and sweeter than in the rest of the day, as if feeling the languor of a peaceful awakening. The concourse of all these objects brings to the senses an impression of freshness which penetrates even to the soul. This has been a half-hour of enchantment which no man can resist; a spectacle so grand, so beautiful, so delicious, leaves no one with a heart untouched.

Full of the enthusiasm which he has experienced, the teacher wishes to communicate it to the child. He fancies he can move him by making him attentive to the sensations by which he himself has been moved. Pure folly! The living spectacle of Nature is in the heart of man; and to see it, it must be felt. The child perceives objects; but he can not perceive the relations which unite them, and can not hear the sweet harmony of their concert. He needs an experience which he has not acquired, and emotions which he has not experienced, in order to feel the composite impression which results at once from all these sensations. If he has not long traversed arid plains, if hot sands have not burned his feet, if the stifling reflections of the sun's rays from the rocks have never oppressed him, how will he enjoy the fresh air of a beautiful morning? How will the perfume of flowers, the charm of the verdure, the humid vapor of the dew, and the soft and peaceful step on the lawn enchant his senses? How will the song of birds cause him a rapturous emotion, if the accents of love and pleasure are still unknown to him? With what transports will he see the dawn of a beautiful day, if his imagination cannot paint for him those with which it may be filled? Finally, how will he be affected by the beautiful spectacle of Nature, if he does not know the hand that has taken care to adorn it?

Do not address to the child discourses which he cannot understand. Let there be no descriptions, no eloquence, no figures of speech, no poetry. Neither sentiment nor taste is now at stake. Continue to be simple, clear, and dispassionate; the time will come, only too soon, for assuming a different language.

As soon as Émile comes to know what life is, my first care shall be to teach him how to preserve it. So far I have not distinguished classes, ranks, or fortunes; nor shall I distinguish them scarcely more in the sequel, because man is the same in all conditions. A rich man does not have a larger stomach than a poor man, and it digests no better than his; the arms of the lord are neither longer nor stronger than those of his slave; a great man is no larger than a common man; and, finally, natural needs being everywhere the same, the means of providing for them ought everywhere to be equal. Adapt the education of man to man, and not to that which he is not. Do you not see that in striving to educate him exclusively for one condition you are making him useless for every other? and that, if it please Fortune, you have labored only to make him unhappy? What is there more ridiculous than a man once a great lord, but now poor, who retains in his misery the prejudices of his birth? What is there more abject than an impoverished rich man, who, recollecting the contempt shown to poverty, feels that he has become the lowest of men? The sole resource of one is the trade of public cheat, and of the other that of a cringing valet with this fine phrase, *"It is necessary for me to live."*

You place confidence in the actual state of society without reflecting that this state is subject to inevitable revolutions, and that it is impossible to foresee or prevent that which may confront your children. The great become small, the rich become poor, the monarch becomes a subject. Are the blows of Fortune so rare that you can count on being exempt from them? We are approaching a state of crisis and a century of revolutions.* Who can answer to you for what you will then become? Whatever men have made, men may destroy; there are no ineffaceable characters save those which Nature impresses, and Nature makes neither princes, nor millionaires, nor lords. What, then, will that satrap do in his fallen state whom you have educated only for grandeur? What will that extortioner do in his poverty who knows how to live only on gold? What will that pompous imbecile do, deprived of everything, who can make no use of himself, and who employs his existence only in what is foreign to himself? Happy he who then knows how to turn away from the station which he quits, and can remain a man in spite of Fortune! Praise as much as you will that conquered king who, in his fury, would be buried under the ruins of his throne; for myself I despise him. I see that he owes his existence solely to his crown, and that if he were not king he would be nothing at all. But he who loses his crown and does without it, is then superior to it. From the rank of a king, which a craven, a villain, or a madman might occupy as well, he ascends to the state of man which so few men know how to fill. He then triumphs over Fortune and braves her; he owes nothing save to himself alone; and when all that remains to him to show is himself, he is not a cipher, but is something. Yes, I would a hundred times rather be the King of Syracuse as a schoolmaster at Corinth, and the King of Macedon as a clerk at Rome,† than an unfortunate Tarquin, not knowing what to do with himself if he cannot reign.

The man and the citizen, whichever he may be, has no other valuable to give to society than himself, all his other valuables being there without his will; and when a man is rich, either he does not enjoy his riches, or the public enjoys them also. In the first case, he steals from others that of which he deprives himself; and in the second, he gives them nothing. So the entire social debt remains with him as long as he pays only with his property. "But," you say, "my father served society while gaining this

---

*I hold it to be impossible for the great monarchies of Europe to last much longer; all have achieved brilliancy, and every state in this condition is in its decline. I have for my opinion reasons more cogent than this maxim; but this is not the time to declare them, and they must be evident to all.

†Alexander, the son of Perseus, last King of Macedonia, was the secretary of a Roman magistrate.

property." Be it so; he has paid his own debt, but not yours. You owe more to others than as though you were born without property; you were favored in your birth. It is not just that what one man has done for society should release another from what he owes it; for each one, owing his entire self, can pay only for himself, and no father can transmit to his son the right of being useless to his fellows; yet that is what he does, according to you, in leaving him riches, which are the proof and reward of labor. He who eats in idleness what he himself has not earned, steals; and a land-holder whom the state pays for doing nothing does not differ from a brigand who lives at the expense of travelers. Outside of society, an isolated man, owing nothing to anyone, has a right to live as he pleases; but in society, where he necessarily lives at the expense of others, he owes them in labor the price of his support; to this there is no exception. To work, then, is a duty indispensable to social man. Rich or poor, powerful or weak, every idle citizen is a knave.

Now, of all the occupations which can furnish subsistence to man, that which approaches nearest to the state of Nature is manual labor; of all the conditions the most independent of fortune and of men, is that of the artisan. The artisan depends only on his labor. He is free—as free as the husbandman is a slave; for the latter is dependent on his field, whose harvest is at the discretion of others. The enemy, the prince, a powerful neighbor, may take away from him this field; on account of it he may be harassed in a thousand ways; but wherever there is a purpose to harass the artisan, his baggage is soon ready; he folds his arms and walks off. Still, agriculture is the first employment of man; it is the most honorable, the most useful, and consequently the most noble that he can practice. I do not tell Émile to learn agriculture, for he knows it. All rustic employments are familiar to him; it is with them that he began, and to them he will ever be returning. I say to him, then, Cultivate the heritage of your fathers. But if you lose this heritage, or if you have none, what are you to do? Learn a trade.

"A trade for my son! My son an artisan! My dear sir, are you serious?" More serious than you are, madam, who would make it impossible for him ever to be anything but a lord, a marquis, a prince, or perhaps, one day, less than nothing; but on my part I wish to give him a rank which he can not lose, a rank which will honor him as long as he lives. I wish to raise him to the state of manhood; and whatever you may say of it, he will have fewer equals by this title than by all those which he will derive from you.

The letter kills and the spirit makes alive. It is important to learn a trade, less for the sake of knowing the trade than for overcoming the prejudices which despise it. You say you will never be compelled to work for a living. Ah, so much the worse—so much the worse for you! But never mind; do not work from necessity, but work for glory. Condescend to the state of the artisan in order to be above your own. In order to put fortune

and things under subjection to you, begin by making yourself independent of them. In order to reign by opinion, begin by reigning over opinion.

Recollect that it is not an accomplishment that I demand of you, but a
trade, a real trade—an art purely mechanic, where the hands work more
than the head, which does not lead to fortune, but with which one can
dispense with fortune. In families far above the danger of lacking for
bread, I have seen fathers carry foresight so far as to add to the duty of
instructing their children the duty of providing them with the knowledge
from which, whatever may happen, they may gain the means for living.
These provident fathers think they are doing a great deal; but they are
doing nothing, because the resources which they fancy they are economiz-
ing for their children depend on that very fortune of which they wish to
make them independent. So that with all those accomplishments, if he
who has them does not chance to be in circumstances favorable for making
use of them, he will perish of hunger just as soon as though he had none of
them.

But instead of resorting for a livelihood to those high knowledges which
are acquired for nourishing the soul and not the body, if you resort, in case
of need, to your hands and the use which you have learned to make of
them, all difficulties disappear, all artifices become useless; you have
resources always ready at the moment of need. Probity and honor are no
longer an obstacle to living. You no longer need to be a coward and a liar
before the great, compliant and cringing before knaves, the base pimp of
everybody, borrower or thief, which are almost the same thing when one
has nothing. The opinions of others do not affect you; you have no one's
favor to court, no fool to flatter, and no porter to conciliate. That rogues
manage great affairs is of little importance to you; this will not prevent you
in your obscure mode of life from being an honest man and from having
bread. You enter the first shop whose trade you have learned: "Foreman, I
am in need of employment." "Fellow-workman, stand there and go to
work." Before noon comes you have earned your dinner, and if you are
diligent and frugal, before the week has passed you will have the where-
withal to live for another week; you will have lived a free, healthy, true,
industrious, and just man. It is not to lose one's time to gain it in this way.

I insist absolutely that Émile shall learn a trade. "An honorable trade, at
least," you will say. What does this term mean? Is not every trade honorable that is useful to the public? I do not want him to be an embroiderer, a
gilder, or a varnisher, like Locke's gentleman; neither do I want him to be
a musician, a comedian, or a writer of books.* Except these professions,

---

*"You yourself are one," some one will say. I am, to my sorrow, I acknowledge; and my
faults, which I think I have sufficiently expiated, are no reasons why others should have
similar ones. I do not write to excuse my faults, but to prevent my readers from imitating
them.

and others which resemble them, let him choose the one he prefers; I do not assume to restrain him in anything. I would rather have him a cobbler than a poet; I would rather have him pave the highways than to decorate china. But, you will say, "Bailiffs, spies, and hangmen are useful people." It is the fault only of the government that they are so. But let that pass; I was wrong. It does not suffice to choose a useful calling; it is also necessary that it does not require of those who practice it qualities of soul which are odious and incompatible with humanity. Thus, returning to our first statement, let us choose an honorable calling; but let us always recollect that there is no honor without utility.

This is the spirit which should guide us in the choice of Émile's occupation, though it is not for us to make this choice, but for him; for, as the maxims with which he is equipped preserve in him a natural contempt for useless things he will never wish to consume his time in work of no value, and he knows no value in things save that of their real utility. He must have a trade which might serve Robinson in his island.

By causing to pass in review before a child the productions of Nature and art, by stimulating his curiosity and following it where it leads, we have the advantage of studying his tastes, his inclinations, and his propensities, and to see glitter the first spark of his genius, if he has genius of any decided sort. But a common error, and one from which we must preserve ourselves, is to attribute to the ardor of talent the effect of the occasion, and to take for a marked inclination toward such or such an art the imitative spirit which is common to man and monkey, and which mechanically leads both to wish to do whatever they see done without knowing very well what it is good for. The world is full of artisans, and especially of artists, who have no natural talent for the art which they practice, and in which they have been urged forward from their earliest age, either through motives of expedience, or through an apparent but mistaken zeal which would have also led them toward any other art if they had seen it practiced as soon. One hears a drum and thinks himself a general; another sees a house built and wishes to be an architect. Each one is drawn to the trade which he sees practiced, when he believes it to be held in esteem.

But perhaps we are giving too much importance to the choice of a trade. Since we have in view only manual labor, this choice is nothing for Émile, and his apprenticeship is already more than half done, through the tasks with which we have occupied our time up to the present moment. What do you wish him to do? He is ready for everything. He already knows how to handle the spade and the hoe; he can use the lathe, the hammer, the plane, and the file; the tools of all the trades are already familiar to him. All he has to do in addition is to acquire of some of these tools such a prompt and facile use as to make him equal in speed to good workmen using the same tools, and on this point he has a great advantage over all others; he has an agile body and flexible limbs, which can assume all sorts of attitudes without difficulty and prolong all sorts of movements without effort. Moreover, he has accurate and well-trained organs; all the machinery of the arts is already known to him. For the duties of master-workman all he lacks is habit, and habit is acquired only with time. To which of the trades whose choice it depends on us to make will he give sufficient time in order to make himself expert in it? This is the only question in the case.

Give to the man a trade which befits his sex, and to a young man a trade which befits his age; every sedentary and domestic occupation which effeminates and softens the body is neither pleasing nor adapted to him. A young lad should never aspire to be a tailor.

Work in metals is useful, and even the most useful of all. However, unless some special reason inclines me to it, I would not make of your son a farrier, a locksmith, or a blacksmith; I would not like to see him in his shop the figure of a Cyclops. So also I would not have him a mason, and still less a shoe-maker. All trades must be practiced, but he who can choose ought to have regard for cleanliness, for this is not a matter of opinion; on this point the senses decide for us. Finally, I would have none of those stupid trades whose operatives, without ingenuity and almost automata, never exercise their hands save at one kind of labor, such as weavers, stocking-makers, and stone-cutters. Of what use is it to employ men of sense at these trades? They are machines in charge of another machine.

All things considered, the trade which I would rather have be to the taste of my pupil is that of cabinet-maker. It is cleanly, it is useful, and it may be practiced at home; it keeps the body sufficiently exercised; it requires of the workman skill and ingenuity, and in the form of the products which utility determines, elegance and taste are not excluded. But if, perchance, the genius of your pupil is decidedly turned toward the speculative sciences, then I would not blame you for giving him a trade adapted to his inclinations; that he learn, for example, to make mathematical instruments, spy-glasses, telescopes, etc.

When Émile learns his trade I wish to learn it with him, for I am convinced that he will never learn anything well save what we learn together. We then put ourselves in apprenticeship, and we do not assume to be treated as gentlemen, but as real apprentices, who are not such for the sport of the thing. Why should we not be apprentices in real earnest? The Czar Peter was a carpenter at the bench and a drummer in his own army; do you think that this prince was not your equal by birth or by merit? You understand that I am not saying this to Émile, but to you, whoever you may be. Unfortunately, we can not spend all our time at the bench. We are not only apprenticed workmen, but we are apprenticed men; and our apprenticeship to this last trade is longer and more difficult than the other. How, then, shall we proceed? Shall we have a master of the plane one hour a day, just as we have a dancing-master? No; we shall not be apprentices, but disciples; and our ambition is not so much to learn cabinet-making as to rise to the position of cabinet-maker. I am therefore of the opinion that we should go, at least once or twice a week, to spend a whole day with the master workman; that we should rise when he does; that we should be at work before he comes; that we should eat at his table, work under his orders, and that, after having had the honor to sup with his family we, if we wish, should return to rest on our hard beds. This is how we learn several trades at once, and how we employ ourselves at manual labor without neglecting the other apprenticeship.

If I have been understood thus far, it ought to be plain how, with the habitual exercise of the body and labor of the hands, I insensibly give to my pupil a taste for reflection and mediation in order to counterbalance in him the indolence which would result from his indifference for the judgments of men and from the repose of his passions. He must work as a peasant and think as a philosopher in order not to be as lazy as a savage. The great secret of education is to make the exercises of the body and of the mind always serve as a recreation for each other.

IV. ÉMILE FROM FIFTEEN TO TWENTY

How swift is our passage over this earth! The first quarter of life has slipped away before we know its use, and the last quarter also slips away after we have ceased to enjoy it. At first we do not know how to live; soon we are no longer able to live; and in the interval which separates these two useless extremities three quarters of the time which remains to us is consumed in sleep, in labor, in suffering, in constraint, in troubles of every description. Life is short, less through the brevity of the time that it lasts than because of this brief period, we have almost nothing for enjoying it. It matters not that the moment of death is far removed from that of birth, for life is always too short when this space is badly filled.

We have two births, so to speak—one for existing and the other for living; one for the species and the other for the sex.

But man in general is not made to remain always in a state of infancy. He passes out of it at a time prescribed by Nature; and this critical moment, though very short, has lasting influences.

As the tempest is announced from afar by the roaring of the sea, so this stormy revolution is foretold by the murmur of the rising passions; a rumbling agitation warns us of the approach of danger.

Here is the second birth of which I have spoken; it is here that man really begins to live, and nothing human is foreign to him. So far our cares have been but child's play; it is only now that they assume a real importance. This epoch, where ordinary education ends, is properly the one where ours ought to begin.

Our passions are the principal instruments of our conservation, and it is therefore an attempt as vain as it is ridiculous to wish to destroy them; it would be to control Nature and reform the work of God. If God were to tell man to destroy the passions which he has given him, God would and would not, he would contradict himself. But he has never given this senseless order; nothing like it is written in the human heart; and whatever God wishes a man to do he does not cause it to be told to him by another man, but he says it to him himself, he writes it in the depths of his heart.

The source of our passions, the origin and basis of all the others, the only one which is born with man and never leaves him while he lives, is the love of self. This passion is primitive, innate, anterior to every other, and of which, in some sense, all the others are but modifications. In this sense all of them, so to speak, are natural; but the most of these modifications have foreign causes without which they would never have existed, and these very modifications, far from being advantageous to us, are harmful; they change the primitive object and go counter to their purpose. It is then that man finds himself estranged from Nature and in contradiction with himself.

Love of one's self is always good and always in conformity with order. Each one being especially charged with his own conservation, the first and the most important of all his cares is and ought to be to guard it with ceaseless vigilance; and how shall he do this unless he takes the greatest interest in it?

It is therefore necessary that we love ourselves in order to preserve ourselves. We must love ourselves more than anything else; and, through an immediate consequence of the same feeling, we love that which preserves us. Every child becomes attached to his nurse. Romulus must needs feel an attachment for the wolf that suckled him. Whatever favors the well-being of an individual attracts him, and whatever harms him repels him; and this is but a blind instinct. That which transforms this instinct into a feeling, attachment into love, and aversion into hatred, is the manifest intention of hurting us or of doing us good.

The first feeling of a child is to love himself, and the second, which is derived from the first, is to love those who come near him; for in the state of weakness in which he is he knows no one save through the care and assistance which he receives. At first, the attachment which he has for his nurse and his governess is but habit. He seeks them because he has need of them and finds it well to have them; it is rather knowledge than benevolence. It requires much time for him to comprehend that they are not only useful to him, but that they wish to be so. It is then that he begins to love them.

A child is then naturally inclined to benevolence because he sees that everything which approaches him is brought to assist him, and he derives from this observation the habit of feeling favorably disposed toward his species; but in proportion as he extends his relations, his needs, and his active or passive dependencies, the feeling of his relations to others is aroused and produces that of duties and preferences. Then the child becomes imperious, jealous, deceptive, and vindictive. If he is constrained to obedience, not seeing the utility of what he is commanded to do, he attributes it to caprice or to the intention of tormenting him, and he rebels. If he himself is obeyed, the moment anything resists him he sees in it a rebellion, an intention of resisting him; and he beats the chair or table for having disobeyed him. The love of self (*amour de soi*), which regards only ourselves, is content when our real needs are satisfied; but pride (*amour-propre*), which makes comparisons, is never satisfied, and could not be, because this feeling, by preferring ourselves to others, also requires that others prefer ourselves to them—a thing which is impossible. This is how the gentle and affectionate passions spring from the love of self, while the malevolent and irascible passions spring from self-love. Thus, that which makes man essentially good is to have few needs and to compare himself but little with others; while that which makes him essentially bad is to have many needs and to pay great deference to opinion. On this principle is easy to see how we may direct to good or to evil all the passions of children and of men. It is true that, not being able to live always alone, they will find it difficult to live always good. And this very difficulty will necessarily increase with their relations; and it is particularly in this that the dangers of society render art and care the more indispensable to us for preventing in the human heart the depravation which springs from its new needs.

The study proper for man is that of his relations. While he knows himself only through his physical being, he ought to study himself through his relations with things, and this is the occupation of his childhood; but when he begins to feel his moral nature, he ought to study himself through his relations with men, and this is the occupation of his entire life, beginning at the point we have now reached.

As soon as man has need of a companion, he is no longer an isolated being, his heart is no longer alone. All his relations with his species, and all the affections of his soul, are born with her. His first passion soon causes the rise of others.

The instructions of nature are tardy and slow, while those of men are almost always premature. In the first case, the senses arouse the imagination; and in the second, the imagination arouses the senses and gives them a precocious activity which can not fail to enervate and enfeeble, first the individual, and then, in the course of time, the species itself. A more general and a more trustworthy observation than that of the effect of climate is that puberty and sexual power always come earlier among educated and refined people than among ignorant and barbarous people.

Children have a singular sagacity in discerning through all the affectations of decency the bad manners which it conceals. The refined language which we dictate to them, the lessons of propriety which we give them, the veil of mystery which we affect to draw before their eyes, are so many spurs to their curiosity. From the manner in which we go about this, it is clear that what we feign to conceal from them is only so much for them to learn; and of all the lessons which we give them this is the one which they turn to the largest account.

If the age at which man acquires the consciousness of his sex differs as much through the effect of education as through the action of nature, it follows that we may accelerate or retard this age according to the manner in which children are educated; and if the body gains or loses consistency in proportion as we retard or accelerate this progress, it also follows that the more we strive to retard it the greater the vigor and power which a young man will acquire. I am now speaking of purely physical effects; but we shall soon see that these are not the only ones.

From these reflections I draw the solution of this question so often asked, whether it is best to enlighten children at an early hour on the objects of their curiosity, or whether it is not best to satisfy them with modest but false explanations. I do not think it necessary to do either. In the first place, this curiosity does not come to them unless we have paved the way for it. We must then proceed in such a way that they will not have it. In the second place, questions which we are not compelled to answer do not require us to deceive the one who asks them; it is much better to impose silence on him than to make him a reply which is false. This law will cause him little surprise if we have taken care to subject him to it in things which are indifferent. Finally, if we decide to reply to them, let it be done with the greatest simplicity, without mystery, without embarrassment, and without a smile. There is much less danger in satisfying the curiosity of the child than in exciting it.

Let your replies always be grave, short, decided, and without ever seeming to hesitate. I need not add that they ought to be true. We can not teach children the danger of lying to men without feeling, as men, the greater danger of lying to children. One single falsehood told by a teacher to his pupil, and known to be such, would forever ruin all the fruits of an education.

An absolute ignorance of certain things is perhaps what is most advisable for children; but let them learn at an early hour that which it is impossible always to conceal from them. It is necessary either that their curiosity be not awakened in any way, or that it be satisfied before the age when it is no longer a danger. In this matter your manner of treating your pupil will depend much on his particular situation, on the society in which he moves, and on the circumstances by which it is foreseen he will be surrounded. It is important in such cases to trust nothing to chance; and if you are not sure of keeping him in ignorance of the difference of the sexes up to his sixteenth year, take care that he learn it before the age of ten.

In your dealings with children I would not have you affect a language which is too refined; nor that you make long *détours*, which they perceive, in order to avoid giving to things their real names. In these matters good manners always have great simplicity; but imaginations sullied by vice make the ear fastidious, and are ever forcing us to adopt refinements of expression. Gross terms are of no consequence; it is lewd thoughts which must be shunned.

Though modesty is natural to the human species, children are naturally destitute of it. Modesty is born only with the knowledge of evil; how, then, shall children who neither have nor ought to have this knowledge have the feeling which is the effect of it? To give them lessons in modesty and honor is to teach them that there are things that are shameful and dishonorable, and to give them a secret desire to know these things. Sooner or later they succeed in this, and the first spark which touches the imagination will most certainly accelerate the conflagration of the senses. Whoever blushes is already guilty; true innocence is ashamed of nothing.

I see but one good means of preserving the innocence of children; and this is, that all those who surround them respect and love it. Without this all the prudence which we try to make use of with them comes to naught sooner or later; a smile, a wink, a chance gesture, tell them all that we seek to conceal from them; it suffices for them in order to learn it to see that we have designed to keep it from them. The nice turns of expression which genteel people use among themselves, taking for granted knowledge which children ought not to have, are wholly out of place with them; but when we truly honor their simplicity we easily adopt, in speaking to them, that simplicity of language which befits them. There is a certain artlessness of language which becomes innocence and is pleasing to it; this is the true tone which turns aside a child from a dangerous curiosity. By speaking to him of everything in simple terms, we do not allow him to suspect that there is anything more to say to him. In giving to coarse words the displeasing ideas which befit them, we smother the first fire of the imagination; we do not forbid him to pronounce these words and to have these ideas; but without his thinking of it we give him a repugnance for recalling them. And from what embarrassment would not this artless liberty save those who, drawing it from their own heart, always say that which must be said, and always say it just as they have felt it!

Your children read; and in their reading they acquire knowledge which they would not have had if they had not read. If they study, the imagination becomes inflamed and sharpened in the silence of the study chamber. If they live in the world, they hear a strange jargon and see examples by which they are strongly impressed. They have been so thoroughly persuaded that they are men, that in all that men do in their presence they at once try to ascertain how all this may be adapted to their use; it must necessarily be that all the actions of others serve them as a model when the judgments of others serve them as a law. The domestics who are made to wait on them and who are consequently interested in pleasing them, curry favor with them at the expense of good morals; and giggling governesses address conversation to them at four years which the most shameless would not dare to hold at fifteen. These nurses soon forget what they have said, but the children never forget what they have heard. Licentious conversation leads to dissolute manners; a vile servant makes a child debauched, and the secret of one serves as a guarantee for that of the other.

Would you put order and control into the nascent passions? Lengthen the time during which they are developed, to the end that they may have the time to adjust themselves in proportion as they come into being. Then it is not man who ordains them, but Nature herself, and your only care is to let her arrange her work. If your pupil were alone you would have nothing to do; but everything that surrounds him inflames his imagination. The torrent of prejudices hurries him on, and in order to rescue him you must push him in a contrary direction. Feeling must restrain the imagination, and reason must put to silence the opinions of men. The source of all the passions is the sensibility; the imagination determines their inclination. Every being who feels his relations must be affected when these relations are altered, and when he imagines, or thinks he imagines, those which are better adapted to his nature. These are the errors of imagination which transform into vices the passions of all limited beings, even of angels, 'if they have passions; for they must needs know the nature of all beings in order to know what relations are most consonant with their own.

This, then, is the sum of all human wisdom in the use of the passions: 1, to feel the true relations of man both in the species and in the individual; 2, to order all the affections of the soul according to these relations. The first feeling of which a young man who has been carefully educated is susceptible is not love, but friendship. The first act of his nascent imagination is to teach him that he has fellow-creatures, and the species affects him before the sex. Here is another advantage of prolonged innocence; it is to profit by the nascent sensibility for sowing in the heart of the young adolescent the first seeds of humanity, an advantage all the more precious as it is the only time of life when the same cares can have a real success.

Would you excite and nourish in the heart of a young man the first movements of the nascent sensibility, and turn his character toward benevolence and goodness? Do not cause pride, vanity, and envy to germinate in him; through the deceptive image of the happiness of men, do not at first expose to his eyes the pomp of courts, the pageantry of palaces, and the attractions of the theatre; do not take him about in social circles and brilliant assemblies; do not show him the exterior of grand society until after having put him in a condition to form an estimate of it in itself. To show him the world before he knows men is not to form him, but to corrupt him; it is not to instruct him but to deceive him.

Men are by nature neither kings, nor grandees, nor courtiers, nor millionaires; all are born naked and poor; all are subject to the miseries of life, to chagrins, evils, needs, and sorrows of every sort; and, finally, all are condemned to death. This is what man truly is; this is that from which no mortal is exempt. Begin, then, by studying that which is most inseparable from human nature, that which most truly constitutes humanity. At the age of sixteen the adolescent knows what it is to suffer, for he himself has suffered; but he hardly knows that other beings also suffer. To see without feeling is not to know and, as I have said a hundred times, the child, not imagining what others feel, knows no ills save his own; but when the first development of the senses enkindles in him the fire of imagination, he begins to know himself in his fellows, to be affected by their complaints, and to suffer with their sorrows. It is then that the sad picture of suffering humanity ought to carry to his heart the first feeling of tenderness which he has ever experienced.

We work in concert with Nature, and while she is forming the physical man, we are trying to form the moral man; but our progress is not the same. The body is already robust and strong while the soul is still languishing and feeble, and notwithstanding all that human art can do, temperament always precedes reason. It is to hold the one and to excite the other that we have so far devoted all our care, so that as far as possible man might always be one. While developing the disposition we have diverted his nascent sensibility; we have regulated it by cultivating the reason. Intellectual objects modify the impressions of sensible objects. By ascending to the principle of things we have withdrawn him from the empire of the senses. It was easy to rise from the study of Nature to the search for its author.

When we have reached this point what new holds we have gained on our pupil! What new means we have of speaking to his heart! It is only then that he finds his real interest in being good and in doing good, with no regard to men, and without being forced to it by the laws; in being just between God and himself; in performing his duty, even at the cost of his life, and in maintaining purity of heart, not only for the love of order to which each always prefers the love of self, but for the love of his Creator which is mingled with this very love of self, in order that he may finally enjoy the lasting happiness which the repose of a good conscience and the contemplation of that Supreme Being promise him in the other life, after having made a good use of this. Depart from this, and I see nothing but injustice, hypocrisy, and falsehood among men; and the individual interest which, in competition, necessarily prevails over everything else, teaches each of them to adorn vice with the mask of virtue. Let all other men consult my happiness at the expense of their own; let everything have reference to me alone; let the whole human race die, if necessary, in pain and in wretchedness, in order to spare me a moment of sorrow or of hunger: such is the inward language of every unbeliever who reasons. Yes, I will maintain it as long as I live: whoever has said in his heart there is no God, and speaks differently, is but a liar or a fool.

The true moment of nature finally comes, as it necessarily must. Since man must die, he must reproduce himself in order that the species may endure and the order of the world be preserved. When, by signs which I have mentioned, you have a presentiment of the critical moment, instantly and forever abandon your former manner with him. He is still your disciple, but he is no longer your pupil. He is your friend—he is a man; henceforth treat him as such.

Émile: The Education of Woman

Sophie ought to be a woman, as Émile is a man—that is, she should have whatever is befitting the constitution of her species and of her sex, in order to fill her place in the physical and moral world. Let us then begin by examining the conformities and the differences between her sex and ours.

All that we know with a certainty is that the only thing in common between man and woman is the species, and that they differ only in respect of sex. Under this double point of view we find between them so many resemblances and so many contrasts, that it is perhaps one of the wonders of Nature that she could make two beings so similar and yet constitute them so differently.

These correspondences and these differences must needs have their moral effect. This consequence is obvious, is in conformity with experience, and show the vanity of the disputes as to the superiority or the equality of the sexes; as if each of them, answering the ends of Nature according to its particular destination, were not more perfect on that account than if it bore a greater resemblance to the other! With respect to what they have in common they are equal; and in so far as they are different they are not capable of being compared. A perfect man and a perfect woman ought no more to resemble each other in mind than in features; and perfection is not susceptible of greater and less.

In the union of the sexes each contributes equally toward the common end, but not in the same way. Hence arises the first assignable difference among their moral relations. One must be active and strong, the other passive and weak. One must needs have power and will, while it suffices that the other have little power of resistance.

This principle once established, it follows that woman is especially constituted to please man. If man ought to please her in turn, the necessity for it is less direct. His merit lies in his power; he pleases simply because he is strong. I grant that this is not the law of love, but it is the law of Nature, which is anterior even to love.

Plato, in his Republic, enjoins the same exercises on women as upon men, and in this I think he was right. Having excluded private families from his ideal state, and not knowing what to do with the women, he sees himself compelled to make men of them. This great genius had arranged everything, foreseen everything, and had anticipated objections which perhaps no one would have thought of making; but he has poorly resolved one which has been raised against him. I do not speak of that ordained community of wives, the censure of which, so often repeated, proves that those who make it have never read him; but I speak of that civil intermingling which everywhere confounds the two sexes in the same employments, the same duties, and can not fail to engender the most intolerable abuses; I speak of that subversion of the sweetest feelings of nature, sacrificed to an artificial feeling which can not exist save through them. Just as though a natural power were not necessary in order to form conventional ties! As though the love we have for our neighbors were not the basis of that which we owe the state! As though it were not through the little community, which is the family, that the heart becomes attached to the great! And as though it were not the good son, the good husband, and the good father, who makes the good citizen!

The moment it is demonstrated that man and woman are not and ought not to be constituted in the same way, either in character or in constitution, it follows that they ought not to have the same education. In following the directions of Nature they ought to act in concert, but they ought not to do the same things; their duties have a common end, but the duties themselves are different, and consequently the tastes which direct them. After having tried to form the natural man, let us also see, in order not to leave our work incomplete, how the woman is to be formed who is befitting to this man.

Would you always be well guided? Always follow the indications of Nature. All that characterizes sex ought to be respected or established by her. You are always saying that women have faults which you have not. Your pride deceives you. They would be faults in you, but they are virtues in them; and everything would not go so well if they did not have them. Prevent these so-called faults from degenerating, but beware of destroying them.

All the faculties common to the two sexes are not equally divided, but, taken as a whole, they offset one another. Woman is worth more as a woman, but less as a man; wherever she improves her rights she has the advantage, and wherever she attempts to usurp ours she remains inferior to us. Only exceptional cases can be urged against this general truth—the usual mode of argument adopted by the gallant partisans of the fair sex.

To cultivate in women the qualities of the men and to neglect those which are their own is, then, obviously to work to their detriment. The shrewd among them see this too clearly to be the dupes of it. In trying to usurp our advantages they do not abandon their own; but from this it comes to pass that, not being able to manage both properly on account of their incompatibility, they fall short of their own possibilities without attaining to ours, and thus lose the half of their value. Believe me, judicious mother, do not make of your daughter a good man, as though to give the lie to Nature, but make of her a good woman, and you may be sure that she will be worth more for herself and for us.

Does it follow that she ought to be brought up in complete ignorance, and restricted solely to the duties of the household? Shall man make a servant of his companion? Shall he deprive himself of the greatest charm of society? The better to reduce her to servitude, shall he prevent her from feeling anything or knowing anything? Shall he make of her a real automaton? No, doubtless. Nature, who gives to women a mind so agreeable and so acute, has not so ordered. On the contrary, she would have them think, and judge, and love, and know, and cultivate their mind as they do their form: these are the arms which she gives them for supplementing the strength which they lack, and for directing our own. They ought to learn multitudes of things, but only those which it becomes them to know. Whether I consider the particular destination of woman, or observe her inclinations, or take account of her duties, everything concurs equally to indicate to me the form of education which befits her.

On the good constitution of mothers depends, in the first place, that of children; on the care of women depends the early education of men; and on women, again, depend their manners, their passions, their tastes, their pleasures, and even their happiness. Thus the whole education of women ought to be relative to men. To please them, to be useful to them, to make themselves loved and honored by them, to educate them when young, to care for them when grown, to counsel them, to console them, and to make life agreeable and sweet to them—these are the duties of women at all times, and what should be taught them from their infancy. So long as we do not ascend to this principle we shall miss the goal, and all the precepts which we give them will accomplish nothing either for their happiness or for our own.

Little girls, almost from birth, have a love for dress. Not content with being pretty, they wish to be thought so. We see in their little airs that this care already occupies their minds; and they no sooner understand what is said to them than we control them by telling them what people will think of them. The same motive, very indiscreetly presented to little boys, is very far from having the same power over them. Provided they are independent and happy, they care very little of what will be thought of them. It is only at the expense of time and labor that we subject them to the same law.

From whatever source this first lesson comes to girls, it is a very good one. Since the body is born, so to speak, before the soul, the first culture ought to be that of the body; and this order is common to both sexes. But the object of this culture is different; in one this object is the development of strength, while in the other it is the development of personal charms. Not that these qualities ought to be exclusive in each sex, but the order is simply reversed: women need sufficient strength to do with grace whatever they have to do; and men need sufficient cleverness to do with facility whatever they have to do.

The extreme lack of vigor in women gives rise to the same quality in men. Women ought not to be robust like them, but for them, in order that the man who shall be born of them may be robust also. In this respect the convents, where the boarders have coarse fare, but many frolics, races, and sports in the open air and in gardens, are to be preferred to the home where a girl, delicately reared, always flattered or scolded, always seated under the eyes of her mother in a very close room, dares neither to rise, to walk, to speak, nor to breathe, and has not a moment's liberty for playing, jumping, running, shouting, and indulging in the petulance natural to her age; always dangerous relaxation or badly conceived severity, but never anything according to reason. This is the way in which the young are ruined both in body and in heart.

Whatever obstructs or constrains nature is in bad taste, and this is as true of the ornaments of the body as of the ornaments of the mind. Life, health, reason, and comfort ought to take precedence of everything else. There is no grace without freedom. Delicacy is not languor, and one need not be sickly in order to please. We excite pity when we suffer; but pleasure and desire seek the freshness of health.

Children of the two sexes have many amusements in common, and this ought to be so. Is not the same thing true of them when grown? They have also individual tastes which distinguish them. Boys seek movement and noise—drums, tops, carts; but girls perfer what appeals to the sight and serves for ornament—mirrors, trinkets, rags, and especially dolls. The doll is the especial amusement of this sex; and in this case the girl's taste is very evidently determined by her destination. The mechanics of the art of pleasing consists in dress, and this is all of this art that children can cultivate.

Observe a little girl spending her time with her doll, constantly changing its attire, dressing and undressing it hundreds of times, continually seeking for new combinations of ornaments, well or badly selected, no matter which; the fingers lack deftness, the taste has not been formed, but the disposition is already seen. In this endless occupation the time goes on without notice; the hours pass but she takes no note of them; she even forgets to eat, and has a greater hunger for dress than for food. But, you will say, she dresses her doll, but not herself. Doubtless. She sees her doll, but does not see herself; she can do nothing for herself; she has not been developed; she has neither talent nor strength; she is all absorbed in her doll, and on it she expends all her coquetry. She will not always devote herself to it, but waits the moment when she shall be her own doll.

Here, then, is a very decided primitive taste, and you have only to follow it and regulate it. It is certain that the little one wishes with all her heart that she might adorn her doll and adjust its sleeve, its neckerchief, its furbelows, its lace; but in all this she is made to depend so rigorously on the pleasure of others that it would be very much easier for her to owe everything to her own industry. Thus appears the reason for the first lessons which are given her; they are not tasks which are prescribed for her, but kindnesses which we feel for her. And, in fact, almost all little girls learn to read and write with repugnance; but as to holding the needle, they always learn this willingly. The imagine themselves already grown, and take pleasure in thinking that these talents will one day be of service in adorning them.

Once opened, this first route is easy to follow; sewing, embroidery, and lace-work will come of themselves. Tapestry is not so much to their liking; and as furniture is not connected with the person, but with mere opinion, it is too far out of their reach. Tapestry is the amusement of women; young girls will never take very great pleasure in it.

This voluntary progress will easily extend itself to designing, for this art is not immaterial to that of dressing with taste; but I would not have it applied to landscape, and still less to portrait painting. Foliage, fruits, flowers, draperies, and whatever may serve to give an elegant outline to attire, and to make for one's self a pattern for embroidery when one can not be found to the taste—this is sufficient for them. In general, if it is important for men to restrict their studies to knowledge of practical use, this is still more important for women; for as the life of the latter, though less laborious, is, or ought to be, more devoted to their duties, and is more interrupted by different cares, it does not allow them to devote themselves by choice to any talent to the prejudice of their duties.

Whatever may be said on the subject jokingly, the two sexes are equally endowed in respect of good sense. In general, girls are more docile than boys, and we ought to use even more authority over them, as I shall presently explain; but it does not follow that we are to require of them anything whose utility they can not see. The art of mothers is to show them the utility of everything which they prescribe for them; and this is so much easier as the intelligence of girls is more precocious than that of boys. This rule banishes from their sex, as it does from ours, not only all trifling studies which end in nothing good, and even fail to make those who have pursued them more agreeable to others; but even all those which have no utility for children of that age, and whose utility at a later period of life the child can not foresee. If I would not urge a boy to learn to read, for a stronger reason I would not force young girls to do this before I had made them understand the purpose of reading; and according to the usual manner of showing them this utility we follow our own idea much more than theirs. After all, why is it necessary that a girl should learn to read and write at an early age? Will she have a household to govern so soon? There are very few who will not abuse rather than use this fatal science; and all are a little too curious not to learn it without compulsion when they have the leisure and the occasion for it. Perhaps they ought to learn to cipher before everything else, for nothing offers a more obvious utility at all times, requires longer practice, or gives a stronger defense against error than the art of computation. If the little one could have cherries to her taste only through an arithmetical process, I warrant you she would soon know how to calculate.

Always justify the duties which you impose on young girls, but never fail to impose them. Idleness and indocility are their two most dangerous faults, and when once contracted they are cured with the greatest difficulty. Girls ought to be heedful and industrious, and this is not all: they ought early to be brought under restraint. This misfortune, if it is one for them, is inseparable from their sex; and they never rid themselves of it save to suffer others which are much more cruel. As long as they live they will be subject to the most continual and the most severe restraint—that which is imposed by the laws of decorum. They must early be trained to restraint, to the end that it may cost them nothing; and to conquer all their whims, in order to subject them to the wills of others. If they wish always to be at work, they must sometimes be compelled to do nothing. Dissipation, frivolity, and inconstancy are faults which easily spring from their first tastes which have been corrupted, and then always followed. In order to prevent this abuse, teach them above all else to conquer themselves. By reason of our senseless customs, the life of a good woman is a perpetual combat with herself; and it is just that this sex share the discomfort of the evils which it has caused us.

Prevent young girls from becoming tired of their occupations, and from becoming enamored of their amusements, as it always happens in the common style of education, where, as Fénelon says, all the tedium is put on one side and all the pleasure on the other. The first of these two inconveniences will not occur if we follow the preceding rules, save when the persons who are with them are displeasing to them. A little girl who loves her mother or her aunt will work all day at her side without weariness; her prattle alone will reward her for all her constraint. But if she who governs her is insupportable to her, she will include in the same disgust whatever she does in her presence. It is very difficult for those who are not happier with their mothers than with any one else in the world, ever to turn out well; but in order to judge of their real feelings we must study them and distrust what they say; for they are fawning, dissimulating, and soon know how to disguise themselves. Nor ought they to be ordered to love their mothers; affection does not come through duty, and constraint serves no purpose in this place. Attachment, kind offices, and simple habit will make the mother loved by her daughter if she does nothing to incur her hatred. Even the constraint in which she holds her, when well directed, far from weakening this attachment, will serve only to increase it, because, dependence being a state natural to women, girls feel that they are made to obey.

For the very reason that they have or ought to have little liberty, they carry to excess the liberty which is granted them; extreme in everything, they abandon themselves to their sports with even greater transport than boys do. This is the second of the inconveniences which I just mentioned This transport ought to be toned down, for it is the cause of several vices peculiar to women—as, among others, caprice and infatuation, by which woman is to-day carried away with an object which she will not regard to-morrow. The inconstancy of their tastes is as hurtful as their excess, and both come to them from the same source. Do not deny them gayety, laughter, noise, and sportive diversions; but prevent them from being satiated with one and running to the other; never suffer them for a single moment of their lives to know themselves free from restraint. Accustom them to see themselves interrupted in the midst of their sports, and to be recalled to other things without a murmur. Mere habit is still sufficient for this purpose, because it merely supplements nature.

There results from this habitual restraint a docility which women need during their whole life, since they never cease to be subject either to a man or to the judgments of men, and they are never allowed to place themselves above these judgments. The first and most important quality of a woman in gentleness. Made to obey a being as imperfect as man, often so full of vices, and always so full of faults, she ought early to learn to suffer even injustice, and to endure the wrongs of a husband without complaint; and it is not for him but for herself that she ought to be gentle. The harshness and obstinacy of women serve only to increase the wrongs and the bad conduct of husbands; they feel that it is not with these arms that their wives should conquer them. Heaven has not made them insinuating and persuasive in order to become waspish; has not made them weak in order to be imperious; has not given them so gentle a voice in order to use harsh language; and has not made their features so delicate in order to disfigure them by anger. When they become angry they forget themselves; they often have reason to complain, but they are always wrong in scolding. Each one ought to preserve the tone of his sex. The husband who is too mild may make a woman impertinent; but, unless a man is a brute, the gentleness of a wife reforms him, and triumphs over him sooner or later.

Let daughters always be submissive, but let not mothers always be inexorable. In order to render a young woman docile, it is not necessary to make her unhappy; to render her modest, it is not necessary to brutalize her. On the contrary, I should not be sorry if she were sometimes indulged in a little adroitness, not to escape punishment for her disobedience, but to make her exempt from obeying. It is not proposed to make her dependence painful, but it suffices to make her feel it. Artifice is a talent natural to the sex, and, persuaded that all natural inclinations are good and upright in themselves, I advise the cultivation of this one, as well as of the others; all that is necessary is to prevent its abuse.

As to the truth of this remark, I appeal to every honest observer. I do not wish women themselves to be examined on this point; our annnoying customs may force them to sharpen their temper. I would have the girls examined, the little girls who have only just come into the world, so to speak; compare them with little boys of the same age, and if the latter do not seem dull, thoughtless, and stupid in their presence, I shall be unquestionably wrong.

I know that austere teachers would have young girls taught neither singing, dancing, nor any other accomplishment. This seems to me ludicrous. To whom, then, would they have these things taught? To boys? To whom does it pertain, by preference, to have these talents: to men, or to women? To no one, they will reply; profane songs are so many crimes; the dance is an invention of the devil; a young girl ought to have no amusement save her work and her prayers. Strange amusements these for a child of ten! For myself, I greatly fear that all those little saints who are forced to spend their childhood in praying may spend their youth in something very different, and, when married, may do their best to redeem the time which they lost while girls. I think that we must have regard to what befits age as well as sex; that a young girl ought not to live like her grandmother, but ought to be lively, playful, frolicsome; to sing and dance as much as she pleases, and to taste all the innocent pleasures of her age. The time will come only too soon for being sedate and for assuming a more serious deportment.

We have gone too far in reducing the pleasure-giving talents to arts; they have been systematized too much; everything has been reduced to maxim and precept, and we have made very tedious to young persons what ought to be for them only amusements and pleasant diversions. I can imagine nothing more ridiculous than to see an old dancing-master approach with a grim air young persons who want merely to laugh, and, while teaching them his frivolous science, assume a tone more pedantic and magisterial than if it were their catechism he was teaching. For example, is the art of singing limited to written music? May not one render his voice flexible and accurate; learn to sing with taste, and even to accompany an instrument, without knowing a single note? Is the same kind of singing adapted to all voices? Is the same method adapted to all minds? I shall never be made to believe that the same attitudes, the same steps, the same movements, the same gestures, and the same dances are equally becoming to a little brunette, lively and keen, and to a tall, beautiful blonde with languishing eyes. When, therefore, I see a master giving exactly the same lessons to both, I say that the man follows his routine but understands nothing of his art.

It is asked whether the teachers for young girls should be men, or women. I do not know. I wish that neither might be necessary, but that they might be free to learn what they are so much inclined to learn, and that we might not see constantly going about in our cities so many laced buffoons. I have some difficulty in believing that the deportment of these fellows does not do more harm than good to young girls, and that their jargon, their tone, and their airs do not give to their pupils the first taste for those frivolities, so important for their masters, which they will hardly be slow, following their example, to make their sole occupation.

In the arts which are merely pleasure-giving in their purpose everything may serve to teach young persons—their father, mother, brother, sister, their friends, their governesses, their mirror, and especially their own taste. We ought not to offer to give them lessons, but they should find it necessary to demand them. We should not turn a reward into a task; and it is especially in studies of this sort that the very condition of success is a desire to succeed. However, if formal lessons are absolutely necessary, I shall not decide the sex of those who are to give them.

Through industry and talent the taste is formed; and through the taste the mind is insensibly opened to ideas of the beautiful in all its forms, and finally to the moral notions which are connected with it. This is perhaps one of the reasons why the feeling of propriety and virtue is developed sooner in girls than in boys; for, in order to believe that this precocious feeling is the work of governesses, we must be very badly instructed in their style of lessons and in the progress of the human mind. Talent in speaking holds the first place in the art of pleasing, and it is through it alone that we can add new charms to those to which habit accustoms all the senses. It is the mind which not only vivifies the body, but which in some sort renews it; it is through the succession of feelings and ideas that it gives animation and variety to the features; and it is through the discourse which it inspires that the attention is kept alive and for a long time sustains the same interest on the same object. It is for all these reasons, I presume, that young girls so soon acquire an agreeable prattle, that they throw an accent into their speech even before they are conscious of its meaning, and that men so soon find amusement in listening to them even before they can be understood by their fair listeners. Men watch the first movement of this intelligence in order thus to penetrate the dawn of emotion.

Women have a flexible tongue; they speak sooner, more easily, and more agreeably than men. They are accused also of speaking more. This is proper, and I would willingly change this reproach into a commendation. With them the mouth and the eyes have the same activity, and for the same reason. A man says what he knows, and a woman what is pleasing. In order to speak, one needs knowledge and the other taste; one ought to have for a principal object things which are useful; the other, things which are agreeable. In their forms of conversation the only thing in common should be the truth.

If boys should not be allowed to ask indiscreet questions, for a still stronger reason they should be forbidden young girls, whose curiosity, when satisfied, or when wrongly evaded, has very different consequences, due to their penetration in anticipating the mysteries which are concealed from them, and to their cleverness in discovering them. But, without awaiting their questions, I would have them thoroughly interrogated themselves, would take care to make them talk, and would tease them in order to make them speak easily and to loosen the mind and the tongue, when it could be done without danger. These conversations, always turned into pleasing channels, but managed with art and well directed, would make a charming amusement for that age, and might carry into the innocent hearts of these young persons the first and perhaps the most useful lessons in morals which they will ever learn, by teaching them, through the bait of pleasure and vanity, to what qualities men really accord their esteem, and in what the glory and happiness of a noble woman consist.

It is easy to see that if boys are not in a condition to form any true idea of religion, for a still stronger reason the same idea is above the conception of girls. It is on this very account that I would speak to them the earlier on this subject; for if we must wait till they are in a condition to discuss these profound questions methodically, we run the risk of never speaking to them on this subject. The reason of women is a practical reason, which gives them great skill in finding the means for reaching a known end, but it does not cause them to find the end itself. The social relation of the sexes is admirable. From this association there results a moral personality of which woman is the eye and man the arm, but with such a dependence of one on the other that it is from the man that the woman learns what must be seen, and from the woman that the man learns what must be done. If the woman could ascend to principles as well as the man, and if the man had the same talents for details that she has, always independent of each other, they would live in perpetual discord, and their union could not subsist. But in the harmony which reigns between them everything tends to the common end, and we do not know which contributes the most to it, each follows the impulsion of the other; each obeys, and both are masters.

For the reason that the conduct of woman is subject to public opinion, her belief is subject to authority. Every daughter should have the religion of her mother, and every wife that of her husband. Even were this religion false, the docility which makes the mother and the daughter submit to the order or nature expunges in the sight of God the sin of error. As they are not in a condition to judge for themselves, women should receive the decision of fathers and husbands as they would the decision of the Church.

Not being able to draw from themselves alone the rule of their faith, women can not confine it within the boundaries of evidence and reason, but, allowing themselves to be carried away by a thousand extraneous impulses, they are always on this side or that of the truth. Always extremists, they are all free-thinkers or devotees; none of them are able to combine discretion with piety. The source of the evil is not only in the tendency to extremes which characterizes their sex, but also in the badly regulated authority of our own. The looseness in morals makes this authority despised, and the fear of repentance makes it tyrannical; and this is how we are always doing too little or too much.

Since authority ought to regulate the religion of women, it is not so important to explain to them the reasons which we have for believing as to expound to them with clearness what we believe; for the faith which we have in obscure ideas is the primitive source of fanaticism, and that which we require for absurd things leads to madness or to incredulity.

In the first place, in order to teach religion to young girls, never make it a thing of sadness and constraint for them, and never a task or a duty; consequently, never make them learn by heart anything connected with it, not even their prayers. Be content with saying your own prayers regularly before them, but without forcing them to take part in them. Make them short, according to the precepts of Jesus Christ. Always make them with suitable solemnity and respect; recollect that as we require of the Supreme Being attention in order to listen to us, we are in duty bound to reflect on what we are going to say to him.

It is less important that young girls know their religion so soon than that they know it well, and especially that they love it. When you make it burdensome to them, when you always represent God as angry with them, when you impose on them in his name a thousand painful duties which they never see you fulfill, what can they think, save that to know one's catechism and to pray to God are the duties of little girls, and desire except to be grown up in order to be exempt, just as you are, from all this constraint? Example! Example! Without this we shall never succeed in anything with children.

When you explain to them the articles of faith, let it be in the form of direct instruction, and not by question and answer; they ought never to answer save what they think, and not what is dictated to them. All the replies of the catechism are on the wrong side—it is the pupil who instructs the teacher; they are even falsehoods in the mouths of children, since they explain what they do not understand, and affirm what they are not able to believe.

I wish some man who thoroughly knows the steps of progress in the child's mind would write a catechism for him. This would perhaps be the most useful book that was ever written, and would not be, to my mind, the one which would do the least honor to its author. One thing is very certain: if this book were good, it would bear but little resemblance to those in use.

Such a catechism will be good only when, from the questions alone, the child will make for himself the replies without having to learn them, it being understood that he will sometimes take his turn in asking questions. To make what I wish to say understood, a sort of model would be necessary, and I well know what I lack in order to trace it out.

It is well to recollect that until the age when the reason is illumined, and when dawning emotion causes the conscience to speak, that which is right or wrong for young persons is what the people who surround them have decided to be such. What they are commanded to do is right, what they are forbidden to do is wrong, and here their knowledge ought to end.* From this we see how important it is, and still more so for girls than for boys, to make a choice of the persons who are to approach them and have some authority over them. Finally, the moment comes when they begin to judge of things for themselves, and then it is time to change the plan of their education.

To what condition should we reduce women if we make public prejudice the law of their conduct? Let us not abase to this point the sex which governs us, and which honors us when we have not degraded it. There exists for the whole human species a rule anterior to opinion. It is to the inflexible direction of this rule that all the others are to be referred. It judges prejudice even; and it is only so far as the esteem of men accords with it that this esteem ought to constitute authority for us.

This rule is the inner moral sense. I shall not repeat what I have previously said on this point. It is sufficient for me to remark, that if these two rules do not co-operate in the education of women, it will always be defective. The moral sense, without opinion, will not give them that delicacy of soul which adorns good manners with universal honor; and opinion, without the moral sense, will never produce anything but artificial and immodest women, who substitute appearance in the place of virtue.

It is important, then, to cultivate a faculty which serves as an arbitrator between the two guides, which does not allow the conscience to go astray, and which corrects the errors of prejudice. This faculty is the reason. But at this word how many questions arise! Are women capable of solid reasoning? Is it important for them to cultivate it? Will they cultivate it with

---

*This reflection should have occurred to Rousseau when he composed the dialogue intended to prove that children are incapable of reason—(P.)

success? Is this culture useful to the functions imposed on them? Is it compatible with the simplicity which is becoming to them?

It results from the different ways of approaching and resolving these questions that, going to opposite extremes, some restrict woman to sewing and spinning in her household with her servants, and thus make of her but the head servant of the master; while others, not content with securing her rights, go farther, and make her usurp our own. For, to place her above us in the qualities peculiar to her sex, and to render her our equal in everything else, what is this but to transfer to the wife the primacy which nature gives to the husband?

The reason which leads man to the knowledge of his duties is not very complex; and the reason which leads woman to the knowledge of hers is still simpler. The obedience and fidelity which she owes to her husband, the tenderness and care which she owes to her children, are such natural and obvious consequences of her condition, that she can not, without bad faith, refuse her consent to the inner sense which guides her, nor fail to recognize her duty in the inclination which has not yet been perverted.

If a woman were wholly restricted to the tasks of her sex, and were left in profound ignorance of everything else, I would not indulge in indiscriminate censure; but this would require a very simple and wholesome state of public morals, or a very retired manner of living. In large cities and among corrupt men such a woman would be too easily led astray, and in this philosophical age she must be above temptation; she must know in advance what may be said to her, and what she ought to think of it.

Moreover, subject to the judgment of men, she ought to merit their esteem; she ought, above all, to secure the esteem of her husband; she ought not only to make him love her person, but make him approve her conduct; she ought to justify before the public the choice which he has made, and make her husband honored with the honor which is paid his wife. Now, how shall she go about all this if she is ignorant of our institutions, if she knows nothing of our usages and our social customs, if she knows neither the source of human judgments nor the passions which determine them? When she depends at once on her own conscience and the opinions of others, she must learn to compare these two rules, to reconcile them, and to prefer the first only when they are in opposition. She becomes the judge of her judges; she decides when she ought to submit to them and when she ought to challenge them. Before rejecting or admitting their prejudices she weighs them; she learns to ascend to their source, to anticipate them, and to render them favorable to her; she is careful never to draw censure upon herself when her duty permits her to avoid it. Nothing of all this can be well done without cultivating her mind and her reason.

The search for abstract and speculative truths, principles, and scientific axioms, whatever tends to generalize ideas, does not fall within the compass of women; all their studies ought to have reference to the practical; it is for them to make the application of the principles which man has discovered, and to make the observations which lead man to the establishment of principles. All the reflections of women which are not immediately connected with their duties ought to be directed to the study of men and to that pleasure-giving knowledge which has only taste for its object; for as to works of genius, they are out of their reach, nor have they sufficient accuracy and attention to succeed in the exact sciences; and as to the physical sciences, they fall to that one of the two which is the most active, the most stirring, which sees the most objects, which has the most strength, and which exercises it most in judging of the relations of sensible beings and the laws of nature. Woman, who is weak, and who sees nothing external, appreciates and judges the motive powers which she can set to work to offset her weakness, and these motive powers are the passions of man. Whatever her sex can not do for itself, and which is necessary or agreeable to her, she must have the art of making us desire. She must therefore make a profound study of the mind of man, not the mind of man in general, through abstraction, but the mind of the men who surround her, the mind of the men to whom she is subject, either by law or by opinion. She must learn to penetrate their feelings through their conversation, their actions, their looks, and their gestures. Through her conversations, her actions, her looks, and her gestures she must know how to give them the feelings which are pleasing to her, without even seeming to think of them. They will philosophize better than she can on the human heart, but she will read better than they can in the hearts of men. It is for women to discover, so to speak, an experimental ethics, and for us to reduce it to a system. Woman has more spirit and man more genius; woman observes and man reasons. From this concurrence there results the clearest light and the most complete science which the human mind can acquire of itself—the surest knowledge, in a word, of one's self and others which is within the scope of our species. And this is the way in which art may incessantly tend to perfect the instrument given by nature.

The Profession of Faith of a Savoyard Priest

I was born a poor peasant, destined by my situation to the business of husbandry; it was thought, however, much more advisable for me to learn to get my bread by the profession of a priest; and means were found to give me a proper education. In this, most certainly, neither my parents nor I consulted what was really good, true, or useful for me to know; but only agreed that I should learn what was necessary to my ordination. I learned therefore what was required of me to learn, I said what was required of me to say, and accordingly was made a priest. It was not long, however, before I perceived too plainly, that, in laying myself under an obligation to be no longer a man, I had committed myself to more than I could possibly perform.

Finding, by sorrowful experience, the ideas I had formed of justice, honesty, and other moral obligations, contradicted in practice, I began to give up most of the opinions I had received, till, at length, the few which I retained, being no longer sufficient to support themselves, I called in question the evidence on which they were established. Thus, knowing hardly what to think, I found myself at last reduced to your own situation of mind; with this difference only, that my lack of faith being the later fruit of a maturer age, it was a work of greater difficulty to remove it.

I was in that state of doubt and uncertainty, which Descartes requires the mind to adopt, in order to enable it to investigate truth. This disposition of mind, however, is too disquieting to last long.

I reflected, therefore, on the unhappy lot of mortals, always floating on the ocean of human opinions, without compass or rudder; left to the mercy of their tempestuous passions, with no other guide than an unexperienced pilot, ignorant of his course, knowing neither whence he came nor whither he is going. I said often to myself, I love the truth; I seek, yet I cannot find it; let anyone show it to me, and I will readily embrace it: why does it hide its charms from an heart formed to adore them?

I have frequently experienced much greater evils; yet no part of my life was ever so constantly disagreeable to me as that interval of unrest and anxiety. Running perpetually from one doubt and uncertainty to another, all that I could derive from any long and painful meditations was uncertainty, obscurity, and contradiction, as well with regard to my existence as my duty.

I cannot understand how any man can be sincerely a skeptic on principle. Such philosophers either do not exist, or they are certainly the most miserable of men. To be in doubt about things which it is important for us to know is a situation too perplexing for the human mind: it cannot long support such incertitude, but will, in spite of itself, determine one way or other, rather deceiving itself than content to believe nothing.

What added further to my perplexity was that of having been educated in a church whose authority admits not of the least doubt. In rejecting one point, I rejected in a manner all the rest; and the impossibility of admitting so many absurd doctrines set me against those which were not so. In being told I must believe all, I was prevented from believing anything, and I knew not where to stop.

In this situation I consulted the philosophers. I turned over their books, and examined their several theories, in all which I found them vain, dictatorial, and dogmatical, even in their pretended skepticism; ignorant of nothing, yet proving nothing; ridiculing one another; only in this last particular, wherein they were all agreed, did they seem to be in the right. Affecting to triumph whenever they attacked their opponents, they lacked everything to make them capable of a vigorous defense. If you examine their reasons, you will find them calculated only to refute; if you count voices, every one is reduced to his own defense; they agree in nothing but disputing. To attend to these philosophers, therefore, was no way to remove my uncertainty.

I decided that the weakness of the human understanding was the first cause of the prodigious variety I found in men's beliefs, and that pride was the second. We have no standard with which to measure this immense machine; we cannot calculate its various workings; we neither know the first cause nor the final effects; we are ignorant even of ourselves; we neither know our own nature nor its principle of action; nay, we hardly know whether man is a simple or a compound being. Impenetrable mysteries surround us on every side; they extend beyond the region of sense; we imagine ourselves possessed of understanding to penetrate them, but we have only imagination. Everyone strikes out a way of his own across this imaginary world; but no one knows whether it will lead him to the point he aims at. We yearn to penetrate, to know everything. The only thing we know not, is to remain ignorant of what it is impossible for us to know. We prefer to determine at random, and believe the thing which is not, than confess that none of us is capable of seeing the thing that is. Being ourselves but a small part of that great whole whose limits surpass our most extensive vision, and concerning which its Creator leaves us to make our idle conjectures, we are vain enough to want to say what the whole is and what we are in relation to it.

But were the philosophers even in a situation to discover the truth, which of them would be interested in so doing? Each of them knows very well that his system is no better founded than those of others; he defends it, nevertheless, because it is his own. There is not one of them, who, really knowing truth from falsehood, would not prefer the latter of his own invention to the former discovered by anybody else. Where is the philosopher who would not readily deceive mankind, to increase his own reputation? Where is he, who secretly seeks any other object than that of distinguishing himself from the rest of the human race? Provided he raises himself above the vulgar, and carries away the prize of fame from his rivals, what more does he ask? The essential point is to think differently from the rest of the world. Among believers, the philosopher is an atheist, and among atheists he affects to be a believer.

The first fruit I gathered from these reflections was to learn to confine my inquiries to those things in which I was immediately interested, to remain contented in a profound ignorance of the rest, and not to trouble myself so far as even to doubt what it did not concern me to know.

I could see, moreover, that instead of clearing up any unnecessary doubts, the philosophers only served to multiply those which most tormented me while they resolved absolutely none. I therefore turned to another guide, and said to myself, "Let me consult my inner light, which will deceive me less than I may be deceived by others; then, at least, the errors I fall into, will be my own, and I shall grow less depraved in the pursuit of my own illusions, than in giving myself up to the deceptions of others."

Taking a retrospect, then, of the several opinions which had successively prevailed with me from my infancy, I found, that, although none of them was so evident as to produce immediate conviction, all had nevertheless different degrees of probability, and that my innate sense of truth and falsehood leaned more or less to each. On this first observation, proceeding to compare, impartially and without prejudice, these different opinions with each other, I found that the first and most common was also the most simple and most rational; and that it wanted nothing more to secure universal suffrage than the circumstance of having been last proposed. Let us suppose that all our philosophers, ancient and modern, had exhausted all their whimsical systems of power, chance, fate, necessity, atoms an animated world, sensitive matter, materialism, and all the rest of it; and after, them let us imagine the celebrated Dr. Clarke enlightening the world, by displaying the Being of Beings, the Supreme and Sovereign disposer of all things. With what universal admiration, with what unanimous applause would not the world receive this new system, so great, so sublime, so proper to elevate the soul, to lay the foundations of virtue, and at the same time so striking, so enlightened, so simple, and, as it appears to me, pregnant with less incomprehensibilities and absurdity than any other system whatever! I reflected that unanswerable objections might be made to all systems, because the human understanding is incapable of resolving every problem. No proof could be brought exclusively of any system. Ought not that system, then, which explains everything to be preferred, when attended with no greater difficulties than the rest?

The love of truth, therefore, being all my philosophy, and my method of philosophizing the simple and easy rule of common sense, which dispensed with the vain subtlety of argumentation, I re-examined by this rule all the knowledge I was possessed of; I resolved to admit as evident every thing to which I could not in the sincerity of my heart refuse my assent; to admit also as true all that appeared to have a necessary connection with the former, and to leave everything else as uncertain, without rejecting or admitting it, determined not to trouble myself about clearing up any point which did not tend to utility in practice.

But after all, who am I? What right have I to judge of these things? And what is it that determines my conclusions? If they are formed in direct consequence of external impressions I trouble myself to no purpose in these investigations. It is necessary therefore to examine, to know what instruments are made use of in such researches, and how far I may rely on them.

In the first place, I know that I exist, and have senses through which I receive impressions. This is a truth so striking that I am compelled to acquiesce in it. But have I in myself a distinct sense of my existence, or do I only know it from my various sensations? This is my first doubt, which at present it is impossible for me to resolve: for being continually affected by sensations, either directly from the objects of them, or from the memory, how can I tell whether my consciousness is or is not something foreign to those sensations, and independent of them?

My sensations are all internal, as they make me sensible of my own existence; but the cause of them is external and independent, for they affect me without my consent, and do not depend on my will for their production or annihilation. I conceive very clearly, therefore, that the sensation which is internal, and its cause or object which is external, are not one and the same thing. Thus I know that I not only exist, but that other beings exist as well as myself; to wit, the objects of my sensations; and even if these objects were nothing but ideas, it is certain that these ideas are no part of myself.

Now, everything that I perceive out of myself, and which acts on my senses, I call matter; and all those portions of matter which I conceive united in individual beings, I call bodies. Thus all the disputes between the idealists and materialists signify nothing to me; their distinctions between the appearance and reality of bodies are chimerical.

Hence I have already acquired as certain a knowledge of the existence of the universe as of my own. I next reflect on the objects of my sensations; and, finding in myself the faculty of comparing them with each other, I perceive myself endowed with an active power with which I was before unacquainted.

To perceive is only to feel or be sensible of things; to compare them is to judge of their existence; to judge of things, and to be sensible of them, are very different. Things present themselves to our sensations as single and detached from each other, such as they barely are in the seamless web of nature: but in our intellectual comparison of them they are removed, transported, as it were, from place to place, and put beside each other to enable us to pronounce concerning their difference and similitude. The characteristic faculty of an intelligent, active being, is, in my opinion, that of giving a sense to the word "exist." In beings merely sensitive I have searched in vain for the force of intellect; nor can I conceive it to be in their nature. Such passive beings perceive every object single, or by itself; or if two objects present themselves, they are perceived as united into one. Such beings having no power to place them side by side, they cannot compare them or judge of their separate existence.

To see two objects at once, is not to see their relations to each other, nor to judge of their difference; just as to see many objects, though distinct from one another, is not to reckon their number. I may possibly have in mind the ideas of a great stick and a little one, without comparing those ideas together, or judging that one is smaller than the other; just as I may look at my hand without counting my fingers.* The comparative ideas of greater and less, as well as numerical ideas of one, two, and three, are certainly not sensations, although the understanding produces them only from our sensations.

It has been claimed, that sensitive beings distinguish sensations one from the other by the actual difference there is between those sensations. This, however, demands an explanation. When such sensations are different, a sensitive being is supposed to distinguish them by their difference; but when they are alike, he can then only distinguish them because he perceives one without the other: for otherwise, how can two objects exactly alike, be distinguished in a simultaneous sensation? Such objects must necessarily be blended together and taken for one and the same; particularly according to that system of philosophy in which it is claimed that the sensations which are representative of extension are not themselves extended.

---

*M. de la Condamine tells us of a people, who knew how to reckon only as far as three: yet these people, having hands, must necessarily have often seen their fingers without ever having counted five.

When two comparative sensations are perceived, they make both a joint and separate impression, but their relation to each other is not necessarily perceived in consequence of either. If the judgment we form of this relation were indeed a mere sensation, excited by the objects, we should never be deceived in it, for it can never be denied that I truly perceive what I feel.

How, therefore, can I be deceived in the relation between these two sticks, particularly, if they are not parallel? Why do I say, for instance, that the small one is a third of the length of the large one, when it is in reality only a fourth? Why is not the image, which is the sensation, conformable to its model, which is the object? It is because I am active when I judge, the operation which forms the comparison is defective, and my understanding, which judges relations, mixes its errors with the truth of those sensations which represent objects.

Add to this a reflection, which I am certain you will think striking when you have duly weighed it: this is, that if we were merely passive in the use of our senses, there would be no communication between them, so that it would be impossible for us to know that the body we touched with our hands and the object we saw with our eyes, were one and the same. Either we should not be able to perceive external objects at all, or they would appear to exist as five perceptible substances, of which we should have no method of ascertaining the identity.

Whatever name be given to that power of the mind which assembles and compares my sensations—call it attention, meditation, reflection, or what you please—certain it is, that it exists in me, and not in the objects of those sensations: it is I alone who produce it, although it be experienced only as a result of the impressions made on me by those objects. Without being so far master over myself as to perceive or not perceive at pleasure, I am still more or less capable of examining the objects perceived.

I am not, therefore, merely a sensitive and passive, but an active and intelligent being; and, whatever philosophers may pretend, I lay claim to the honor of thinking. I know only that truth depends on the existence of things, and not on my understanding which judges of them; and that the less such judgment depends on me, the nearer I am certain of approaching the truth. Hence my rule of relying more on feeling than reason is confirmed by reason itself.

Being thus far assured of my own nature and capacity, I begin to consider the objects about me, regarding myself, with a kind of trembling, as a creature thrown on the wide world of the universe, and, as it were, lost among an infinite variety of other beings without knowing anything of what they are, either in themselves or with regard to me.

Everything that is perceptible to my senses is matter, and I deduce all the essential properties of matter from those sensible qualities which make it perceptible and are inseparable from it. I see it sometimes in motion and at other times at rest;* hence I infer that neither motion nor rest are essential to it; but motion being an action is clearly the effect of a cause, of which rest is simply the absence. When nothing acts on matter it does not move; and for the very reason that it is equally indifferent to motion and rest, its natural state is to be at rest.

Again, I perceive in bodies two kinds of motion; namely, a mechanical or communicated motion, and a spontaneous or voluntary one. In the first, the moving cause is external to the body moved and in the second it exists within it. I shall not conclude, however, that the motion of a watch, for example, is spontaneous; for, if nothing should act upon it but the spring, that spring would not wind itself up again when once down. For the same reason, also, I will not admit the spontaneous motion of fluids, nor even of fire itself, which, in melting solids, causes their fluidity.

You will ask me if the motions of animals are spontaneous? I will freely answer, I cannot positively tell, but analogy speaks in the affirmative. You may ask me farther, how I know there is any such thing as spontaneous motion? I answer, very well, because I feel it. I will to move my arm, and accordingly it moves without the intervention of any other immediate cause. It is in vain to endeavor to reason me out of this feeling; it is more powerful than any rational evidence, you might as well attempt to convince me that I do not exist.

If the actions of men were not spontaneous, and there were no such spontaneous action in what happens on earth, we should be the more at a loss to conceive what is the first cause of all motion. For my part, I am so fully persuaded, that the natural state of matter is a state of rest, and that it has in itself no principle of activity, that whenever I see a body in motion, I instantly conclude either that it is an animated body, or that its motion is being communicated to it. My understanding will by no means acquiesce in the notion that unorganized matter can move of itself, or be productive of any kind of action.

The visible universe, however, is composed of inanimate matter,[†] which appears to have nothing in its composition of that unity or that feeling, which is common to the parts of an animated body; while it is certain that we ourselves, as parts thereof, have no sense of our existence in the whole. The universe, moreover, is in motion, and since its movements are all regular, uniform, and subjected to constant laws, nothing

---

*This rest may be said to be only relative; but as we perceive degrees in motion, we can very clearly conceive one of the two extremes, which is rest; and this we conceive so distinctly, that we are even induced to take that for absolute rest which is only relative. Now, motion cannot be essential to matter, if matter can be conceived to exist at rest.

†I have made the strongest efforts I am able, to conceive the existence of a living molecule or primary element, but in vain, The idea of matter, perceiving without organs of perception, appears to me contradictory and unintelligible. To reject or adopt this notion, it is necessary we should first comprehend it; and I must confess I am not so happy.

appears therein similar to that liberty which is evident in the spontaneous motion of men and animals. The world, therefore, is not an huge self-moving animal; it receives its motions from some foreign cause, which we do not perceive. I am so strongly persuaded within myself of the existence of this cause, that it is impossible for me to observe the rising and setting of the sun, without conceiving that some force must urge it forward; or if it is the earth itself that turns, I cannot but believe that some hand must turn it.

If it be necessary to admit general laws that have no apparent relation to matter, from what fixed point must that inquiry set out? Those laws, being nothing real, or substantial, must have some prior foundation equally unknown. Experience and observation have taught us the laws of motion; these laws, however, determine effects only, without displaying their causes and therefore are not sufficient to explain the system of the universe. Descartes could form a model of the heavens and the earth with dice, but he could not give the first impulsion to those dice, nor bring into play his centrifugal force without the assistance of a rotatory motion. Newton discovered the law of gravity, but gravity alone would soon have reduced the universe into one solid mass. Therefore, he found it necessary to add a projectile force in order to account for the elliptical movement of the heavenly bodies. Could Descartes tell us by what physical law his vortices were put and kept in motion? Could Newton produce the hand that first impelled the planets in the tangent of their respective orbits?

The first causes of motion do not exist in matter; bodies receive motion, and communicate motion to each other, but they cannot originally produce it. The more I observe the action and reaction of the powers of nature acting on each other, the more I am convinced that they are merely effects, and that we must always go back to some volition as the first cause. For to suppose there is a progression of causes to infinity, is to suppose there is no first cause at all. In a word, every motion that is not produced by some other, must be the effect of a spontaneous voluntary act. Inanimate bodies have no action but motion, and there can be no real action without volition. Such is my first principle. I believe, therefore, that a will gives motion to the universe, and animates all nature. This is my first article of faith.

In what manner volition produces physical and corporeal action, I know not, but I know from experience within myself that it does so. I will to act, and the action immediately succeeds: I will to move my body, and my body instantly moves; but the idea that an inanimate body, lying at rest, should move itself or produce motion, is incomprehensible. The will is known to me by its acts, and not by its essence. I know will as motivating cause, but to conceive matter producing motion would be to conceive an effect without a cause, in other words, to conceive absolutely nothing.

It is no more possible for me to conceive how the will moves the body than to conceive how sensations affect the mind. I do not even know why one of these mysteries ever appeared more explicable than the other. For my own part, whether at the time I am active or passive, the means of union between the two substances appears to me absolutely incomprehensible. Is it not strange that the philosophers have eliminated this incomprehensibility, only to confound the two substances together, as if operations so different could be better explained as the effects of one subject than of two?

General and abstract ideas are the source of our greatest errors. The jargon of metaphysics never discovered a simple truth, but it has filled philosophy with absurdities of which we are ashamed as soon as they are stripped of their pompous language. Tell me truly, my friend, if, when you are told of a blind, unintelligent power being diffused throughout all nature, any precise idea is conveyed to your understanding? It is imagined that something is meant by those vague terms, "universal force" and "necessary motion" that convey no meaning? The idea of motion is nothing more than the idea of passing from one place to another, nor can there be any motion without some particular direction; for no individual being can move several ways at once. In what sense, then, can matter necessarily move? Has all the matter of which bodies are composed, a general and uniform motion, or has each atom a particular motion of its own? In the former case, the whole universe must form one solid and indivisible mass; in the latter case, it must constitute a diffused and incoherent fluid, without any possibility of two atoms ever being united. What can be the direction of the common motion of all matter? Is it in a right line upwards or downwards, to the right or to the left? Again, if every atom or particle of matter revolved only on its axis, none of them would change its place, and there would be no motion communicated; and even in this case such a revolving motion would have to be given direction. To ascribe to matter motion in the abstract is to use meaningless words; and if we give matter any determinate motion, we must of necessity pre-suppose the cause that determines it. The more I multiply particular forces, the more new causes I have to explain, without ever finding one common agent that directs them. So far from being able to conceive any regularity or order in the fortuitous concourse of elements, I cannot even conceive the nature of their concurrence; and an universal chaos is more inconceivable than universal harmony. I easily comprehend that the mechanism of the world cannot be perfectly known to the human understanding; but, whenever men undertake to explain it, they ought at least to speak in such a manner that others may understand them.

If matter being put in motion reveals to me the existence of a will as the first active cause, then this matter being subjected to regular laws of motion, reveals the existence of an intelligence: this is my second article of faith. To act, to compare, to choose, are the operations of an active, thinking being; such a being, therefore, exists. Do you proceed to ask me, where I discover his existence? I answer, Not only in the revolutions of the celestial bodies, not only in myself; but in the flocks that feed on the plain, in the birds that fly in the air, in the stone that falls to the ground, and in the leaf that trembles in the wind.

I can judge the physical order of things, despite my ignorance of their final cause, because, in order to reach such a judgment, I have only to compare the several parts of the visible universe with each other, study their mutual concurrence and reciprocal relations, and observe the general result of the whole. I do not know why the universe exists, but I can nevertheless see how it is modified, I cannot fail to perceive that intimate connection by which the several beings it is composed of afford each other mutual assistance. I resemble, in this respect, a man who sees the inside of a watch for the first time, and is captivated with the beauty of the work, although ignorant of its use. I know not, he may say, what this machine is good for, but I see that each part is made to fit some other; I admire the artisan in every part of his workmanship, and am certain that all these wheels act thus in concert to some common end which I cannot see.

But let us compare the partial and particular ends, the means whereby they are achieved, and their connections of every kind; then let us appeal to our inner light; what man in his senses could refuse to acquiesce in such testimony? To what unprejudiced view does not the visible arrangement of the universe proclaim the supreme intelligence of its author? How much sophistry does it not require to disavow the harmony of created beings, and that admirable order in which all the parts of the system concur to the preservation of the whole? You may talk to me as much as you please of combinations and chances; what end will it answer to reduce me to silence, if you cannot persuade me of the truth of what you advance? And how will you strip me of that involuntary feeling, which continually contradicts you? If organized bodies are fortuitously combined in a thousand ways, before they assume settled and constant shapes; if at first there came to be formed stomachs without mouths, feet without heads, hands without arms, and imperfect organs of every kind, which have perished for want of the necessary faculties of self-preservations; how comes it that none of these abortive products has engaged our attention? Why has nature at length come to obey laws to which she was not at first subjected? I confess that I ought not to be surprised that any possible thing should happen, when the rarity of the event is compensated by the great odds that it did not happen. And yet if anyone was to tell me that a number of printer's types, jumbled promiscuously together, had disposed themselves in the order of the letters composing the *Aeneid* of Virgil, I would not deign to take one step to verify or disprove such a story. It may be said that, I forget the number of chances; but pray how many chances must I suppose to render such a combination in any degree probable? I can see enough to conclude that the odds are an infinite number to one against the poem being the effect of chance. Add to this, that the product of these combinations must be always of the same nature as the elements combined; hence life and organization never can result from a blind concourse of atoms, nor will the chemist, with all his art in compounds, ever find perception and thought at the bottom of his crucible.

I believe, therefore, that the world is governed by a wise and powerful Will. I see it, or rather I feel it; and this is important for me to know. But is the world eternal, or is it created? Are things derived form one self-existent principle? or are there two, or more? And what is their essence? Of all this I know nothing, nor do I see that it is of any consequence I should. That Being whose will is his deed, whose principle of action is in himself; that Being, in a word, whatever it be, that gives motion to all the parts of the universe, and governs all things, I call GOD. To this term I annex the ideas of intelligence, power, and will, which I have gathered from the order of things; and to these I add that of goodness, which is a necessary consequence of the foregoing; but I have no better knowledge of the Being to whom I give these attributes. He remains at an equal distance from my senses and my understanding; the more I think of him, the more I am confounded; I know with certainty that he exists, and that his existence is independent of any of his creatures; I know also that my existence is dependent on his, and that everything I perceive is in the same situation. I see the Deity in all his works; I feel him within me, and behold him in every object around me, but I no sooner endeavor to contemplate what he is in himself, I no sooner inquire where he is, and what is his substance, than he eludes the strongest efforts of my imagination and my troubled mind grasps nothing.

For this reason I shall never take it upon myself to argue about the nature of God, beyond what I am obliged to by the relation he appears to stand in to myself. There is so great a temerity in such speculations, that a wise man will never enter on them without trembling and being fully conscious of his incapacity to proceed far on so sublime a subject: for it does less injury to the Deity to entertain no ideas of him at all, than to harbor those which are depreciating and unjust.

After having discovered those of his attributes by which I am convinced of his existence, I return to myself, and consider the place I occupy in that order of things which is directed by him, and subjected to my examination. Here I find my species stand incontestably in the first rank since man, by virtue of his will and the instruments he has to put it into execution, has a greater power over the bodies by which he is surrounded, than they, by mere physical impulse, have over him. By virtue of his intelligence also, I find that man is the only created being here below that can take a general survey of the whole system. Is there one creature, except man, who knows how to observe all others, to weigh, to calculate, to foresee their motions, their effects, and to join, if I may so express myself, the feeling of a common existence to that of the individual? What is there so very ridiculous in supposing every thing made for man, when he is the only created being who knows how to relate all things to himself?

It is true then that man is lord of creation, that he is, at least, sovereign over the habitable earth; for not only does he subdue all other animals, and even dispose of the elements at his pleasure by his industry; but he alone among terrestrial beings knows how to subject the earth to his convenience, and even to appropriate to his use, by contemplation, the very stars and planets he cannot reach. Let anyone show me an animal of another species who knows how to make use of fire, or has faculties to admire the sun. What! am I able to observe, to know other beings and their relations; am I capable of discovering what is order, beauty, virtue, of contemplating the universe, and of elevating my ideas to the hand that governs the whole? Am I capable of loving what is good and doing it, and yet put myself in the same category as the beasts? Abject soul, it is your gloomy philosophy alone that renders you at all like them. Or, rather, it is in vain that you would debase yourself; your own genius rises up against your principles; your benevolent heart gives the lie to your absurd doctrines, and even the abuse of your faculties demonstrates their excellence in spite of yourself.*

I, who have no system to maintain, who am only a simple, honest man, attached to no party, with no desire to be the founder of any sect, and contented with the situation in which God has placed me, I see nothing in the world, except the Deity, better than my own species; and were I left to choose my place in the order of created beings, I see none that I could prefer to that of man.

No material can be self-active, and I perceive that I am so. It is useless to dispute with me on so clear a point; my own feeling carries with it a stronger conviction than any argument that reason could urge against it. I have a body, on which other bodies act and which acts reciprocally on them. This reciprocal action is indubitable; but my will is independent of my senses. I can either consent or resist; I am either vanquished or victor, and I perceive clearly within myself when I act according to my will, and when I submit to be governed by my passions. I have alway the power to will, though not always the force to execute it. When I yield to any temptation, I act from the impulse of external objects. When I reproach myself for my weakness in so doing, I listen only to my own will. I am a slave in my vices, and free in my remorse. The feeling of my liberty is effaced only when I do wrong, and when I prevent the voice of the soul from being heard in opposition to the laws of the flesh.

---

*These words are addressed to Helvétius, whose book *L'Esprit* had argued that man is only a more complicated kind of beast.

All the knowledge I have of volition is derived from a feeling of my own; and the understanding is known no better. When I am asked, what is the cause that determines my will? I ask in my turn, what is the cause that determines my judgment? For it is clear that these two causes make but one and if we realize that man is active in forming his judgment of things, and that his understanding is only a power of comparing and judging, we shall see that his liberty is but a similar power, derived from the same source. He chooses the good as he judges the true, and in the same way that he makes a false judgment, he makes a bad choice. What then is the cause that determines his will? It is his judgment. And what is the cause that determines his judgment? It is his faculty of intelligence, his power of judging; the determining cause lies in himself. Beyond this, I know nothing of the matter.

Doubtless I am not free not to will my own good, or to will my own evil: but my liberty consists in this very circumstance, that I am incapable of willing anything harmful to me, or at least what appears so, unless some alien factor interferes in my determination. Does it follow from this that I am not my own master, because I am incapable of assuming another being, or of divesting myself of what is essential to my existence?

The principle of all action lies in the will of a free being; we can go no farther, in search of its source. It is not the word 'freedom' that has no signification; it is the word 'necessity'. To suppose any act or effect, which is not derived from an active principle is indeed to suppose effects without a cause. It is to enter a vicious circle. Either there is no first impulse or every first impulse has no prior cause; nor can there be any such thing as will without freedom. Man is, therefore, a free agent, and as such animated by an immaterial substance; this is my third article of faith. From these three first, you may easily deduce the others, without my continuing to number them.

It is the abuse of our faculties which makes us wicked and miserable. Our cares, our anxieties, our griefs, all come from ourselves. Moral evil is incontestably our own work and physical evil would in fact be nothing, did not our vices render us sensible of it. It is not for our preservation that nature makes us sensible of our needs? Is not pain of body an indication that the machine is out of order, and a warning for us to provide a remedy? And as to death—do not the wicked render both our lives and their own miserable? Who wants to live forever? Death is a remedy for all the evils we inflict on ourselves; nature will not let us suffer perpetually. To how few evils are men subject, who live in savage simplicity? They hardly experience disease or passions; they neither foresee death, nor suffer from the apprehension of it; when it approaches, their miseries render it desirable, and it is to them no evil. If we could be content with being what we are, we should have no inducement to lament our fate; but we inflict on ourselves a thousand real evils in our search for imaginary happiness.

Those who are impatient under trifling pains must expect to suffer much greater ones. In our efforts to re-establish by medicines a constitution we have impaired by the irregularities of our way of life, we add to the evil we feel, the greater one we dread; our tears of death anticipate its horrors and hasten its approach. The faster we endeavor to flee from death, the more we feel it; thus are we in terror as long as we live, and die blaming nature for those evils which we bring upon ourselves by doing outrage to nature's laws.

Inquire no longer, man, who is the author of evil: behold him in yourself. There exists no other evil in nature than what you either do or suffer, and you are equally the author of both. A general evil could exist only in disorder; but, in the system of nature, I see an established order which is never disturbed. Particular evil exists only in the feeling of the suffering being: and this feeling is not given to man by nature he gives it to himself. Pain and sorrow have but little hold on those who, unaccustomed to reflection, have neither memory nor foresight. Take away our fatal improvements; take away our errors and our vices, take away, in short, everything that is the work of man, and all the rest is good.

If the soul is immaterial, it may survive the body; and if so, Providence is justified. Had I no other proof of the immateriality of the soul than the oppression of the just, and the triumph of the wicked in this world, that alone would prevent my having the least doubt of it. So shocking a discord amidst the general harmony of things, would naturally make me look for the cause. I should say to myself, we do not cease to exist with this life; everything re-assumes its order after death. I should, indeed, be embarrassed to ask myself where man is to be found, when all his physical properties are destroyed. At present, however, there appears to me no difficulty in this question, as I acknowledge the existence of two different substances. It is very plain that during my corporeal life, when I perceive only by means of my senses, whatever is not submitted to their cognizance must escape me. When the union of the body and the soul is broken, I conceive that the one may be dissolved, and the other preserved entire. Why should the dissolution of the one necessarily bring about that of the other? On the contrary, being so different in their natures, their union provokes a state of violence, and when it is broken they both return to their natural situation: the active and living substance regains all the force it had employed in giving motion to the passive and dead substance to which it had been united. Alas! my failings make me all too sensible that man is but half alive in this life, and that the life of the soul commences at the death of the body.

But what is that life? Is the soul immortal in its own nature? My limited comprehension is incapable of conceiving anything that is unlimited. Whatever we call infinite is beyond my understanding. What can I deny, or affirm, what arguments can I employ on a subject I cannot conceive? I believe that the soul survives the body so long as is necessary to justify Providence in the good ordering of things; but who knows that this will be for ever? I can readily conceive how material bodies wear away, and are destroyed by the separation of their parts, but I cannot conceive a like dissolution of a thinking being; and since I cannot imagine how it can die, I assume it does not die at all. This assumption is both consoling to me and not unreasonable, so why should I be afraid to entertain it?

I feel that I have a soul: I know it both from thought and sensation: I know that it exists, without knowing its essence; I cannot reason, therefore, about ideas which I do not possess. One thing, however, I know very well, which is, that the identity of my being can be preserved only by the memory, and that to be in fact the same person, I must remember having existed. Now I cannot recollect, after my death, what I was during life, without recollecting also my perceptions, and consequently my actions; and I doubt not but this remembrance will one day constitute the happiness of the just, and the torments of the wicked. Here below, the violence of our passions absorbs the innate sense of right and wrong, and stifles remorse. The mortification and disgrace, also, under which virtue labors in the world, prevents our being sensible of its charms. But, when we come to be delivered from the delusions of sense, we shall enjoy the contemplation of the Supreme Being, and those eternal truths of which he is the source; when the beauty of the natural order of things shall strike all the faculties of the soul, and when we are employed solely in comparing what we have really done with what we ought to have done, then will the voice of conscience re-assume its sonority and strength; at that also the pure delight which arises from a consciousness of virtue, or the bitter regret of having debased ourselves by vice, will determine the lot which is severally prepared for us.

After having thus deduced, from the impressions of perceptible objects, and that inner feeling which leads me to judge causes according to the light of nature the most important truths I need to know, it remains for me to inquire what principles I ought to draw from them, for my conduct in life, what rules I ought to prescribe to myself, in order to fulfil my destiny on earth, according to the design of him who placed me here. Following my own method, I deduce these rules not from the lofty principles of philosophy but find them written in indelible characters on my heart. I have only to consult myself concerning what I ought to do; all that I feel to be right, is right; whatever I feel to be wrong, is wrong: conscience is the ablest of all casuists, and it is only when we are trafficking with her, that we have recourse to the subtleties of logical ratiocination. The first of our cares is that of ourselves; yet how often have we not been told by the inner voice that to pursue our own interest at the expense of others is to do wrong! We sometimes imagine that we are obeying the impulse of nature, just as we are resisting it: in listening to the voice of our senses, we turn a deaf ear to the dictates of our hearts; the active being obeys, the passive being commands. Conscience is the voice of the soul, the passions are the voice of the flesh. It is surprising that these two voices should sometimes conflict with each other; or can it be doubted, when they do, which ought to be obeyed? Reason deceives us all too often, and has given us all too much right to distrust her conclusions; but conscience never deceives us; she is man's truest and safest guide. Conscience is in the soul, while instinct is in the body. Whoever obeys conscience walks in the true path of nature, and need not fear to be misled.

Bibliography

COLLECTED WORKS IN FRENCH

Gagnebin, Bernard and Raymond, Marcel et al. (eds.). *Oeuvres complètes de Jean-Jacques Rousseau*. Paris: Bibliothèque de la Pléiade, 1959– (in progress).
Launay, Michel (ed.). *J.-J. Rousseau: Oeuvres complètes*, 3 vols. Paris: Editions du Seuil, 1971.
Leigh, R.A. (ed.). *J.-J. Rousseau: Correspondance complète*. Geneva: Banbury and Oxford, The Voltaire Foundation, 1965– (in progress).

WORKS TRANSLATED INTO ENGLISH

Citizen of Geneva: Selected Letters of J.-J. Rousseau. Trans. Charles W. Hendel. New York: Oxford University Press, 1937.
Confessions. Trans. J.M. Cohen. Baltimore: Penguin, 1953.
A Dictionary of Music. Trans. William Waring. London: J. Robinson, 1771.
A Discourse on the Origin of Inequality. Trans. Maurice Cranston. New York: Viking-Penguin, 1984.
A Discourse on the Sciences and the Arts, in *The First and Second Discourses*, Trans. R. and D. Masters. New York: St Martin's Press, 1964.
Émile. a Treatise on Education. Trans. Barbara Foxley. New York: E.P. Dutton, 1911.
Essay on the Origin of Languages, *The First and Second Discourses and Essay on the Origin of Languages*. Trans. Victor Gourevitch. New York: Harper and Row, 1986.
The Government of Poland. Trans. Willmore Kendall, 1972.
Julie, or the New Eloise. Trans. and abridged, Judith H. McDowell, University Park: The Pennsylvania State University Press, 1968.
Letter to M. d'Alembert on the Theatre. Trans. as *Politics and the Arts*, Allan Bloom, Glencoe, IL: The Free Press, 1960.
Letters on the Elements of Botany. Trans. Thomas Martyn. Twickenham, England: The Felix Gluck Press, 1979.
The Reveries of the Solitary Walker. Trans. Charles E. Butterworth, New York: New York University Press, 1979.
The Social Contract. Trans. Maurice Cranston. Baltimore: Penguin, 1968.

BIOGRAPHIES

Cranston, Maurice. *Jean-Jacques: The Early Life of Jean-Jacques Rousseau*. New York: W. W. Norton, 1983.

Crocker, Lester G. *Jean-Jacques Rousseau*. 2 vols. New York: Macmillan Company, 1973.

Green, F.C. *Jean-Jacques Rousseau: A critical study of his Life and Writings*. New York: Cambridge University Press, 1955.

Guêhenno, Jean. *Jean-Jacques Rousseau*, 2 vols. Trans. John and Doreen Weightman. New York: Columbia University Press, 1966.

Hendel, Charles W. *Jean-Jacques Rousseau: Moralist*. New York: Oxford University Press, 1934.

Josephson, Matthew. *Jean-Jacques Rousseau*. London: Victor Gollancz, 1932.

Morley, John. *Rousseau*. New York: The Macmillan Company, 1886.

Mowat, R.B. *Jean-Jacques Rousseau*. London: Arrowsmith, 1938.

COMMENTARIES

Blanchard, William H. *Rousseau and the Spirit of Revolt*. Ann Arbor: University of Michigan Press, 1967.

Broome, J.H. *Rousseau: A Study of his Thought*. London: Edward Arnold, 1963.

Cameron, David. *The Social Thought of Rousseau and Burke*. London: Weidenfeld and Nicolson, 1973.

Carter, Christine J. *Rousseau and the Problem of War*. New York: Garland Publishing, 1986.

Cassirer, Ernest. *The Question of J.-J. Rousseau*. Trans. Peter Gay. Bloomington: Indiana University Press, 1963.

Chapman, John W. *Rousseau: Totalitarian or Liberal?* New York: Columbia University Press, 1956.

Charvet, John. *The Social Problem in the Philosophy of Rousseau*. New York: Cambridge University Press, 1974.

Cobban, Alfred. *Rousseau and the Modern State*. London: Allen and Unwin, 1934.

Coleman, Patrick. *Rousseau's Political Imagination*. Geneva: Droz, 1984.

Cranston, Maurice and Peters, R.S. (eds.). *Hobbes and Rousseau*. New York: Doubleday, 1972.

de Beer, Sir Gavin. *Jean-Jacques Rousseau and His World*. London: Thames and Hudson, 1972.

Durkheim, Emile. *Montesquieu and Rousseau*. Trans. Ralph Mannheim. Ann Arbor: University of Michigan Press, 1960.

Einaudi, Mario. *The Young Rousseau*. Ithaca, NY: Cornell University Press, 1962.

Ellenburg, Stephen. *Rousseau's Political Philosophy*. Ithaca, NY: Cornell University Press, 1976.

Ellis, Havelock. *From Rousseau to Proust*. London: Constable, 1936.

Ellis, Madeleine B. *Julie: A Synthesis of Rousseau's Thought* (1748–1759). Toronto: University of Toronto Press, 1949.

Fralin, Richard. *Rousseau and Representation* New York: Columbia University Press, 1978.

Gay, Peter. *The Enlightenment: and Interpretation*, 2 vols. New York: Knopf, 1966. Bibliographical chapters devoted to Rousseau.

———. *The Party of Humanity: Essays in the French Enlightenment*. New York: Knopf, 1964.

Gildin, Hilail. *Rousseau's Social Contract*. Chicago: University of Chicago Press, 1982.

Gough, J.W. *The Social Contract*. New York: Oxford University Press, 1957.

Grimsley, Ronald. *Jean-Jacques Rousseau; A Study in Self-Awareness*. New York: Oxford University Press, 1961.

———. *The Philosophy of Rousseau*. New York: Oxford University Press, 1973.

———. *Rousseau and the Religious Quest*. Oxford: The Clarendon Press, 1968.

Hall, J.C. *Rousseau: An Introduction to his Political Philosophy*. New York: St Martin's Press, 1973.

Hamilton, James F. *Rousseau's Theory of Literature*. York, S.C.. French Literature Press, 1979.

Hampson, Norman. *Will and Circumstance: Montesquieu, Rousseau and the French Revolution*. London: Duckworth, 1983.

Harvey, Simon et al. (eds.). *Reappraisals of Rousseau*. Manchester, England: Manchester University Press, 1980.

Havens, George R. *Jean-Jacques Rousseau*. Boston: Twayne Publishers, 1978.

Leigh, R.A. (ed.). *Rousseau After 200 Years*. New York: Cambridge University Press. 1980.

Lemos, Ramon. *Rousseau's Political Philosophy*. Atlanta: University of Georgia Press, 1977.

Levine, Andrew. *Rousseau and the Politics of Autonomy*. Boston: University of Massachusetts Press, 1976.

Mason, John Hope (ed.). *The Indispensable Rousseau*. New York: Quartet Books, 1979.

Masters, Roger D. *The Political Philosophy of Rousseau*. Princeton: Princeton University Press, 1968.

Miller, James. *Rousseau: Dreamer of Democracy*. New Haven: Yale University Press, 1984.

Robinson, Philip E.J. *Jean-Jacques Rousseau's Doctrine of the Arts*. New York: Peter Lang, 1984.

Schwartz, Joel. *The Sexual Politics of J.-J. Rousseau*. Chicago: University of Chicago Press, 1984.

Shklar, Judith N. *Men and Citizens: A Study of Rousseau's Social Theory*. New York: Cambridge University Press, 1969.

Spurlin, Paul M. *Rousseau in America*. Athens: University of Alabama Press, 1969.

Talmon, J.L. *The Origins of Totalitarian Democracy*. London: Secker and Warburg, 1952.

Volpe, Salvano della. *Rousseau and Marx*. Trans. John Fraser, London, Lawrence and Wishart, 1978.

Wright, E.H. *The Meaning of Rousseau*. New York: Oxford University Press, 1929.

Wokler, Robert. *The Social Thought of J.-J. Rousseau*. New York: Garland Publishing, 1986.

BIBLIOGRAPHY

Chanover, P., "Rousseau: A pedagogical bibliography," *French Review*, XLVI (1973).

Sénelier, Jean. *Bibliographie générale de Jean-Jacques Rousseau*. Paris: Presses Universitaires de France, 1950. Standard bibliography of Rousseau; lists translations as well as original French texts.

ARTICLES

Allers, Ulrech S., "Rousseau's Second Discourse," *Review of Politics*, XX (1958).

Baczko, Bronislaw, "Rousseau and Social Marginality," *Daedalus*, CVII (1978).

Barber, Benjamin R., "Rousseau and the Paradoxers of the Dramatic Imagination," *Daedalus*, CVII (1978).

Benda, H.J., "Rousseau's Early Discourses," *Political Science*, V (1953).

Bloch, J.H., "Rousseau and Helvétius," *Journal of the History of Ideas*, XL (1979).

Bloom, Allan, "The Education of Democratic Man: Émile," *Daedalus*, CVII (1978).

Burgelin, Pierre, "The Second Education of Émile," *Yale French Studies*, XXVIII (1961–2).

Burns, J.H., "Rousseau Revisited," *Political Studies*, XII (1964).

Cantor, P.A., "The Metaphysics of Botany: Rousseau and the New Criticism of Plants," *Southwest Review*, LXX (1985).

Carter, Richard B., "Rousseau's Newtonian Body Politic," *Philosophy and Social Criticism*, VII (1980).

Cell, Howard R., "Breaking Rousseau's Chains," *University of Ottawa Quarterly*, XLIX (1979).

Cobban, Alfred, "New Light on the Political Theory of Rousseau," *Political Science Quarterly*, LXVI (1951).

Cranston, Maurice, "A Revolution in Music: Rousseau and Rameau," *The Great Ideas Today* (1986).

———, "Rousseau and the Ideology of Liberation," *The Wilson Quarterly*, VII (1983).

———, "Rousseau's Social Contracts," *The Great Ideas Today* (1985).

Crocker, G., "Order and Disorder in Rousseau's Social Thought," *Proceedings of the Modern Language Association*, IXCIV (1979).

Davies, A.F., "Rousseau and the Politics of Sensibility," *Australian Journal of Political History*, VI (1960).

de Jouvenel, Bertrand, "Rousseau: Pessimistic Evolutionist," *Yale French Studies* XXVIII (1961–2).

Doone, John B. Jr., "Rousseau's Theory of Natural Law," *Journal of the History of Ideas*, XXXIII (1972).

Eckstein, W., "Rousseau and Spinoza," *Journal of the History of Ideas*, V (1944).

Ellis, Madeleine B., "Jean-Jacques Rousseau: Biographical Problems," *Romantic Review*, XXXVIII (1948).

Featherstone, Joseph, "Rousseau and Modernity," *Daedalus*, CVII (1978).

Fellows, Otis, "Buffon and Rousseau," *Proceedings of the Modern Language Association*, LXXV (1960).

Fetscher, Iring, "Rousseau's Conception of Freedom," *Nomos*, IV (1962).

Friedrich, C.J., "Law and Dictatorship in the *Contrat social*," *Revue Philosophique*, CXLI (1951).

Gossman, Lionel, "The Innocent Art of Confession," *Daedalus*, CVII (1978).

———, "Rousseau's Idealism," *Romantic Review*, LII (1961).

———, "Time and History in Rousseau," *Studies in Voltaire and the Eighteenth Century*, XXX (1964).

Gourevitch, Victor, "Rousseau on the Arts and Sciences," *Journal of Philosophy*, LXIX (1972).

Graubard, S., (ed), "Rousseau for Our Time," *Daedalus*, CVII (1978).

Havens, G.R., "Diderot, Rousseau and the *Discours sur l'inégalité*," *Diderot Studies*, III (1961).

Hoffman, Stanley, "Rousseau on War and Peace," *American Political Science Review*, LVII (1963).

Howard, Dick, "Rousseau and the Origin of Revolution," *Philosophy and Social Criticism*, VI (1979).

John, G., "The Moral Education of Émile," *Journal of Moral Education*, XI (1981).

Keller, A.C., "Plutarch and Rousseau's First Discourse," *Proceedings of the Modern Language Association*, LIV (1939).

Kelly, G.A., "Rousseau, Kant and History," *Journal of the History of Ideas*, XXIX (1968).

Kessen, William, "Rousseau's Children," *Daedalus*, CVII (1978).

Kisch, Eve, "Rameau and Rousseau," *Music and Letters*, XXII (1941).

Lough, J., "The Earliest Refutation of the *Contrat social*," *French Studies*, XXIII (1969).

McAdam, James I., "Rousseau and the Friends of Despotism," *Ethics*, LXXIV (1963).

McNeil, Gordon, "The Anti-Revolutionary Rousseau," *American Historical Review*, LVIII (1953).

Manuel, Frank E., "A Dream of Eupsychia," *Daedalus*, CVII (1978).

Masters, Roger D., "Jean-Jacques is Alive and Well," *Daedalus*, CVII (1978).

Mercken-Spaas, G., "The Social Anthropology of Rousseau's Emile," *Studies in Voltaire and the Eighteenth Century*, CXXXII (1975).

Paul, Charles B., "Music and Ideology," *Journal of the History of Ideas*, XXXII (1971).

Plamenatz, John, "Pascal and Rousseau," *Political Studies*, X (1962).

Riley, Patrick, "Rousseau as a Theorist of Federalism," *Publius*, III (1973).

Rosenberg, Aubrey, "Rousseau's *Lévite d'Ephraim* and the Golden Age," *Australian Journal of French Studies*, XV (1978).

Schwartz, Benjamin I., "The Rousseau Strain in the Contemporary World," *Daedalus*, CVII (1978).

Sherover, Charles M., "Rousseau's Civil Religion," *Interpretations*, VIII (1980).

Shklar, Judith N., "Rousseau and Equality," *Daedalus*, CVII (1978).

———, "Rousseau's Images of Authority," *American Political Science Review*, LVIII (1964).

Silverthorne, M.J., "Rousseau's Plato," *Studies in Voltaire and the Eighteenth Century*, CVVI (1973).

Skillen, Anthony, "Rousseau and the Fall of Social Man," *Philosophy* LX (1985).

Starobinski, Jean, "The Accuser and the Accused," *Daedalus*, CVII (1978).

——, "The Illness of Rousseau," *Yale French Studies*, XXVIII (1961–2).

Strauss, Leo, "On the Intention of Rousseau," *Social Research*, XIV (1947).

Tanner, Tony, "Julie and '*la Maison paternelle*,' " *Daedalus*, CV (1976).

Taylor, Eric, "Rousseau's Conception of Music," *Music and Letters*, XXX (1949).

Teichgraeber, Richard F., "Rousseau's Argument for Property," *History of European Ideas*, II (1981).

Waldman, T., "Rousseau on the General Will and the Legislator," *Political Studies*, VIII (1960).

Wilkins, B.T., "The nature of Rousseau," *Journal of Politics*, XXI (1959).

Williams, David, "The Influence of Rousseau on Public Opinion," *English Historical Review*, XLVIII (1933).

Wokler, Robert, "The Influence of Diderot on the Political Theory of Rousseau," *Studies in Voltaire and the Eighteenth Century*, CXXXII (1975).

——, "Perfectible Apes in Decadent Culture," *Daedalus*, CVII (1978).

——, "Rousseau and Rameau on Revolution," *Studies in the Eighteenth Century*, VI, Canberra (1979).